D1477188

'This definitive account of British nursing during the Great War and vivid conveyance of the personal experience of combat nursing is placed within the context of the war's chaos and confusion. Yvonne McEwen's international profile as one of the finest historians of women's experience of war can only be enhanced by this opus to scholarship.'

Professor John S. G. Wells, Head of the School of Health Sciences,
Waterford Institute of Technology

'McEwen's work weaves the personal and political together, simultaneously unravelling complicated professional relationships. Her interpretation is embedded in the overarching context of women's roles in medicine, warfare and society. The skilful discovery and use of primary sources amplifies the participants' voices, making this work authoritative, authentic and absolutely fascinating.'

Joanne Murray, The Legacy Center, Drexel University College of Medicine

To the memory of my beloved Grandmother Elizabeth Doherty
who knew first-hand the trauma of war

In the Company of Nurses

The History of the British Army Nursing Service in the Great War

Yvonne McEwen

EDINBURGH
University Press

© Yvonne McEwen, 2014

Edinburgh University Press Ltd
The Tun – Holyrood Road
12 (2f) Jackson's Entry
Edinburgh EH8 8PJ
www.euppublishing.com

Typeset in 10.5/13pt Sabon by
Servis Filmsetting Ltd, Stockport, Cheshire
Printed and bound in Malta by
Gutenberg Press

A CIP record for this book is available from the British Library

ISBN 978 0 7486 7911 9 (hardback)
ISBN 978 0 7486 7912 6 (webready PDF)

Contents

Figures

Acknowledgements

FIRSTLY, MY SINCERE THANKS to Colonel Wendy Spencer, past Director of the Army Nursing Service, who commissioned the book, and to Major Judy Evans, Regimental Secretary, now retired; without their vision and support the book would not have been considered.

The support of Colonel David Bates, Director, Army Nursing Services and the Trustees of the Queen Alexandra's Royal Army Nursing Corps Association is gratefully acknowledged. There was great enthusiasm from the Corps when the book was first suggested and a meeting with nurses recently returned from tours of duty in Iraq and Afghanistan inspired the title. As I listened to their stories, I knew I was in the company of dedicated nurses and I felt admiration, respect and gratitude that nurses of such calibre were there for the country and our troops when they were needed. This book is as much about today's nurses as it is about the military nurses who served a hundred years ago; the spirit, humanity and dedication prevail.

The assistance of Catherine, Derek and Rob at the Army Medical Services Museum was very helpful, particularly when I was trying to establish the whereabouts of many of the Corps' documents and papers, and I am very grateful to them.

The team at Edinburgh University Press have been extremely kind and helpful throughout the preparation of this book and have shown remarkable patience; to Ellie Bush, Carla Hepburn, Ian Davidson and Eddie Clark, I thank you sincerely. I would particularly like to acknowledge the support of my commissioning editor, John Watson; I count myself very fortunate to have such a terrific advisor and advocate.

For their cooperation and assistance and, where appropriate, permission to quote from their documents, I am grateful to: The London Hospital Archive, London; Bristol University Archives and Special Collections, Bristol; Wellcome Trust, London; Imperial War Museum, Department of Collections, London; British Red Cross Society, London; The National Library of Scotland, Edinburgh; The Royal College of Nursing Archives and Special Collections, Edinburgh; The Royal College of Surgeons, Edinburgh; The Royal College of Physicians, Edinburgh; Lothian Health Archives, Edinburgh; National Archives, Kew; Parliamentary Archives, London; Gayle, Cengage Learning, Digital Archive, Women, War and Society 1914–1918; CEF Books, Ottawa, for kind permission to quote from *Lights Out!* by K. Wilson. Every effort has been made to contact copyright holders but if there are omissions, I apologise; they will be acknowledged in future editions.

My sincere thanks to the Carnegie Trust for the Universities of Scotland for their generous financial assistance, and to Drexel College of Medicine Archives and Legacy Centre for the Gloeckner Research Fellowship. Thanks also to the University of Edinburgh and particularly Professor Douglas Cairns, without whose support the book would not have gone beyond the discussion phase.

I would particularly like to express my thanks to the Luard, Brander and Gameson families for their great kindness and for their permission to quote from the private papers of K. E. Luard, M. Brander and L. Gameson.

To my very dear family and friends, who were often the subject of neglect when I was working on 'the book', thank you for keeping up your long-suffering tradition. Thanks also to Alistair who, despite many years of instruction, is still trying patiently to help me master the computer; his assistance has been invaluable in the production of this book and it is much appreciated. And to Sheila Crilly, who for thirty years has been there for me in everything I have written; without her input I would never have finished the book. Our friendship has survived many a 'constructive comment and suggestion'.

Finally, for Ben, who missed many planned walks but has forgiven me, my thanks for his company and comfort throughout.

Abbreviations

AANS	Australian Army Nursing Service
ABS	Advanced Dressing Station
AMS	Army Medical Services
ANS	Army Nursing Service
AOD	Army Ordnance Department
AT	Ambulance Train
BH	Base Hospital
BJN	*British Journal of Nursing*
BRCS	British Red Cross Society
CANC	Canadian Army Nursing Corps
CB	Crisis Beds
CCS	Casualty Clearing Station
CO	Commanding Officer
COA	Court of Adjustment
COE	Court of Enquiry
DAH	Disordered Action of the Heart
DAMS	Director of Army Medical Services
DDMS	Deputy Director of Army Medical Services
DI	Dangerously Ill
DORA	Defence of the Realm Act
FA	Field Ambulance
GH	General Hospital
HS	Hospital Ship
LOC	Lines of Communication
MEF	Mediterranean Expeditionary Force
MiD	Mentioned in Dispatches
MM	Military Medal
MO	Medical Officer
MOP	Ministry Of Pensions
MRC	Medical Research Committee
NT	*The Nursing Times*
NYDN	Not Yet Diagnosed (Nerves)
OStJJ	Order of St John of Jerusalem
QAIMNS	Queen Alexandra's Imperial Military Nursing Service
QAIMNSR	Queen Alexandra's Imperial Military Nursing Service Reserve
RAMC	Royal Army Medical Corps

RAP	Regimental Aid Post
RRC	Royal Red Cross
SI	Seriously Ill
SS	Shell Shock
SSRTN	Society for State Registration of Trained Nurses
TAT	Temporary Ambulance Train
TFNS	Territorial Force Nursing Service
VAD	Voluntary Aid Detachment
VC	Victoria Cross
WO	War Office

Introduction

THE FIRST GUNSHOT WAS like no other and it produced a war like no other; the war was epic in size and tragedy and one hundred years later we are still fascinated by it. The number of books written on the subject can best be described as phenomenal and the involvement of the British Expeditionary Force (BEF) in the global conflict has been extensively covered in everything from referenced works to coffee-table publications. Central to the combat effectiveness of the BEF was the work of the Army Medical and Nursing Services.

In Britain, the latter has been the subject of historical neglect as there is a dearth of original research into the professional, personal and political lives of the women employed in the military nursing services. At the outbreak of the Great War there were fewer than 400 trained nurses in the Queen Alexandra's Imperial Military Nursing Service (QAIMNS), but by the end of the hostilities, 23,931 trained and untrained nurses, including 2,894 Dominion and USA nurses, had served with the Imperial Nursing Service.[1]

In nearly one hundred years, the number of publications on the work of the QAIMNS is best described as scant, and research-based monographs are negligible. The first post-war book to examine the work of the Army Nursing Services in the Great War was *Reminiscent Sketches*, which was compiled from submissions sent by Anne Beadsmore Smith, Matron-in-Chief, QAIMNS, to Lady Norman, Chairwoman of the Women's Work Sub-Committee at the Imperial War Museum in 1919.[2] In her letter to Lady Norman, Miss Beadsmore Smith explained the background to the submissions:

> I am now enclosing the sketches written by members of our Service in accordance with your request. So far these are all the sketches which Dame Maud McCarthy forwarded from France. I hope, however, to have some more of other theatres of war at a later date. I hope these are what you wanted. I think some are quite interesting.[3]

Unfortunately, as far as can be ascertained, there were no further submissions from the other theatres of war, thus leaving a paucity of information on the work of the QAIMNS in Macedonia, Mesopotamia, Palestine, North Russia, Italy and East Africa. However, the relatively few sketches submitted by Anne Beadsmore Smith have consistently featured in publications on the QAIMNS in the Great War.

In 1923, Elizabeth Haldane published *The British Nurse in Peace and War*, which covers the work of Florence Nightingale, the struggle for professional recognition, the formation of the QAIMNS, the Territorial Force Nursing

Service (TFNS) and the rise of the Voluntary Aid Detachments (VADs). It also covers military nursing in the First World War.[4]

Thirty years later, Ian Hay (Major-General John Hay Beith) attempted to write a history of the Army Nursing Service but encountered difficulties with the hierarchy of the service during the preparation of the manuscript. The book was eventually published under the title *One Hundred Years of Army Nursing* and covers the Nightingale period through to the Second World War. It is not a referenced work and relies primarily on the original First World War sketches. Despite Ian Hay being well recognised for the power of his prose, there is a feeling that the book is not all that it could have been, and for whatever reason, a grand ambition was thwarted. This could have been due to a breakdown in relationships that developed between the author and the Corps.[5]

Under the Famous Regiments series in 1975, Juliet Piggott published *Queen Alexandra's Royal Army Nursing Corps*. The book covers much of the same ground as Ian Hay's book and draws on the same sources. It is a light-touch history of the Army Nursing Service with no original research on the professional or personal aspects of the nurses' lives.[6] In *The Roses of No Man's Land* Lynn MacDonald draws on personal interviews, diaries and letters to tell the story not just of the professional and volunteer nurses in the First World War but also the doctors, stretcher-bearers, chaplains and soldiers in British and American units. When published in 1980, the book was an immediate success and thirty-four years later it is still in print. It was one of the earliest First World War history books to be compiled from statements from those who served.[7] In 2001, Eric Taylor published *Wartime Nurse* and the content covers army nursing from the Crimea Campaign to the Korean War. Eric Taylor cites nurses' narratives from the Imperial War Museum collections as well as the nursing journals of the time. Unlike Lynn MacDonald's book, Eric Taylor covers much of the same material and eras as the Hay and Piggott publications.[8] To mark the centenary of the Queen Alexandra's Royal Army Nursing Corps (QARANC) in 2002, an illustrated history of the Corps was commissioned, entitled *Sub Cruce Candida*. The book consists of photographs, and extracts taken from the letters and diaries of Corps members during its hundred-year history. It is a beautifully presented book and the narrative on the evolution of military nursing dates from the establishment of a hospital for the British Garrison at Tangiers in 1662. It is the only book in the listed collection to cite a chronology of British military nursing up to the formation of the Army Nursing Services in 1881.[9] In 2006, *It's a Long Way to Tipperary: British and Irish Nurses in the Great War* was published. It is the first monograph to deal solely with the experiences of British and Irish nurses in the First World War, and contains original research on the health and deaths of nurses as well as extending the nurses' narratives beyond the original First World War collection. Unfortunately, it is not a referenced work.[10] Three years later, *Containing Trauma*, authored by the nurse historian Christine Hallett, examined the work of trained and volunteer nurses. It is a heavily referenced work and draws on multiple sources. The book is not just about British nurses in the First World War; it covers the Australian and Canadian nursing services as well as nurses working in independent and volunteer units outwith the control of the War Office and Army Medical and Nursing Services. In addition to the primary source narratives, the book draws on the fictional and autobiographical writings of socialites, thespians and aspiring writers who rather fancied themselves as volunteer nurses. Because the book is dominated by references, it probably narrows the readership to nurse, health and social historians. The book deals solely with nursing practice and does not contextualise the work of nurses within the larger wartime or professional issues.[11]

In my 2006 book on First World War nursing, I said that nurses provided a 'safe haven ... where traumatised soldiers could express their feelings of fear, despair and shame'. I argued that nurses contributed significantly to the early development of 'physical and psychological trauma care' and that, had the nursing profession been more aware of its wartime historical identity and achievements, it might have been recognised as the foremost authority on trauma care, rehabilitation and survivor issues. I have not altered my opinion, but question now why nurses did not act upon or share their hard-earned experience and why, for the most part, they chose silence over expression. Traditionally, their role was akin to a walk-on part with no lines to say; though war had given them centre stage and a voice, only a few chose to speak during the tragic epic and very few took the opportunity to deliver the lines that were so important to our understanding of the tragedy and the roles played by nurses and their colleagues.

Only one British nurse, Kate Luard, QAIMNS (Reserve), chose to break the silence during the early years of the War and I have written a chapter on her defiance of the Defence of the Realm Act (DORA) in my edited monograph on war corresponding.[12]

The nurses who served during the First World War did not live or practise in a vacuum. They had personal and professional lives and I have tried to represent the, at times, competing and conflicting demands on them. This is not a book about the administrative minutiae of nursing in the First World War; it does not cover uniforms, allowances, transfers, pay contracts or promotions, and while very important to our understanding of the administration of the nursing services, I have chosen to focus on the professional, personal and political issues.

Furthermore, for reasons stated earlier, the book does not cover all the theatres of military operations. The biggest problem in writing this book has been accessing primary sources on the British military nursing service and there were times when the book was near to being abandoned. The First World War archives of the QAIMS were not as extensive as the Corps believed them to be and quite often what did exist was not made readily available to me. It became clear very quickly that it would be impossible to write an Official History on the war work of the QAIMS.

When the Committee for Medical History of the War approached the War Office in 1918 for information on the Nursing Services they were not well received. Major Brereton, who was responsible for compiling the Medical

History, requested Ethel Becher, Matron-in-Chief, QAIMNS, for information on the work of the nursing services which she refused to give him. Subsequent enquiries led to an exchange of letters with the War Office and he was informed that 'Miss Becher could only be made to yield material for the women's section by superior orders from the surgeon general, and she is not in sympathy with the writing of history'.[13] The problem for any historian attempting to write the history of the nursing services started with Miss Becher's refusal. It is impossible to construct a history if the main player will not cooperate. Furthermore, she left no diaries or official papers. An exhaustive archives search has brought little if any information to light on her time in high office. There are no known personal archives of the Matron-in-Chief, and subsequent enquiries have been fruitless. However, the Matron-in-Chief for France and Flanders, Maud McCarthy, kept a War Diary which covers the work of the nursing services in France and Flanders from the beginning of the War until demobilisation. The diaries on first reading are very impressive but when compared with contemporaneous reports they become less agreeable. It is perfectly clear that Maud McCarthy had a very positive image of herself and the service and was not prepared to have anything ruin that perception or reputation; her diary, therefore, is to be read with a degree of caution. As a day-to-day documentation of nursing administration it is indeed impressive but is laced with self-promotion and effusion on the work of the nurses. At the time, almost everyone recognised the professionalism and dedication of the nursing services, and while it was important to maintain a record for posterity it is difficult to reconcile her actions during the War with those less cooperative subsequently. Furthermore, in the absence of the Matron-in-Chief's War diaries and papers, we have a unilateral view of the nursing administration. It is clear from Maud McCarthy's diary that a degree of tension existed between the two women and therefore interpretation of her diary is problematic, as we read only one side of the extensive communications and reports and have no idea how they were perceived or acted upon by the Matron-in-Chief; it is the equivalent of listening to a one-sided conversation or argument.

In addition to the problems with the Matron's diaries and papers, there is a paucity of material from members of the regular and reserve forces. However, I have spent many years working on what does exist and I have come to the conclusion that, even if there had been a vast nursing archive to call upon, the outcome of this book would not have been affected. I have observed it is not what was said in letters, diaries, memoirs and autobiographies; it is the unsaid that has proved to be much more interesting and worthy of further investigation.

From 1915 to 2014, over 140 English language books and pamphlets have been published on First World War nursing. Within the historiography, the work of the Imperial Military Nursing Service is generally under-represented and quite often mythologised. This is particularly true of the long-held shibboleths which prevail about the personal and professional relationships that existed between the military and volunteer nurses. Additionally, although visual iconography is strongly represented, confusion still prevails over the uniforms worn by the different services. The military nurses' starched white veils, grey uniforms, scarlet or grey and scarlet tippets, redolent of clothing worn by the female religious orders which for centuries dominated nursing and care-giving, are contrasted with the blue dress and white bibbed apron with the red cross motif and the close caped head covering of the volunteer nurses. The painting by Sir William Lavery on the cover of this monograph was chosen for a variety of reasons, not least because of its fine illustration of the distinguishing uniforms worn by the military and volunteer nursing services.

The two nurses in Lavery's painting are positioned in front of a large window overlooking the harbour at Le Havre. The volunteer nurse resting back on her hands has adopted a very relaxed look while the other, a member of the Queen Alexandra's Imperial Military Nursing Service Reserve, strikes a very bold, hand-on-hip stance. Both nurses display what is best described as 'attitude'. For the time, their adopted poses would have been frowned upon and considered unprofessional and unfeminine. Perhaps Lavery caught something of the new, liberating times for women, especially nurses, when attitudes towards certain behaviours, gestures and mannerisms became more relaxed, albeit unofficially. However, the subjects are without discernible facial features and their anonymity dominates the painting.

In ancient Rome, the term *damnatio memoriae* – 'damnation of memory' – was used to dishonour those who fell out of favour or were disgraced. It was the practice to remove or defile the features of the individual from statues or illustrations with the intent of erasing their memory from history. Although not the subject of disgrace, Sister Currier and Nurse Billam who posed for Lavery's painting are without facial identity and they are defined only by their uniforms. For whatever reasons, Lavery chose to highlight what they were rather then who they were.

The history of the nursing services in the First World War has never really been in favour with professional historians, although in the past few years there has been a steady growth of literature amongst nurse historians. Even so, for the most part, the personal cost of nursing in those pivotal years of professional development has remained under-researched. The physical and psychological cost of their labours, and the loss of life within their ranks, are seldom recognised or commemorated. In fact, it could be argued that certain aspects of the nurses' war experiences were not to be memorialised and resulted *de facto* in *damnatio memoriae*. Therefore I hope this book – published in the centenary of the First World War – will go some way to rectifying the historical neglect of the personal cost for many nurses, and serve as a reminder that they too made the ultimate sacrifice for 'The Great War and Civilisation'.

NOTES

1. *Hansard*, HC Debates, 14 April 1919, vol. 114, cc2542–4.
2. *Reminiscent Sketches*, John Bale and Danielsson, 1922.

3. Beadsmore Smith, A. Letter to Lady Norman, Women at Work Collection, Imperial War Museum, BRCS 25.1/7.
4. Haldane, E. (1923), *The British Nurse in Peace and War*, London: John Murray.
5. Hay, I. (1953), *One Hundred Years of Army Nursing*, London: Cassell.
6. Piggott, J. (1975), *Queen Alexandra's Royal Army Nursing Corps*, London: Leo Cooper.
7. MacDonald, L. (1984), *The Roses of No Man's Land*, London: Papermac.
8. Taylor, E. (2001), *Wartime Nurse*, Robert Hale.
9. Gruber, E. and Searle, G. (2002), *Sub Cruce Candida*, Camberley: QARANC Association.
10. McEwen, Y. (2006), *It's a Long Way to Tipperary; British and Irish Nurses in the Great War*, Dunfermline: Cualann.
11. Hallett, C. (2009), *Containing Trauma*, Manchester: Manchester University Press.
12. McEwen, Y. T. and Fisken, F. (2012), *War, Journalism and History: War Correspondents in the Two World Wars*, Oxford: Peter Lang.
13. Brereton, T. S., Letter re: Ethel Becher to Women at Work Committee, Women's War Work Collection, Imperial War Museum, BRCS 25.3/7.

BOOK I

In the Lap of the Gods

Pitiless Mars was now dealing grief and death to both sides with impartial hands. Victors and vanquished killed and were killed and neither side thought of flight. In the halls of Jupiter the gods pitied the futile anger of the two armies and grieved that men had so much suffering.

Virgil

1

Magic, Miracles and Myth:
The Genesis of Military Nursing

THE QUEEN ALEXANDRA'S IMPERIAL Military Nursing Service (QAIMNS) was established by Royal warrant in 1902, but its predecessor, the Army Nursing Service (ANS), was formed in 1881. The small cadre of nurses that constituted the ANS were the pioneers of British professional military nursing and they regarded themselves as the guardians, and natural inheritors, of Florence Nightingale's Crimea achievements. However, the role of the military nurse did not evolve after the first salvo was fired in the Crimea: its origins date from antiquity. The long-held shibboleth that Florence Nightingale was the mother of military nursing is based on a false premise; six years before Nightingale's foray to the Crimea, a Hungarian nurse, Zsuzsanna Kossuth, was serving as Chief Nurse of the Hungarian Army and Head of the Hungarian National School of Nursing.[1]

It is unfortunate that the Nightingale legend has come to dominate the historiography of care-giving in warfare, since all the available evidence indicates that men and women had been nursing combatants for centuries, some with great reputation and distinction.

Florence Nightingale had a large presence in the politics of military and public healthcare reform but the importance of her role as a nurse in the Crimea campaign has to some extent been overstated. She became known as 'The Lady with the Lamp' but this romanticised epithet belies the fact that she did very little nursing at this time. In reality, her role was akin to a nursing administrator and purveyor. Moreover, it was not an already distinguished nursing career or a national reputation that made her suitable for the position to which she was appointed; it was the result of personal contacts and patronage.

On 12 October 1854, *The Times*' Constantinople correspondent, Thomas Chenery, not as commonly believed William Howard Russell, filed a dispatch relating to the lack of medical arrangements at the Crimea. He wrote:

> It is with feelings of surprise and anger that the public will learn that no sufficient medical preparations have been made for the proper care of the wounded. Not only are there not sufficient surgeons – that, it might be argued, was unavoidable – not only are there no dressers and nurses – that might be a defect of system for which no one is to blame – but what will be said when it is known that there is not even linen to make bandages for the wounded?[2]

In support of this impassioned dispatch from Chenery, *The Times* ran an editorial appealing for funds to be raised for the care and comfort of the sick and
wounded. Over the next few days the newspaper was able to report that donations of money had been promised, including an offer from Sir Robert Peel, son
of the former Prime Minister. In a second dispatch to *The Times*, Chenery wrote:

> The worn-out pensioners who were brought out as an ambulance corps are totally
> useless, and not only are surgeons not to be had, but there are no dressers or nurses to
> carry out the surgeon's directions and to attend on the sick during intervals between
> his visits. Here the French are greatly our superiors. Their medical arrangements are
> extremely good, the surgeons are numerous, and they also have help of the Sisters of
> Charity, who have accompanied the expedition in incredible numbers. These devoted
> women are excellent nurses.[3]

The day after Chenery's second dispatch, *The Times* printed a letter signed 'A
Sufferer by the Present War'. The anonymous writer raised a question about the
number of 'able-bodied and tender-hearted English women who would joyfully
and with alacrity go out to devote themselves to nursing the sick and wounded'.[4]

Clearly the War Office was embarrassed by the revelations in *The Times* and
army commanders were furious about newspaper interference in army affairs.
It was uncommon for military leaders to be held publicly accountable for their
strategy and prosecution of warfare, and they were particularly sensitive to what
they believed to be unwarranted criticism, particularly from the press. During
the first six months of the Crimean campaign various government enquiries were
held into what was, and continued to be, wrong with the management of the
campaign. With further revelations in *The Times* from letters written by soldiers
and their families about the appalling lack of casualty care arrangements, urgent
action was needed.

Sidney Herbert, who was Secretary of State at War and a personal friend
of Florence Nightingale, wrote to her about the situation in the Crimea and
asked her to consider taking charge of the nursing arrangements. In his letter,
he claimed that her personal qualities, her knowledge and power of administration, and, 'among greater things, your rank and position in Society give you
advantages in such a work which no other person possesses'. In addition to
highlighting her credentials for the position, he addressed the recruitment of
suitable women to accompany her to the Crimea. Appealing to her sense of duty,
and perhaps even vanity, Herbert wrote:

> There is but one person in England that I know of who would be capable of organis-
> ing and superintending such a scheme; and I have been several times on the point of
> asking you hypothetically if, supposing the attempt was made, you would undertake
> to direct it ... The selection of the rank and file nurses would be very difficult ... and
> the difficulty of finding women equal to the task ... and requiring, besides knowledge
> and goodwill, great courage.[5]

Florence Nightingale rose to Sidney Herbert's challenge and the nation's
need. Her place in history was secured. While there can be little doubt that

Florence Nightingale showed great courage and tenacity of spirit by accepting the position offered by Herbert, in theory and in practice she possessed neither great knowledge nor experience of military nursing and healthcare. Contrary to popular belief, Miss Nightingale was not, as Herbert had stated in his letter, 'equal to the task', though in fairness to her position, there were few, if any, men or women at that time equipped with the skills and knowledge needed to combat the effects of the diseases and injuries that befell the armies.

The healthcare conditions and nursing arrangements in the Crimea were, without doubt, a challenge to Florence Nightingale's limited nursing knowledge and experience. However, the lessons learned from what she was unable to achieve in caring for the sick and wounded would later encourage her to formulate ideas on healthcare reform which she believed would ameliorate suffering in future conflicts and improve the day-to-day health of the army and civilians.[6]

Almost forty years after her experiences in the Crimea, Florence Nightingale reflected on her achievements, and in particular on the establishment of a training school for nurses which opened on 15 June 1860 at St Thomas's Hospital in London. 'The Lady with the Lamp' had secured herself a place in the nation's affections and, as a result, the training school had been established by public subscription. In 1892, Nightingale wrote:

> There comes a crisis in the lives of all social movements. This has come in the case of nursing in about thirty years. For nursing was born about thirty years ago. Before it did not exist, though sickness was as old as the world.[7]

Miss Nightingale was mistaken; men and women had been delivering care to the sick, injured and destitute for centuries. In times of warfare there was a long-established, though informal, practice of men and women supplying care and comfort for armies and navies. It was, perhaps, more a question of semantics as to what constituted 'nursing' and how it differentiated, if at all, from care-giving in the evolutionary practice of medical science and military medicine.

War is a vile business, and throughout history women have always had a role to play; it has never been purely male-dominated, as some believe. It is a truism that women have often been the cause and instigators of warfare as well as its victims; they have also been military leaders and combatants. Moreover, women have a distinct advantage over men in as much as they can both produce and become warriors.

The Classics remind us of the multiple roles that women played in support of, or within, the military. Herodotus in the *Histories* cites Artemisia, a senior naval commander, who fought in the Battle of Salamis, and Homer, in the *Iliad*, relates the story of the Amazonian Queen Penthesilea who died by the hand of Achilles at Troy. The Amazonian queens Antiope and Hippolyte were said to have fought with or against Theseus and Achilles.[8]

In the history of ancient Greece, the women of Sparta bred sons proudly, if not enthusiastically, for warfare. There was no place for weakling babies and new-born Spartan boys who were deemed to be weak were abandoned to die on the slopes of Mount Taygetus. When a Spartan male reached his seventh year, he was handed over by his mother to train for a life of discipline, hardship and warfare. This action did not imply lack of maternal affection; women and their sons were trained to subordinate their feelings for the common goal of the state – 'conquer or die'. It has been claimed that Spartan women were in great demand as nurses, though there is no firm evidence to support this assertion. However, by breeding warriors Spartan women were also creating potential casualties of war and it would not be surprising if indeed Spartan women were sought out for their nursing skills. After all, since, traditionally, the Greeks waged war every six months, producing and caring for warriors would be considered essential.[9]

Although the evidence of care-giving in classical antiquity is scanty and incomplete, it is known that women were care-givers in both civilian and military life. One of the earliest references to the healing arts in warfare can be found in Homer's epic poem the *Iliad*, where a detailed description is given of the physical and psychological consequences of warfare. Within the text, Homer cites in great detail at least 150 different types of wound inflicted by swords, spears and arrows. Throughout the poem, he refers to the medical and nursing care given to warriors by fellow combatants, or the *Iatros* – the doctor. The poem also suggests that women had a role to play in caring for the battle casualties, referring to Agamede, daughter of Augeas, King of Epeans, who knew the healing power of every herb and who, in caring for the wounded at Troy, 'prepared the gentle bath and washed their gory wounds'.[10]

Homer was clearly insightful into the treatment of war wounds and how they were inflicted. The poem includes one of the earliest recorded instances of the staged care of battlefield casualties. For example, injured warriors were transported from the scene of battle to barracks, *klisiai* – wooden huts or nearby ships – for treatment. Subsequently, men and women, most likely slave-nurses, cared for them, carrying out ritual chants and incantations while washing and tending to the wounds.

In the initial treatment, the *Iatros* or slave-nurse washed wounds with wine or vinegar. The Greeks were right in believing that wine had beneficial values though its constituent parts would be unknown; wine contains polyphenol compounds, such as malvoside, which when applied to wounds reduces infection. Furthermore, the acetic acid in vinegar is an effective antiseptic. In some types of wounds a pad soaked in wine was covered with a dry sponge and leaves and bound onto the wounds. The leaves had no therapeutic value but their application stopped the evaporation of the wine from the dressing and sponge. The Greek practice was to apply drugs directly onto wounds and, because it was believed it kept wounds cool and dry, there was a preference for bitterroot. They also used myrrh, frankincense and cinnamon as healing agents, and Herodotus, commonly known as the 'father of history', refers in detail in his *Histories* to sources of resin-based therapies. He cites the use of myrrh on battle wounds: when the commander of a Greek ship fighting the Persians was 'ill hacked about with wounds', the warriors on board the ship 'tended his wounds with myrrh'.[11]

When a wound or wounds required suturing to prevent infection, the suture was covered in copper oxide and honey, an antibacterial remedy passed on from the Egyptians.

The Greeks did not know how to amputate gangrenous limbs and the limb was left to rot. They referred to gangrene as *melasmos* – blackening. Surprisingly, according to the Hippocratic collection, the injured or wounded could survive providing the dead tissue was removed from the bone, the appropriate diet was given and the patient was nursed in the proper position.

The wounds of war were many and varied and there is no evidence that the Greeks knew how to prioritise care; but as recorded in the Hippocratic collection many warriors had lingering deaths, not necessarily because of delays in care, but because of a lack of medical knowledge. One case describes a warrior struck in the abdomen by an arrow who 'developed terrible abdominal pains and started vomiting bile', after which he was 'temporarily relieved of the pain' but developed a 'great thirst and fever then died within seven days of wounding'. A second example records the wounding of a warrior by a javelin. He was struck in the back but initially did not complain of any pain: on the third day the warrior 'developed a sharp pain in his abdomen'; on the fourth day he was 'restless with the pain becoming intense'; and on the fifth day he died. A third case records in distressing detail the prolonged death of a warrior struck in the back with an arrow. According to the *Iatros*, the warrior:

> Had a wound barely worth mentioning, because it did not go deep. But before long, after the arrow was pulled out, he was arched back by convulsions like those of opisthotonos; and the jaws locked; if he took some fluid into the mouth and tried to swallow it came back through the nostrils; and the other signs became worse.[12]

In all probability what the *Iatros* described was tetanus, commonly known as lockjaw.

The death and disability outcomes of prolonged warfare must surely have been calamitous for the soldiers, their families and for the Greek armies. It is therefore difficult to understand why the Greeks prohibited women from campaigns. It is evident from the types and severity of wounds that warriors required some form of nursing care. Sadly, apart from the Homeric descriptions of caregiving in battle, there is little evidence to enlighten us on the role of women. Perceived wisdom of the time claimed the presence of women would soften warriors engaged in the hardship and endurance of the battlefield and there could be no place for them in warfare. It is clear, however, from the Homeric poems that, in spite of an edict banning women, they were in attendance at Troy.

Furthermore, if there was no place for them on military campaigns, the *Iliad* highlights that women certainly had influence on the military. After all, this is a story about a war which broke out because of a woman, with female gods becoming more closely involved in the direction of the war. The rivalry and arguments between the deities led to the deaths of the main protagonists, Hector and Achilles, and the destruction of Troy.

For centuries, many scholars believed the Trojan War was the creation of Greek imagination. But in the late nineteenth century archaeological evidence discovered a few miles off the Aegean coast supported a theory that Troy was not a mythical place but had actually existed. Nonetheless, the tragedy of Troy, be it myth or fact, has given to us, through Homer's epic poem, an incredible description of camaraderie, loyalty, duty, physical and psychological wounding, and care-giving in warfare at its most noble.[13]

In the Greek mythical medical tradition, the great god Apollo gave his son Asklepious to the centaur, Chiron, to be cared for and educated in the healing arts. The curative powers of Asklepious became legend and when he married Epione their several children all became healers. Within the *Iliad*, Homer refers to the physician sons of Asklepious, Machaon and Podaleirios, who accompanied the Greek army to the Trojan War. The four daughters of Asklepious, Hygiea, Panacea, Iaso and Aegle, were also skilled in the healing arts. In Greek society the female deities of healing were numerous. Artemis-Hecate, the moon goddess of healing and succour, and her daughters, Medea and Circe, were skilled medical herbalists; Artemis-Hecate herself was considered to be a specialist in children's diseases, and Zeus, father of all the Gods, called her the 'nurse mother'. Hygiea, the goddess of health, presided over the great temple at Epidourus while Demeter, Persephone, Artemis and Eileithyia were primarily concerned with the health of women and children and with pain relief and conditions of the eye. In the Thebes Archaeological Museum there are 3,000-year-old votive tablets from grateful men and women extolling the healing powers of Demeter and Persephone.

In ancient Greek culture Arête was the goddess of virtue, and to possess *arête* was to have courage and strength in the face of adversity. The Greeks believed that individuals should strive to achieve *arête*, as it was also associated with excellence and perfection. To attain *arête* was to live up to one's full potential.

In the Homeric poems, *arête* is frequently associated with bravery but more often with effectiveness. Men and women of *arête* are persons who use their strength, bravery and wit to achieve healthy, meaningful and fulfilled lives. The Greek women who established themselves as skilled medical practitioners were definitely possessed of *arête*. Olympios of Thebes was the author of a treatise on prescriptions; Salpe wrote on remedies for diseases in women; and Satira was considered an expert on the treatment of fevers. Numerous texts refer to Greek women as healers, care-givers and medical herbalists, and further evidence of their roles in the healing arts can be found on carvings, amphorae, bas-reliefs and epigraphs.[14]

It was, however, the Asclepiadae, the physician-priests of the temples of Asklepious, that are credited with the establishment of early Greek medicine. It has been estimated that, throughout Greece, at least three hundred temples were erected to the cult of Asklepious. The most famous, if not the most important, healing place for sick or wounded pilgrims was established at Epidaurus, for it was there on Mount Titthion that the great god of medicine, Asklepious, was born. The Asklepian temples were established for the sick, infirm and wounded to seek the help of the gods of good health. However, admission to the temples was selective; only people with conditions that were deemed curable were received into them. Also, as it was claimed that births and deaths within the locality of the temples had a polluting effect, women approaching confinement and people about to die were placed outside the temple gates.[15]

In ancient Greek text there are no references to hospitals as such, but recorded as places of care-giving and healing are the *xenodochion*, *iatrion* and *abaton*. The *xenodochion*, a form of municipal inn or hostel, was a temporary resting place for strangers, the sick and the poor. The *iatrion* was a combination of publicly or privately owned dispensary and clinic. The *abaton* were not places for physical treatment but dream temples where the sick and wounded would consult with the Dream Oracle. The *abaton* were housed within the Asklepian temples and could accommodate 120 persons, with one section for women, another for men. There are references to women of the *abaton* called *Kanephoroi* and the *Arrephoroi*, who were said to be the priestesses of the temple. It is not known if they had any kind of care-giving role but scholarly interpretation of the visual representation of *Kanephoroi* and *Arrephoroi* suggests they carried baskets of remedies for the sick and wounded. There is, however, debate among classicists regarding the function of these women.[16]

The *abaton* were, in effect, religious spas where therapy consisted of relaxation, baths, music and aesthetic appreciation of the surroundings, for *abaton* were built in places of beauty. As night fell the sick and injured would wait for curative messages from the gods to be delivered in their dreams. It is probable that nocturnal visions and messages came from the administration of some kind of dream-inducing drug, hallucinogen, hypnotic or by suggestion. There is evidence to suggest the Greeks were quite familiar with the narcotic properties of opium, henbane and hemlock.

From preserved evidence of the time, there are details of the type of health problems or wounds 'cured' at the temples. In one case, a soldier had been wounded in battle by an arrow piercing his lung. For over a year the wound suppurated, filling, it was stated, sixty-seven basins with pus. The soldier sought help in the *abaton* and in a vision, while sleeping, he saw a god extract the arrowhead from his lung. According to the ancient inscription, when morning came the soldier walked out of the temple holding the arrowhead in his hand.

In another recorded case a soldier had been blinded by a spearhead which remained lodged in his eye; in his temple dream, a god pulled out the spear then restored his vision.[17] However improbable the cases may seem to the twenty-first-century reader, there is little difference, if any, between Bronze Age mystic cures and modern-day faith-healing and psychoanalytical dream interpretation. For the Greeks, the *abaton* held out a promise that the Dream Oracle would be sympathetic and, through the guidance and wisdom of the male and female gods, the sick and wounded would be delivered relief from their pain and suffering.

Despite the mysticism that prevailed in the healing arts there is evidence to suggest that the Greeks considered nursing to be both a skill and a science. The Greek physician Aretaeus gave detailed instructions on the management of the sickroom and the sickbed. He advised on heating, lighting and ventilation; he suggested decor colours should be soothing and restful, and that different kinds of conditions required specific types of beds and bed-clothing. Celsus emphasised the need for a strict regime of fluid replacement in the fevered patient and, as the patient's condition improved, the need for the patient to be placed on a restricted, light diet. He also recommended the type of bed-clothing needed to control body temperature. Another example of the Greeks' perception of nursing and care is the insightful treatise on care-giving by Rufus of Ephesus, in which he discussed the psychological conditions that can accompany physical sickness and the relationship between carer and patient, and also recorded his recommendations on the care needs of the elderly.[18]

Florence Nightingale, in her much-exalted *Notes on Nursing,* claimed that 'nursing ought to signify the proper use of fresh air, light, warmth, cleanliness, quiet, and the proper selection and administration of diet'.[19] Clearly, centuries before the publication of her work, the Greeks had pioneered the art of nursing the sick.

It was not the Greeks, however, who were the forerunners in the healing arts; the practice of healing had long been established in India, Ceylon, Egypt, Babylon and Assyria. In the ancient sacred text of India, the Vedas, the scriptures and folklore not only describe the healing arts but counsel care-givers on preventative medicine. Within the Vedas are discussions covering medicine, surgery, poisons, insanity, wounds, massage and the care of children. From these entries it is clear that women were not restricted in their roles.

In the days of Vedic culture, when men and women held equal status in many matters, some women even participated in battles. According to the collection of Hindu hymns dating from 2000 BC or even earlier, known as the Rig Veda, Queen Vishplah, wounded on the field of battle, had to undergo a limb amputation. The sacred book tells us that not only did she recover but also, once her wound healed, she was fitted with a prosthetic leg. This is a remarkable tale of a warrior queen, and it raises questions about the sophistication of surgery, rehabilitation, the development of prosthetics and the accepted role of women as combatants.[20]

In Assyria, it was in the temples to the female gods of Ishtar and Gula that mortals directed their litanies and incantations in pursuance of good health. The goddess of medicine, Ishtar, was also referred to as the weeping goddess, for it was said she had great sympathy for suffering; unsurprising, for she was also the goddess of war. Gula was the goddess of death and resurrection, and was also referred to as the 'chief physician'. Pre-dating the Greeks, women as goddesses and mortals in Egypt played an important role in health. Isis, the great goddess of medicine, was also renowned for mummifying the dismembered body of her slain husband Osiris, who died at the hands of his brother Seth. Her sisters,

Nephthys and Neith, were worshipped for the powers they possessed to control nocturnal pains in mortals. The goddess Sekhmet was known as a bone-setter. But it was mortal women, not deities, who underwent medical instruction.

Egyptian physicians, male or female, were called *Swnw*, pronounced, it is believed, 'Soo-noo'. Egyptian women were allowed to attend medical training and had access to the royal medical schools. Many opportunities were made available to them once their training was complete. Near the mouth of the Nile, at Sais, a women's college was built to specialise in the teaching and practice of gynaecology and obstetrics. An inscription found by archaeologists which supports the establishment of this college reads: 'I have come from the school of medicine at Heliopolis, and have studied at the women's school at Sais where the divine mothers have taught me how to cure diseases.'[21]

Herodotus claimed that Egyptian women were expert in the use of the scalpel and in setting broken bones, and ancient Egyptian wall paintings depict women lancing boils, circumcising babies, operating and dressing wounds. According to Amelia Edwards, the Victorian Egyptologist, the Egyptians seemed to pride themselves on their skills in the art of healing, which was held in such high esteem that Egyptian royalty made it their subject of study.[22] Cleopatra, arguably the most famous Egyptian queen, has been credited with writing several volumes on the diseases that affect women. The queens Mentuhotep and Hatshepsut were also said to be gifted physicians. While it was acceptable for female rulers to undertake a medical education, in practice it was the plebeian class of women which ministered to the sick and injured, and among them were skilled dispensers and pharmacists. The *Swnw* used emetics, diuretics and sedatives. In surgery and on wounds they pioneered the use of wound-closure, fractured limbs were set with splints and bandages, haemorrhage was controlled by cautery, and they developed theories on antisepsis and infection control.[23] In relative isolation from the rest of the world, Egyptian civilisation flourished along the banks of the Nile but this did not stop engagement in internecine conflicts or military incursions into neighbouring regions. It was providential that the Egyptians pioneered surgery, asepsis, wound-closure, cautery and splinting, for such skills were necessary in brutal battles where wounds sustained in hand-to-hand combat had devastating effects on the human body.

In a mass grave dated around 2000 BC, the bodies of sixty Egyptian soldiers were found preserved sufficiently well to identify the wounds they had sustained – mace injuries, gaping wounds, and arrows still embedded.

In an excavated surviving fragment written around 1200 BC, the life and death of a soldier is disturbingly described:

> He is taken to be a soldier as a child of a reed's length ... He rises in the morning only to receive castigation, and will be wounded with bloody wounds. He is accoutred with weapons in his hand, and stands in the battlefield. A lacerating blow is dealt his body; a double blow descends on his skull. He receives a shattering blow to his eyes and nose ... He is beaten like a papyrus and battered with castigations.[24]

The term 'beaten like a papyrus' suggests the soldier was beaten to a pulp. Given the ferocity of frequent conflicts and the wounds inflicted, the development of surgical and wound-management techniques by the Egyptians was essential.

It is not possible to say with certainty that advances in wound management and surgery were a direct result of military campaigns, but we do know that the first recorded use of a suture was around 1100 BC and that it was used by an embalmer on the abdomen of a mummy. In six of the forty-eight cases recorded on the Smith papyrus, the surgeon is advised to 'draw together the wounds', thus implying some form of apparatus for closing wounds. It is demonstrated through papyri and carvings that Egyptians used a variety of methods for the closure of surgical and combat wounds, for instance clamps, bandages, gum strips and beeswax. To control wound infection different properties were applied such as honey, malachite or chrysocolla. Because of its hypertonic effect, honey draws water from bacterial cells, thus inhibiting bacterial growth. Malachite and chrysocolla contain copper and, while copper is toxic, it has proven to be a successful therapy if used in small quantities. The celebrated Greek physician, pharmacologist and botanist, Dioscorides, concluded that chrysocolla had the ability to clean and heal wounds and reduce scarring, but he also advised that it caused vomiting and it was strong enough to poison the patient. The ancient Egyptians could not know the scientific principles behind the use of honey and copper but they were aware of the therapeutic values.

Two of the most highly sought-after remedies, frankincense and myrrh, were difficult to obtain because they came from southern Arabia and the Horn of Africa. In Egyptian medical papyri they are referred to as healing balms, and were desired for health and spiritual wellbeing. Such was the status of myrrh as a healing agent that an Egyptian army officer on campaign, in a dispatch to the Pharaoh Amenophis, requested 'more troops, and myrrh for medicine'. In the Ebers papyrus the use of myrrh as a topical application is recommended, it being stated that for a neck wound myrrh balm should be applied directly and secured with a dressing. The Egyptians had great faith in the healing power of myrrh, using it to clean wounds and believing it could prevent the spread of infection. Additionally, they thought myrrh could arrest the development of gangrene. Conversely, since it was thought myrrh had mystical powers as well as a practical application, it was burned in ritual worship. Despite their pioneering methods in the management of health, surgery and wound care, the Egyptians still favoured the intervention of their gods. They believed that chanting during the application or removal of bandages, reciting sacred incantations during the administration of medicines, and the breath of a god into wounds were the ultimate panacea for redemptive healing.[25]

The Romans also, like the Egyptians and the Greeks, worshipped numerous deities, again believing they had the power to control health and wellbeing. Minerva was the great medical goddess, as well as being the virgin goddess of warriors. It was claimed that, without her favour, no soldier of the

Roman armies would start for Gaul. The Roman goddesses were as numerous as the diseases they were supposed to cure; for example, we know of Scabies, Genitamana, Fecunditas, Nascia, Angitia, Angina and Angerona. Additionally, Carna had charge of all male and female internal organs while fevers were the responsibility of Febris and Cloacina.

According to Celsus, the medical encyclopaedist, among the mortal practitioners of health there were many fine female healers who on their daily rounds were accompanied by nurses or slaves assisting with operations, midwifery, urine collection, cupping and leech therapy. Celsus was an admirer of the women herbalists and healers of Rome and described some of the instruments they used in their practice. Among their curative paraphernalia he claims there were forceps, scalpels, instruments for removing arrow tips and lance heads, bone elevators, drills for trephining the skull, catheters, spatulas, curettes and suturing needles.

These Roman women, in their provision of healthcare, were involved in surgery, obstetrics, gynaecology, paediatrics, pharmacy, dispensing and nursing.[26] And their practice was not confined primarily to the conditions and diseases of women; the best of nursing care and medical knowledge was for the soldiers of Rome.

It was an approved practice to place sick and wounded soldiers in private homes, and the army relied heavily upon civilians to fulfil the care-giving role. It was stated, however, that the persons involved in caring for sick or wounded legionaries must be of irreproachable character and none were considered more appropriate than the great patrician families; it is known that members of the Fabii family, one of the richest and most powerful houses in Rome, made it their practice to quarter sick and wounded soldiers in their homes.

Little evidence exists unfortunately on the development and practice of Roman military medicine since, because education was the privilege of the few and oral communication predominated, the developments in Greek and Roman medicine went unrecorded. Among historians and archaeologists, there are disputes regarding the evolution of the military medical system, military hospitals and battlefield care.[27]

However, the available evidence does suggest the existence of a medical corps within the Roman army. The brutality of hand-to-hand combat as described by the Greek historian Dionysius of Halicarnassus clearly indicates the necessity for some form of organised medical care:

> Holding their swords straight out, they would strike their opponents in the groins, pierce their sides, and drive their blows through their breasts into their vitals. And if they saw any of them keeping these parts of their bodies protected, they would cut the tendons of their knees or ankles and topple them to the ground roaring and biting their shields and uttering cries resembling the howling of wild beasts ... The Romans, however, being accustomed to many toils by reason of their unabating and continuous warfare, continued to meet every peril in noble fashion.[28]

But the Roman soldier did not always display bravery in the face of battle. In one particular engagement the soldiers refused to fight, feigning wounds as an excuse. Their commander berated them for cowardice and threatened to invoke military law if they would not stand and fight. Dionysius records:

> The soldiers then broke out into disobedience, clamoured against him and bade him lead them out of the enemy's country, alleging that they were no longer able to hold out by reason of their wounds; for most of them had bound up the sound parts of their bodies as if they had been wounded. Hence Appius was obliged to withdraw his army from the enemy's country ... As soon as they were in friendly territory, the consul assembled the troops, and after uttering many reproaches said that he would inflict upon them the punishment ordained against those who quit their posts ... Thereupon the centurions whose centuries had run away and the antesignani who had lost their standards were either beheaded with an axe or beaten to death with rods; as for the rank and file, one man chosen by lot out of every ten was put to death for the rest. This is the traditional punishment among the Romans for those who desert their posts or yield their standards.[29]

Given the vicious nature of the warfare they engaged in, not to mention the retribution meted out for refusing to fight, it would be reasonable to assume the Romans would make provision for the care of the sick and injured.

As the Roman Empire expanded and the army moved further into new territories, it became impossible to dispatch soldiers back to the care of the citizenry; the logistics of caring for the sick and wounded in the outposts of the Empire required Roman military leaders to make more immediate provision for the care of their troops. Furthermore, there was the problem of maintaining morale. Generals were aware that fit and healthy Roman legionaries had to be segregated from sick, injured and dying soldiers. The shared accommodation that existed between healthy and incapacitated soldiers had an adverse effect on courage and morale. The Roman historian, Livy, observed:

> The soldiers were dispirited; all night long they had been kept awake by the groans of the wounded and the dying. Had the enemy attacked the camp before daylight, their fear would have been so great as to cause them to desert their standards; as it was, they were only kept from flight by a feeling of shame, in every other respect they were as good as beaten.[30]

As we know, from the earliest days of the military medical system, it became the practice to place the sick and wounded in the homes of the civilian class and as the army pushed forward, expanding the boundaries of the Roman Empire in the provinces, so these soldiers were quartered with local inhabitants. Territorial acquisition, with all the attendant problems of transportation, administration, efficiency, economy, supplies and the health of the troops, required a reorganisation of the military medical system. The army of the Empire and the army of the Republic were two different entities and it is clear the military medical system evolved with the expansion of the Empire.

It was the Emperor Augustus who formed a professional military medical corps, recognising that key to the expansion of the Empire was the reduction of sickness wastage and injury attrition rates among his seasoned and skilled troops. As part of the army reform Augustus established the Army Medical School, where men wishing to become military physicians had to undertake training. If they failed to meet the standards, they could not serve in the Roman army. Within the medical corps were different types of physicians and care-givers. For example, the Roman army was divided into legions, each of ten cohorts and each cohort numbering six centuries. Within the legions, the military physicians consisted of the *medicus legionaris*, *medicus coorti* and *medicus ordinarii*. The cavalry had its own doctors, *medici alarum*, and the Roman navy had *medici triremes*. All army military physicians were under the command of the *praefectus castrensis*. In the absence of supportive evidence, it is presumed there was also a hierarchical structure among the military physicians, the *medicus legionaris* probably being the most senior.

From the establishment of the Roman Republic to the development of the Roman Empire, the organisational structure of the army significantly altered. It would be more than reasonable, therefore, to assume the medical military structure developed in accordance with the needs of the army, the campaign experiences of military physicians and the medical knowledge at the time.

In addition to the military physicians there were the *milites medici*, who were classed as *immunes*, which meant they were exempt from all military duties other than caring for the sick and wounded, and the *noscomi*, in all probability skilled slaves, who were attached to the military.

Roman military medicine and care-giving was male-dominated. Little mention is made of women attending to sick or wounded soldiers, but this is not surprising as Roman women were generally not referred to unless being acknowledged as ideal wives or loving mothers. However, as we know, there were exceptions, for example the women of the great patrician families, and female physicians cared for sick and wounded soldiers. But the lowly status of female slave-nurses involved in care-giving would render them unworthy of acknowledgement.

Within the military medical system there is evidence to suggest there may have been some form of organised battlefield casualty care. For instance, a practice existed where between eight and ten men in a troop were designated to ride along the battle line and pick up the wounded, and for this purpose their saddles had two stirrups on the left side. These mounted soldiers carried water flasks and bandages, and for each man rescued they received a reward. Aid stations were set up behind the standards, and dressings and bandages were applied by *capsarii*. From the aid station the wounded were transported by horse-drawn wagon to a mobile or stationary military hospital, the *valetudinaria*.[31] The bas-relief on Trajan's column in Rome, which depicts soldiers being bandaged and carried from the battlefield, gives some weight to the limited evidence available on the care of battle casualties.

The *valetudinaria* was a product of military efficiency and, hopefully, humanity. There is, however, considerable debate among historians and archaeologists about the function of the *valetudinaria,* with some believing they were forts, not hospitals, or that the buildings had a multiple purpose.

From archaeological evidence, they were quadrangular in shape, with barrack-like wards surrounding a central courtyard. Again, opinions differ about the function of the rooms within the building, some historians and archaeologists claiming the *valetudinaria* housed treatment rooms, kitchens, baths, latrines, herb gardens, a dispensary and mortuary. Medical instruments found on-site may support the argument that the *valetudinaria* did have a care-giving purpose. What is known, without fear of contradiction, is that Roman military physicians operated on, or otherwise treated, soldiers with a variety of medical accoutrements such as scalpels, drills and probes, forceps, catheters and arrow-extractors, and soldiers requiring surgery were sedated with opium or henbane.[32]

Faced with the distinct possibility of being wounded or maimed in battle, Roman soldiers were not content with the help provided by military physicians; they also sought divine intervention. They believed 'the signs of the gods' could influence military campaigns, and omens presided over logic. Their fate and the success of battles and campaigns, they believed, depended on the gods being appeased and placated.

Mars, the Roman god of war, was the most important of the military gods; festivals were held in March and October to honour him. In March, the beginning of the Roman military year, festivals lasted for three weeks, the centre-piece being a horse race on Rome's Field of Mars. The military year concluded in October with a chariot race on the same field, and the winning horse was sacrificed to thank the god of war for the army's safe deliverance from battle. Nonetheless, prayers and sacrifices were not considered sufficient to ward off wounding and ill health. For health and safety to be assured, talismans and charms were carried by Roman soldiers who believed the fate of their health rested not solely in mortal hands but in the lap of the Gods.[33]

It is evident that in the Bronze Age healthcare and care-giving were primarily driven by superstition. Moreover, it has been said that the sickbed was the cradle of the earliest and most tenacious superstition, and invariably people confused medicine with magic.

However, from the information available about the ancient world, it can be seen that women practised the healing arts with a combination of skill, maternalism and mysticism. While not enjoying the same position in society as men, the female gods, as a conduit, gave women – priestesses, wise women, seers, healers and herbalists – an elevated status and acknowledgement of their ability to bring skill and succour to the health needs of both civilians and soldiers. James Stuart Blackie, the eminent Scottish classicist, noted, 'Nothing was more common in ancient times than the healing skills possessed by women.'

Nevertheless, the contribution by men to care-giving, particularly within the military systems, cannot be underestimated. The educational opportunities made available to Roman military physicians, together with the practical experience they and their nursing assistants gained in dealing with battle casualties, laid the foundations for the establishment of military medicine. They were the architects of everything that followed.

THE CRUSADING SPIRIT

The first organised, coordinated and financed military nursing service was established during the period of the Crusades, which were a series of religiously sanctioned military campaigns waged by much of Christian Europe to prevent Muslim military expansion into Byzantium, the former eastern Roman Empire, and to liberate Jerusalem and the Holy Land from Muslim control. The Crusades to the Holy Land started around 1095 and ended around 1270. However, the Crusader campaigns in Spain and Eastern Europe continued into the fifteenth century.

In 1095, at Clermont in Auvergne, Pope Urban II called a council of French nobles and clergy to discuss the Muslim encroachments. In a powerful speech, he claimed 'all Christendom was disgraced by the triumphs and supremacy of the Moslems in the East' and the Holy Land, which was dear to all Christians, was 'profaned'. The Pope suggested that all Christian kings, instead of waging war against each other, should turn their weapons against the enemies of God and help their Christian brothers and sisters. In his final call-to-arms, the Pope said they were embarking upon a just war and *Deus vult* – it is the will of God – was a fitting battle cry. The enticement to join the Crusade was a promise from the Pope that the defenders of the Holy Land would have remission of all their sins and gain entry to paradise.[34]

The Pope's impassioned plea resulted in a crusading fervour that swept through Europe. Despite his decree that no women, children or monks should take part in the Holy War, they ignored the Papal dictate and with chants of *Deus vult* and 'To Jerusalem' they flocked to follow the Crusaders' banner. What Urban II wanted was an army of knights drawn from the French aristocracy; but what he got was an army that consisted not only of French nobles and their trained knights but also thousands of peasants, petty nobles, priests, prostitutes, doctors and debtors. In their quest to save the Holy Land, the Crusaders were also seeking the promise of everlasting salvation of their souls; it was in effect a salvation army.

Known as the 'Peasants' Crusade', the first Crusade was in disarray from the beginning. Urban II planned an orderly departure of the Crusaders for 15 August 1096, the Feast of the Assumption, but months before the agreed date a number of unexpected peasant armies took the pilgrim's oath and set off for the Holy Land.

It was estimated that 100,000 fighting men – knights and soldiers, and 600,000 pilgrims able to bear arms made their way through Europe and Asia Minor. There was no organised plan or skilled leadership and as the Crusaders travelled through different lands and climates they were beset with many physical and emotional hardships and conflicts. Historical documents make little reference to the type of medical and nursing care given to the Crusaders before they finally reached Jerusalem, but it is known that many nobles travelled with their own personal physicians, and men of medicine were among the Crusaders. It was claimed that within the ranks of the travelling Holy Army, there were women who nursed, and 'Crusaders, weary, thirsty and oppressed with labour and heat, would have sunk into despair if women of the camp had not revived their courage'.[35]

In their missionary zeal the Crusaders swept all before them, murdering and plundering their way to the Holy Land. Before they finally reached the walls of Jerusalem in 1099, thousands had died from climatic conditions, malnutrition, disease or wounds. At the siege of Jerusalem, many more died of battle-related injuries. Whether women actually took up arms during the expedition remains a subject of historical debate. However, it was claimed that in combat 'women were not to be restrained from mingling in the fight; they were everywhere to be seen in these moments of peril and anxiety supporting and relieving their fainting friends'.[36]

Before the Crusades, pilgrims travelled in the Holy Land unhampered and unarmed. Should they become sick or injured, hostels and hospitals were made available to them throughout the pilgrim routes. In Jerusalem, under the auspices of Italian merchants from Amalfi, a monastery and hospitals, or *hospitalias*, were built to receive pilgrims from all faiths or races. The Hospital of St John was established for the care of men and the hospital of St Mary Magdalene looked after the needs of women. According to records of the time, the hospital of St John had eleven male wards and was staffed by male nurses. Conversely, there is little recorded about the staffing and work of the women's hospital. The records show that nuns were delivering the care but only one is named, the Abbess Agnes, a Roman lady. It would appear that no records or personal memoirs of her life and work exist.

The Benedictines, a monastic order, ran the hospitals. Under the supervision of Brother Gerard, they were supported in their work by lay brothers and pilgrims. During the First Crusade, Jerusalem was besieged and Brother Gerard was imprisoned. When Godfrey of Bouillon took the city, Brother Gerard was released and he resumed the management of the hospitals. The slaughter and carnage of that dreadful event do not require retelling but it must have made a great imprint on the minds of those who survived. When Gerard returned to his ministrations, he decided to break away from the Benedictines and adopted the Augustinian Rule. It is unclear why he made this decision but under the Rule of St Benedict, after a year's probation, any man, regardless of rank or background, can enter the monastery and, having joined the order, he must remain a monk for the rest of his days. The monks lived under strict discipline, confined within the monastery walls and forbidden to have communication with the outside world. The three vows of the Benedictine Rule were obedience, stability and conversion in the way of life. These restrictive rules were incompatible with Gerard's vision of delivering physical and spiritual care within and outside the walls of Jerusalem. Whatever influenced Brother Gerard's actions, he had established the autonomous, philanthropic, religious *Fratres Hospitalarii* by 1113. Initially, the *Fratres* did not take on a military role, but the Order was formally recognised in the Bull of Pope Paschal II, *Pie Postulatio Voluntatis*. Following the death of Gerard in 1118, Raymond du Puy, his successor and First Master of the Order, changed its character from monastic-hospitaller to taking on the defensive care of the sick. The Order constituted priests, knights and lay brethren, with the priests and knights bound by the threefold pledge of charity, poverty and obedience. The hospital adopted the policy of *sans frontières*, receiving all who were in need of care – Christians, Muslims and Jews. It was an amalgam of nursing and spiritual care in union with military support that led to the establishment of the Knights Hospitallers of St John of Jerusalem.[37]

The hospital complex in Jerusalem was vast and between the different hospitals there was accommodation for 2,000 patients, a somewhat large bed capacity but perhaps suggesting the maximum available when the hospitals were under pressure to accommodate the outbreak of diseases or accommodate battle casualties. While it may be true the hospitals had the capacity for dealing with large numbers of patients, there is a degree of ambiguity regarding the term hospital as, in the Middle Ages, charitable institutions such as almshouses, hospices, resting places and quasi-medical institutions were called hospitals. Notably, their main function was limited medical and nursing care of the sick, usually the elderly or infirm. The institutions dedicated to the medical and surgical treatment of the sick and injured were the *domus infirmorum* – the infirmary, where doctors, or monks with some medical knowledge and training, treated patients. The hospital of St John of Jerusalem was an infirmary. According to John of Würzburg, a German priest, the hospital complex in Jerusalem was an edifice of vast dimensions incorporating churches, hospitals and a convent for the nursing nuns. Of the work carried out by the brothers and nuns he states,

> There was an enormous multitude of sick people, both men and women, who are tended and restored to health daily at very great expense. When I was there I learned that the whole number of these sick people amounted to two thousand, of whom sometimes in the course of one day and night more than fifty were carried out dead.[38]

Another visitor was Theodorich, a German cleric, who reinforced the size of the hospital and the standard of care.

> What a rich place this is and how excellently it spends money for the relief of the poor, and how diligent in its care for beggars ... we could in no way judge the number of people who lay there but we saw thousands of beds.[39]

Although Theodorich is reinforcing the size of the bed capacity, he is not describing a hospital, but an almshouse, yet his testament does supply evidence of the various types of care-giving facilities that existed within the vast hospital complex.

As a consequence, a number of statutes were drawn up to meet the spiritual and physical needs of the hospital patients, specifying how funds were to be used for the benefit of the sick and injured – the admissions procedure, nursing care and duties, dietary needs and spiritual care – and professional protocols and behavioural rules for doctors, nurses and patients were also listed. Male nurses, called sergeants, carried out the care of the sick and injured, the only exception to the rule being the limited use of nursing nuns who worked in the women's hospital. The following extract from the hospital statutes illuminates some of the work carried out.

- In the hospital, four experienced doctors shall be appointed for the service of the poor. They should be qualified to examine urine and diagnose disease.
- It is ordained how long and how broad the beds in which the sick lie and each bed should have a coverlet and two sheets of its own.
- Each of the sick should have a cloak of sheepskin, cap of wool and boots for going to and coming from the latrines.
- The brethren shall humbly wash the feet and heads of the sick, and cleanse their garments, and make their beds and prepare the food they need, give them drinks, and be obedient in all things for the benefit of the sick.
- Little cradles should be made for the babies of women pilgrims born in the hospital, so they may lie separate and that the baby in its own bed may be in no danger from the restlessness of the mother.
- Let the brethren of the hospital by night and by day cheerfully and gladly tend the sick as their Lords.[40]

In a set of regulations titled 'Concerning the food for the sick, doctors, and the organisation of the Palace of the Sick in Jerusalem', the admission procedure was predicated upon *mea culpa* – confession and atonement, the religious culture of the time believing that the salvation of the soul was a much nobler cause than saving lives or limbs. The perceived wisdom was sins before sickness, penitent before pain.

On admission, the 'redeemed' were given fresh clothing and food. Interestingly, according to the regulations, each patient was given their own feeding utensils but their linen was changed every two months. The patients' diet consisted of white bread, poultry, vegetables, broth and fruits such as apples, pears, figs, grapes and plums, and they were given wine twice a day. Dependent on the patient's condition, there were three categories of medical care available: the general physician *mieges*; the specialist physician *fisicien*; and the surgeon *cyrurgici*. It was the duty of the *fisicien* to deal with the most vulnerable patients, but there is no evidence to support any specialist interventions or knowledge by those who nursed.[41]

From the available evidence it is clear the Crusaders made heavy demands on the hospitals. Out of necessity pilgrim hospitals evolved from delivering the basics of food, rest and spiritual care to providing well-organised and -financed medical services. While there is some compelling evidence on the type of work carried out in the hospitals, conversely there appears to be a paucity of documentation on Crusader battlefield hospitals.

The Crusader armies' chosen method of engagement was to defend fortified positions rather than engage in open battle. In siege warfare, wounding and disability were brought about by a variety of methods and weapons. For close-quarter combat, sword, mace, axe and dagger were used, and projectile weapons constituted the bow, crossbow, javelin and trebuchet stones. Additionally, boiling oil or water were used as deterrents for those attempting to scale the walls of fortifications. Siege warfare meant the construction of siege towers with the resulting falls commonly causing death, or traumatic injuries to the head, spine, pelvis and extremities. When the siege towers were destroyed, those inside were killed by crush injuries or suffocation. It has been argued that the success of attacks was based on six principles: subverting key defenders, installing fear in the defenders by the use of propaganda, sapping the walls, storming the defences, shelling the defences, and starving the population.[42]

William of Tyre, Archbishop of Tyre and Chancellor of the Kingdom of Jerusalem, exemplified this strategy in a chronicle.

> He encircled the town with his forces, assigned the officers of his legions to appropriate stations, and dug in. The catapults and siege engines weakened the fortifications; the continual shooting of arrows tormented the citizens incessantly; and the besieged were given no respite. It was announced, meanwhile, and the news was also spread by rumour, that the city of Edessa, a city faithful to God, was suffering the agonies of a siege at the hands of the enemy of the faith and the foe of the Christian name.[43]

For the defenders and attackers alike, siege warfare must surely have brought about tremendous physical and psychological challenges. However, the defending garrison and the population they were protecting, in addition to sickness, wounding and starvation, faced an added horror of a long siege – disease from putrefying unburied corpses.

Some narrative accounts describe women assisting in the construction of siege works. It is feasible and would have been practical for them to carry out many of the non-combatant support roles such as runners and suppliers. Although unrecorded, it is highly probable that women tended to the sick, wounded and dying. However, a statement from Margaret of Beverley who was in Jerusalem when Saladin besieged it in 1187, supports the suggestion that women played an active role.

> During this siege, which lasted fifteen days, I carried out all of the functions of a soldier that I could. I wore a breastplate like a man; I came and went on the ramparts, with a cauldron on my head for a helmet. Though a woman, I seemed a warrior, though filled with fear, I learned to conceal my weakness … The fighters could have

no rest. I was giving the soldiers at the wall water to drink, when a stone, like a mill-wheel fell near me; I was hit by one of its fragments; my blood ran. But my wound quickly healed, because someone immediately brought medicine, though the scar remains.[44]

Margaret does not say who brought her medicine or what the medicine consisted of, and we can only speculate who was rendering care. It is probably safe to assume it was a woman or a Christian Brother. It was the duty of the monastic community to minister to the sick and injured, and give absolution to the dying; sieges were no exception.

On the care and transportation of battlefield casualties, the writings of Arnold of Villanova are probably among the earliest indicators of the organisation of medieval battlefield medicine. Villanova's *Regimen Almarie* is a miscellany of practical advice on everything from maintaining the health of the army to important logistical and environmental issues, such as suitable locations for army camps; how to identify an uncontaminated water supply; the disposal and burial of human and animal remains; and the care and treatment of combatants.[45]

On the battlefield, Crusader Knights primarily fought on horseback, with the support of foot soldiers. The arrow, lance, sword, spear and mace were the weapons of choice, and the main source of injury. While defensive body armour was used, it was no guarantee against serious or mortal wounding. The Knights and Crusader soldiers wore chain mail (the hauberk) covering the head, chest, abdomen, thighs and shoulders, and in addition they wore padded undergarments, which were meant to dissipate blows and penetration from weapons. The most vulnerable areas were the face, elbows and knees, and from palaeopathology studies it would appear that debilitating and mortal blows were struck in these unprotected parts of the body.[46]

It was part of enemy tactics to fell charging horses by wounding or killing the animal, resulting in life-threatening fractures to the head, neck or spine for the mounted combatant. If the horse fell on top of its rider then death or serious injury could be directly attributed to crushing injuries of limbs and internal organs.

For the combatants who immediately survived their wounds, the chain of evacuation from the battlefield to a treatment facility is unclear. There is no firm evidence to support the existence of casualty collection stations or field hospitals, although reference has been made to the existence of battlefield hospital tents organised by the Order of St John. Yet, from the little evidence that does exist, it would appear that the casualties were removed from the battlefield on pallets or litters and taken to the nearest town or hospital, although wounded combatants presented logistical and moral challenges for armies. In major engagements, the sheer volume of casualties made it impracticable, if not impossible, to move them to safety and care-giving facilities. Armies travelling with their sick and wounded were inevitably slowed down and this made them vulnerable to sustained attacks.[47]

While there is a paucity of evidence on battlefield transportation, evacuation and treatment facilities, there is quite a lot of information on the type of weapons used and the injuries they inflicted. Battlefield injuries primarily consisted of penetrating trauma. The injuries were usually caused by arrow or lance; equally, the combatant could be run through with a sword. Blades caused partial and full thickness lacerations to soft tissues and they could also cut through bone. The mace caused avulsed wounds and crushed bones. Head, spine and crush injuries were not uncommon. In fact, the head and face were the most vulnerable parts of the body.

The treatment of battle wounds was based on the corpus of European medical knowledge, which by the time of the Crusades had entered a dark age. The practice of medicine had been supplanted by superstition, wishful thinking, magic formulae, incantations and a belief in miracles. The support of the saints was more important than a diagnosis by the doctor. In the East, the medical canon was a combination of Greco-Arabian medicine and it flourished under scientific enquiry. The physician Ibn Sina, often known by his Latin name Avicenna, produced a medical textbook, *Canon of Medicine*, that for six centuries dominated the medical schools of Asia and Europe.[48]

It would appear that the treatment of Europeans' wounds changed very little from the Greek and Roman therapies. The antiseptic power of wine and vinegar was still the main agent for wound-cleansing. Bandages held lacerated wounds together, and if the wounds were severe, thread, gut or bone sutures were employed. The use of bone suture is interesting. The procedure consisted of inserting parallel rows of bone needles through both edges of the wound then leaving them *in situ* until tissue union occurred. For the treatment of wounds and abscesses, the poultice was a common therapy. The management of burns was predicated on the presence or absence of blistering. The thirteenth-century Italian surgeon Theodorich Borbognoni advocated that wound contamination could be avoided by ensuring that no foreign body was left in the wound, and that rest, medicine and diet were necessary for the successful outcome of wound-healing. Moreover, Arnold of Villanova recommended the topical application of herbs, particularly polygonum, for wound management, and in addition he suggested the oral administration of wine infused with herbs for those weakened by combat or combat injuries. In order to control bleeding, pressure bandages – sponges soaked in vinegar – or cautery were used. When haemorrhage occurred, tourniquets and cautery were considered the best method of control, and cautery was also employed in the treatment of gangrene.[49]

Head injuries were common and medieval surgical texts devote significant sections on how to diagnose and treat skull fractures. A typical procedure involved making a cross-shaped incision in the scalp and retracting the flaps from the bone to get a clear view of any suspected injury. The bone was cleaned, ink was applied to detect any fracture lines as these would appear darker, and in addition, any bleeding was controlled with a hot cautery iron or vinegar on a sponge. If possible, fragments of bone causing damage to the brain were removed, then the wound was dressed. The ancient practice of trepanning was also used in the management of head injuries. There is evidence to suggest that in bone injuries, manipulation was used to treat dislocations and long bone injuries were managed by realignment of the bone, splints or plaster.[50]

While the chroniclers of the time left some very detailed information on the medical management of combat injuries, there is a dearth of information on the battlefield and hospital nursing care of the sick and wounded. Furthermore, the evidence on the outcomes of combat injuries was seldom recorded unless the injuries related to someone of high rank. Additionally, the treatment of battlefield injuries such as spinal fractures remains unclear.

The use of pain-relieving drugs dates back to antiquity and Avicenna's knowledge was immense. In his *Canon* he wrote, 'the most powerful of the stupefacients is opium'. There can be little doubt that the types of injuries sustained in battles or sieges would require strong analgesia, and sedation if surgery were to be carried out. The drugs most in use were opium, henbane, mandrake and hemlock, and ancient texts make reference to inhaling the vapours of bhang for anaesthetic purposes. There is evidence to suggest that during the Crusades the *spongia somnifera*, the sleeping sponge, was used for anaesthetic purposes. Dangerous drugs such as opium and hemlock were mixed with various fruit juices and seeds and boiled into a sponge. The sponge was applied to the nostrils until the patient fell asleep. After surgery was completed, a sponge soaked in vinegar was passed under the nostrils until the patient was awake. This therapy, however, was highly dangerous as the drugs involved had detrimental effects on breathing, and if administered in high quantity could lead to death.[51]

However, there were no healing balms that could treat prejudice, fanaticism and violence. The religious, romantic image of the Crusades is belied by the fact that they were brutal, violent and barbarous affairs. The 'soldiers of God' may have been driven by a religious zeal to secure Christianity in the Holy Land and in the process save their souls, but for some, particularly the European nobles, the prospect of money, land and power was equally seductive. It was the amalgam of religious, commercial, personal and political ambitions that led to blood-letting on an unprecedented scale for the time. As a consequence, the types of institutions needed for the care and treatment of the Crusaders expanded. While the increase led to an expansion in nursing care, there is little evidence to suggest there was an enhancement of skills and reputation among those who nursed. With the exception of women in the religious orders, men carried out most of the nursing care in the hospitals and infirmaries, and on the battlefields. In the eyes of those who chronicled the Crusades, nursing, although vital, must have been regarded as mundane, unremarkable and therefore unworthy of mention. Aristocratic women are well represented in the history of the Crusades and it has been suggested that some established hospitals and infirmaries but the historical evidence is scant and unconvincing. It is said that Eleanor of Aquitaine, who accompanied her husband Louis VII on the Second Crusade, departed for the

Holy Land with a retinue of women voluntarily recruited to nurse the sick and wounded. In 1248, on a Crusade to Egypt, Hersende, a female physician, accompanied King Louis IX but there is no evidence to suggest she did any more than attend to the King. The daughter of King James I of Aragon, Sancia, was said to have established and worked in hospitals in the Holy Land. There are occasional references to women as healers and herbalists. For example, in a lecture given by the Persian physician Rhazes, titled *On the Factors which Alienate the Public from the Physician*, he cites a patient, unhappy with the care he received from a physician, who sought treatment from 'the women and the vulgar'. Additionally, he refers to the fact that he 'learnt remedies from women and herbalists who had no knowledge of medicine'.[52] If there were women who became established as skilled or exceptional nurses, their stories are unrecorded or lost. It is an unfortunate truism that, during the period of the Crusades, women did not write about women; men recorded most of the information. However, the monastic work of the Hospitallers is the main source of information on care-giving during this violent and turbulent period. Substantial evidence on the secular work of nursing pilgrims and Crusaders is yet to be found.

At the time of the Crusades, European medicine had gone into a decline. It was unsophisticated and, for the most part, the medical knowledge acquired from the writings of Hippocrates, Aristotle and Galen was forsaken and replaced by superstition and magic. The science of medical practice was supplanted by the power of charms, amulets, talismans and sacred relics. Great faith was placed in miracles, not medicine. Only in the East were the works of the great men of medicine valued and improved upon. Nonetheless, for many, pilgrimages to the Holy Land were predicated upon healing miracles, redemptive practice and the hope of finding a holy relic. Moreover, entrepreneurship flourished in tandem with religious fervour and guilt, for at the interface profit met penitent, as flasks of Jordan water or earth from the Mount of Olives enjoyed a high trade value. However, it was the long, exacting search for forgiveness, the Papal guarantees of remission of sins and access to Paradise that brought the Crusaders to the Holy Land and into the care of the first recognised military nursing service, the Knights Hospitallers of St John of Jerusalem.

NOTES

1. Lee, E. (1892), *Some Noble Sisters*, London: James Clarke and Company, pp. 126–36.
2. *The Times*, 12 October 1854.
3. Ibid., 13 October 1854.
4. Ibid., 14 October 1854.
5. Stanmore, Lord (1906), *Sidney Herbert, and Lord Herbert of Lea: A Memoir*, London: John Murray, p. 339.
6. Woodham-Smith, C. (1972), *Florence Nightingale*, London: Constable and Company; Strachey, L. (1918), *Eminent Victorians*, London: Chatto and Windus.
7. British Museum, *Nightingale Papers*, vol. CLXIV, p. 27.

8. Carroll, M. (1907), *Woman in all Ages and in all Countries: Greek Women*, Philadelphia: Rittenhouse Press.

9. Ibid., p. 142.

10. Homer, *Iliad*, Book 11.880.

11. Herodotus, *Histories*, Book 3.107.XX.

12. Majno, G. (1982), *The Healing Hand*, Cambridge, MA: Harvard University Press, pp. 197–200.

13. Strauss, B. (2006), *The Trojan War*, New York: Simon and Schuster.

14. Hurd-Mead, K. C. (1938), *A History of Women in Medicine*, Haddam: The Haddam Press, pp. 28–39.

15. Nutting, M. A. and Dock, L. L. (1907), *A History of Nursing*, vol. 1, New York: G. P. Putnam's Sons, pp. 67–81.

16. Cato, R. (1906), 'Hippocrates and the Newly Discovered Temple at Cos', *The British Medical Journal*, 10 March 1906, pp. 571–4; Walbank, M. B. (1981), 'Artemis Bear-Leader', *The Classical Quarterly*, vol. 31, no. 2, pp. 276–81.

17. Majno, pp. 201–3.

18. Nutting and Dock, pp. 79, 80.

19. Nightingale, F. (1969), *Notes on Nursing*, New York: Dover Publications.

20. Gordon, C. A. (1887), *Medicine in Ancient India*, London.

21. Hurd-Mead, p. 16.

22. Edwards, E. B. (1891), *A Thousand Miles Up the Nile*, London: G. Routledge and Sons.

23. Hurd-Mead, pp. 21–3.

24. Majno, p. 84.

25. Ibid., p. 113.

26. Hurd-Mead, pp. 48–50.

27. Barker, P. (2002), 'The Roman Military Valetudinaria: Fact or Fiction?', in R. Arnott (ed.), *The Archaeology of Medicine*, Oxford: British Archaeological Reports, pp. 69–79.

28. Dionysus of Halicarnassus, *The Roman Antiquities*, 9.50.X.

29. Ibid., XIV.10.

30. Livy, *History of Rome*, 10.X.X.

31. Williams, H. S. and Williams, E. H. (1904), *A History of Science*, vol. 1, London: Harper Brothers, p. 227.

32. Barker, P., pp. 69–80.

33. Lane Fox, R. (2005), *The Classical World: An Epic History of Greece and Rome*, London: Penguin Books, p. 301.

34. Robinson, J. H. (ed.) (1904), *Readings in European History*, vol. 1, Boston: Ginn and Co., pp. 312–17.

35. Mills, C. (1820), *History of the Crusade for the Recovery and Possession of the Holy Land*, vol.1, London: Longman, p. 143.

36. Ibid., p. 252.

37. Mitchell, P. D. (2004), *Medicine in the Crusades*, Cambridge: Cambridge University Press, pp. 61–70.

38. Würzburg, J. (1896), *Description of the Holy Land*, vol. 5, London: Palestine Pilgrim Text Society, p. 44.

39. Theodorich (1896), *Description of the Holy Places*, vol. 5, London: Palestine Pilgrim Text Society, p. 22.
40. Gregg, G. (1963), *The State of Medicine at the Time of the Crusades*, Opening Address, Ulster Medical Society, Medical School, Royal Victoria Hospital, Belfast, 10 October 1963; King, E. J. (1934), *The Rules, Statutes and Customs of the Hospitallers 1099–1310*, London: Methuen.
41. Mitchell, pp. 67–8.
42. Bradbury, J. (1994), *The Medieval Siege*, Woodbridge: Boydell Press.
43. William of Tyre, *Historia rerum in partibus transmarinis gestarum*, XIV, 4–5, *Patrologia Latina* 201, 642–5, translated by James Brundage (1962), *The Crusades: A Documentary History*, Milwaukee: Marquette University Press, pp. 79–82.
44. Michaud (ed.) (1829), *Bibliothèque de Croisades*, vol. 111, Paris: Ducollet, pp. 569–75.
45. McVaugh, M. R. (1992), 'Arnold of Villanova's Regimen Almarie (Regimen Castra Sequentium) and Military Medicine', *Viator*, 23, pp. 201–13.
46. Mitchell, P. D., Nagar, Y. and Ellenblum, R. (2006), 'Weapon Injuries in the 12th Century Crusader Garrison of Vadum Iacob Castle, Galilee', *International Journal of Osteoarchaeology*, 16: pp. 145–55.
47. Mitchell, pp. 58–9.
48. Robinson, V. (1931), *The Story of Medicine*, New York: Tudor Publishing Company, pp. 160–5.
49. Mitchell, P. D. (1999), 'The Integration of Palaeopathology and Medical History of the Crusades', *The International Journal of Osteoarchaeology*, 9, pp. 333–43.
50. Ibid. pp. 336–7.
51. Ford, W. W. (1944), 'A Prelude to Anaesthesia', *The New England Journal of Medicine*, vol. 231, no. 6.
52. Robinson, pp. 152–3.

BOOK II

The Wrath of the Gods

We have seen great deaths and strange,
And many a sorrow of unknown shape,
And nothing of these that is not Zeus.

Sophocles

2

Did the Conflict Breed Conflict?
The Politics of Care-giving, 1914

THE CONCEPT OF VOLUNTARY aid in times of war or national crisis started with the formation of the Red Cross in 1863. In Britain, The National Society for Aid to the Sick and Wounded in War was established in 1870; it eventually became the British Red Cross Society (BRCS) in 1905. The St John Ambulance Association was formed in 1877 under the ancient Order of St John of Jerusalem (OStJJ).

In the twelfth century, the Roman Catholic Order of St John brought its mission to England. Under the rule of Henry VIII, the Catholic Order was dissolved but was revived under the Protestant faith in 1831. The Order was given the royal seal of approval in 1888, when Queen Victoria granted the association a Royal Charter. From its roots in the Crusades, the Order of St John developed into a movement that crusaded for and succeeded in creating community voluntary aid schemes and first-aid training, and was responsible for establishing the first ambulance service in Britain. The *raison d'être* of the Association was, 'Promoting and encouraging all that makes for moral and spiritual strengthening of mankind and all works of humanity and charity for the relief of persons in sickness, distress, suffering and danger without distinction of race, class or creed.'[1]

On 16 April 1913, a conference was held for Nursing Officers of the St John's Ambulance Brigade and the Territorial Branch of the St John's Ambulance Association. With the permission of Colonel Sir Herbert Jekyll, Chancellor of the Order of the Hospital of St John of Jerusalem in England, the conference was hosted in the Chapter Hall of the Order located at St John's Gate, Clerkenwell, London.

In attendance were the great and the good of the Ambulance Brigades and Voluntary Aid Detachments, including Dr James Cantlie, a highly respected physician and a tireless advocate for teaching and the implementation of first-aid programmes in Britain. Also invited were nursing representatives from the War Office, Ethel Hope Becher, Matron-in-Chief of the Queen Alexandra's Imperial Military Nursing Service, and Principal Matron Maud McCarthy (QAIMNS). The conference was chaired by Lady Perrott, Superintendent-in-Chief of the St John's Ambulance Brigade and a pioneer of voluntary aid. In her welcome speech and introductory remarks Lady Perrott acknowledged the presence of the Matron-in-Chief: 'Miss Becher has shown her interest in our work and has

kindly come here today and in so doing has given us great pleasure and encouragement.' Then, in a somewhat prophetic comment, Lady Perrott added, 'I feel
these are anxious days and no one knows when we may be called upon to serve
our country.' She then proceeded to address issues on training for the Brigade
and Voluntary Aid Detachments, as well as commenting on uniforms, discipline
and *esprit de corps*. On the latter she said, 'Germany always sets us an example
with their devotion to the Fatherland, and hence their success, and we need the
same in the Order of St John.'[2]

Lady Perrott did not have long to wait. By the summer of 1914 the country
was heading for war and the spirit of cooperation between the regular and
volunteer nursing services and the War Office would be sorely tried and tested.

On 5 August 1914, *The Times* carried the headline 'War Declared'.[3]

After weeks of political brinkmanship trying to avert a war in Europe, on 4
August the British Foreign Secretary, Sir Edward Grey, had delivered an ulti-
matum to Germany which demanded its termination of military action against
neutral Belgium or face war with Britain. On the same day, newspapers were
already predicting the outcome of the faltering negotiations. *The Daily Mail*
editorial stated:

> The shadow of an immense catastrophe broods over Europe today. All hope of peace
> has disappeared with a crash ... Our duty is to go forward into the valley of the
> shadow of death with courage and faith – with courage to suffer, with faith in our
> God and country.[4]

According to *The Times*, the position in Europe was 'one of breathless antici-
pation of the beginning of hostilities on a large scale. France and Russia await
with evident anxiety the decision of Great Britain as to her attitude towards the
crisis.'[5] *The Daily News*, which had been so adamant that Britain should not be
embroiled in a European war, had to concede: 'Let us fight, if we must, without
bitterness and without malice, so that when the tragedy is over we may make
an honourable peace.'[6] Scotland's national newspaper, *The Scotsman*, predicted
that stoicism would prevail: 'At any moment Great Britain may be at war with
the German Powers. Her people will accept this destiny with quiet and enduring
courage.'[7]

Following days of newspaper speculation, and the declaration of hostilities
finally announced, the nursing press responded. *The Nursing Times* editorial pro-
phetically lamented, 'What was nominally a quarrel between Austria and Serbia
has led to a European Armageddon', and predicted, 'The conflict will be terrible,
and every soldier will be required for fighting and every nurse for the care of the
wounded.' In a spirit of patriotism and professional determination, it concluded,
'The call has come and the nurses are ready.'[8] Its rival, *The British Journal of
Nursing*, arguably the most politically astute within the nursing press, declared:

> The call to arms which has reverberated through this country with such sudden
> urgency since our last issue has its echo in the equally urgent call to trained nurses to
> be prepared to respond to any summons to place their services at the disposal of the

sick and wounded ... There is probably not a woman in the country who does not desire to place her services at its disposal, and time will show the many ways in which women's work can be utilised, but, in the supreme care of the moment, the provision for the sick and wounded, it is to trained nurses the call is made.[9]

The emphasis of the editorial was on 'trained nurses' – not 'volunteers' – caring for the casualties. Within the first few days of war being declared, however, the drama and excitement of the evolving situation led to women from a variety of social backgrounds, many with little or no nursing experience, volunteering to nurse the anticipated casualties within the British Expeditionary Force (BEF). Nursing in peacetime was rarely exciting and the day-to-day ministrations of caring for the sick and injured brought little financial reward or public recognition. Despite the exigencies of war, the civilian nurse leadership feared that the consequences of supplementing the military and civilian professional nursing services with volunteer nurses could be a diminution of skill and perhaps unemployment for nurses post-war. Wider political concerns were also expressed. Prior to the outbreak of the First World War, key figures within the nursing leadership and many trained nurses were active suffragists. The nurse campaigners combined their demands for professional recognition with the right to vote and many trained nurses felt that the long-delayed Nurse Registration Bill could be prejudiced by increasing the numbers of semi-skilled or unskilled nurses within the ranks of the profession. They also believed that volunteer nurses from aristocratic and privileged backgrounds could not identify with the needs of professional middle-class women; the 'ladies of position' who ran the local and regional Voluntary Aid Detachments and sat on the National Committees were ardent anti-feminists and their political aspirations, or perhaps the lack of such aspirations, were a complete antithesis to the expectations and demands of the trained nurses seeking professional recognition as well as economic and political liberation. It was not surprising, therefore, that trained nurses expressed concerns about volunteers whose motives for nursing were founded simply in wartime altruism. The whole system of nurse practice and training left the public, including nurses themselves, in a state of confusion. There was no easy way to distinguish between the training, quality and calibre of women who claimed to be nurses. The outbreak of war made a bad situation worse.[10]

Notwithstanding the professional anxieties, *The Nursing Mirror and Midwives' Journal* took a more balanced view of the situation and advised trained nurses and potential volunteers not to get carried away with the excitement of the war fever gripping the country. It also urged caution against gossip and the reliability of the press, advising that nurses should not become 'bewildered by the strife of tongues, the unreliability of news or demoralised by the contradictory reports of victories or defeats'.[11]

However, particular groups of professional nurses were called upon to mobilise for war service: these were the Queen Alexandra's Imperial Military Nursing Service (QAIMNS), Queen Alexandra's Imperial Military Nursing

Service (Reserve) (QAIMNSR), Queen Alexandra's Royal Naval Nursing Service (QARNNS) and the Territorial Force Nursing Service (TFNS). Within days of the outbreak of hostilities, representatives of the military and civilian nursing services were summoned to the War Office.

The War Office: for some, the name evoked thoughts of great men and stirring deeds; for many, it was an institution steeped in the traditions of incompetence, idleness and intransigence. It was a department of the British Government responsible for the administration of the army, and its formation dated back to the seventeenth century. During the Crimean War, a Colonel Lefroy, whose impressive title was Confidential Adviser to the Secretary of War on Scientific Matters, described the War Office as:

> A rickety clumsy machine, with a pin loose here and a tooth broken there and a make-shift somewhere else, in which the forces of Hercules may be exhausted in a needless friction before the hands are got to move, so in our Executive, with the Treasury, the Horse Guards, the War Department, the Medical Department, all out of gear, but required to move together before a result can be attained.[12]

Years after the conflicts in the Crimea, Egypt and the Sudan, and the war in South Africa, little if anything had changed in the methods or psychology of the War Office. It appeared the effectiveness of the bureaucratic war machine was still undermined by persistent clashes between civil servants and the military authorities. The problems were long-standing and Sidney Herbert, appointed Secretary at War in 1852, complained that War Office mandarins possessed a capacity for 'spoiling, interfering and delaying', with their favourite method apparently being 'excessive minuting'. This was evidenced by the fact that, in one particular case, it took seventeen months and one very large file of minutes to decide on matters relating to the welfare of the War Office cat.[13] There was an excessive, some might have thought ridiculous, number of memoranda, such as one issued in 1913 instructing personnel to desist from repairing army type-writers: 'No person or persons are authorised to do any repairs whatsoever to HM typewriters unless specially asked to do so, as much inconvenience has been caused to the British Army through voluntary effort.' But a year later it was widespread voluntary effort that would sustain the war effort.

However, some of the memos relating to the nursing service bordered on the absurd and on one occasion a memorandum was discussed in parliament. Apparently, members of the Imperial Nursing Service were issued with instructions forbidding them to attend dances in the stations they belonged to, and if they did attend, they were not allowed to dance. If they disobeyed the Order, they would forfeit two months towards promotion. In the House of Commons, Colonel John Seely, Liberal MP, confirmed, 'Dancing is prohibited for the members of Queen Alexandra's Imperial Nursing Service except when on leave of absence and away from their stations. This Order was issued two years ago, and copies were duly distributed.' In a tongue-in-cheek response, Captain Faber MP enquired, 'Will the right hon. Gentleman state whether that Order was issued on account of the "Turkey Trot" or the "Bunny Hug"?' Colonel Seely was unimpressed: 'No, Sir. I do not think so, because the Order was issued two years ago when these dances were, fortunately, not invented.'[14]

However, despite some of the strange directives that emanated from the War Office, its edifice belied the internal machinations, absurdities and strife. Located on Horse Guards Avenue in Whitehall, the magnificent neo-Baroque building had a thousand rooms across seven floors, linked by two and a half miles of corridors. It had taken five years to build at a cost of £1.2 million. The structure was trapezium in shape with four distinctive domes, designed more for ornamentation than function; a description that equally could have applied to the War Office.

In this great structure on 9 August 1914, representatives from the military and civilian nursing services congregated in the office of Ethel Hope Becher, Matron-in-Chief of the Queen Alexandra's Imperial Military Nursing Service, and awaited their mobilisation orders. According to Maud McCarthy, Principal Matron at the War Office, after waiting all day for news, the message was delivered to the women in the evening by a Staff Officer. Upon entering the office of the Matron-in-Chief, he expressed the nurses' orders in two words: 'Carry on.'[15]

The mobilisation was implemented under the direction of Ethel Hope Becher. Described as formidable, Ethel Becher was tall, stately, graceful and possessed a strong, resourceful character. The daughter of Colonel Arthur William Reddie Becher, a cavalry officer in the Indian Army, and granddaughter of General Sir Arthur Mitford Becher, she was well schooled in the ways of the army. Privately educated, she subsequently trained as a nurse at the London Hospital. The Matron there, Eva Luckes, equally formidable, described Ethel Hope Becher as 'exceptionally capable' and noted that as a Ward Sister she managed her wards with 'marked ability, and kept them and her subordinates in excellent order'. Furthermore, Eva Luckes observed, 'She was such a smart Sister in many respects that some people were inclined to doubt whether the comfort and happiness of her patients were not occasionally sacrificed for the sake of the appearance of her wards', although those serving under her were never of that opinion for she was well respected as a nurse and manager. However, there was a part of Ethel Becher's disposition which did concern the Matron of the London Hospital, and she noted this in a confidential file:

> EHB has a very excitable temperament, and was occasionally subject to outbursts of temper and lack of self-control that was much to be deplored. Her manners were somewhat abrupt and occasionally unpleasant enough to do the better side of her nature much injustice. On one occasion I felt it right to speak to EHB very seriously on her occasional lack of self-control, pointing out the bad example it afforded to those working under her, and how this weakness detracted from her unquestionable gifts, both as a nurse and ward manager. She was very hurt and indignant at the time but there was a marked improvement from that time onward.[16]

In 1899, a month after the start of the war in South Africa, when Ethel Becher applied for a position in the Army Nursing Service Reserve, concerns about her temperament were put aside, for, in a letter of reference, Eva Luckes wrote that she had 'great faith in her organising skills and her unwavering steadfastness of purpose'.

Moreover, Luckes predicted that when Ethel Becher gained experience of army nursing, and acquired knowledge from the expedition to South Africa, she could 'scarcely imagine anyone better qualified to suggest suitable reforms in the Army Nursing Service if the opportunity for introducing much needed improvements should ultimately occur in connection with war nursing in the South African War'.[17]

Following her nursing experiences in South Africa, Ethel Becher decided to make a career in the Army Nursing Service. It was a wise decision; by 1910 she had become the third holder of the much-coveted position of Matron-in-Chief of the Queen Alexandra's Imperial Military Nursing Service.

When war broke out in August 1914, Ethel Becher had been within a month of retiral and it was anticipated that Maud McCarthy, Principal Matron at the War Office, would be her successor. However, civil members of the Nursing Board had suggested that for reasons of continuity and experience Ethel Becher should remain in post for the duration of the War. In some quarters the proposal was most unwelcome, with supporters of Maud McCarthy agitating for a change of leadership. Earlier in 1914, an attempt had been made by civil members of the Board to grant an extension to Ethel Becher's term in office. The Nursing Board minutes raised several concerns explaining why, at that time, it would be unwise to lose such an experienced Matron-in-Chief. Their main concern was the suitability of a particular candidate to hold a senior nursing position in the War Office. Additionally, they claimed continuity between the Nursing Board and the Matron-in-Chief, Director General and Deputy Director General was necessary when new personnel were about to be appointed into those senior nursing and medical administrative posts. It is clear the arguments were not based solely on administrative concerns, but were influenced by the politics of preference for a new Matron-in-Chief. The Nursing Board minutes stated:

> In the event of Miss McCarthy the Principal Matron now at Head-Quarters being selected to succeed Miss Becher, it would be necessary to bring Principal Matron, Miss Oram, home from South Africa, a lady considered quite unfit to succeed Miss McCarthy. The majority of Civil Members of the Board being comparatively recent appointments, it would be awkward changing the Matron-in-Chief at a time when a new Director General and Deputy Director General of the Army Medical Services were about to come into office. Miss Becher had shown exceptional ability and administrative capacity during her term in office. The Director General designate, Surgeon General Sloggett, who, it is understood, has expressed himself as opposed to Miss Becher's extension and in favour of Miss McCarthy being selected to succeed her, can know but little of either of these ladies.[18]

The outgoing Director General of the Army Medical Services and Chairman of the Army Nursing Board, Sir Launcelotte Gubbins, was not impressed with the arguments. Responding in a firm written response to the Board's deliberations, he wrote:

> I dissent from their recommendations on the following grounds. There would be no intention of bringing Miss Oram home from South Africa; she is due to retire next year and I entirely agree that she is unfit for employment at Head-Quarters. The majority of Civil Members of the Board have had considerable experience on the Board … and the Nursing Service has been so well organised that it is now a going concern, and there would be no difficulty in carrying on even if the executive were entirely new. I do not agree that Miss Becher has shown exceptional ability or administrative capacity, and of this I think the Director General under whom she immediately served for the past four years ought to be a better judge than the civil members who are only brought in contact with her at Board or Sub-committee meetings.[19]

Additionally, he cited the fact that when it was proposed that Miss Sidney Browne, first Matron-in-Chief of the Queen Alexandra's Imperial Military Nursing Service, should have her term of office extended, it had been agreed then by the Nursing Board that it would be 'inexpedient to create a precedent for the extension to 5 years of the tenure of future Matrons-in-Chief'. He also commented that 'The post of Matron-in Chief is the one prize in the Nursing Service; it is much sought after and to debar a deserving member, even for a year, would be felt as a hardship.' His arguments concluded:

> The alternative to Miss Becher's extension and passed by unanimous resolution of the Board, namely the recommendation of Miss McCarthy and Miss Wilson for the post of Matron-in-Chief and Principal Matron, respectively, will provide a staff at Head Quarters of two exceedingly capable and level headed administrators, and I have not the slightest fear of the future of the Nursing Service in their hands.[20]

Despite Miss McCarthy and Miss Wilson being informed by the Secretary of State that they were successful in their respective promotions, to the consternation of Sir Launcelotte Gubbins the Nursing Board referred the matter back to the Secretary of State for War, stating:

> They [the Nursing Board] consider this extension of the Matron in Chief's term of office essential for the proper carrying on of the work, especially so, as there is to be a new Director General and a new assistant Director General neither of whom know anything of the work. This is a matter on which the signatories are entitled to give an opinion, and one about which, in all its aspects, they feel competent to judge.[21]

The Nursing Board requested that Ethel Becher's contract be extended by one year; the Secretary of State in consultation with the Director General granted an extension until September 1914. With the outbreak of war in August, Ethel Becher was retained as Matron-in-Chief.

One week into the conflict, working from room 360 at the War Office and assisted by a small cadre of military and civilian support staff, Ethel Becher set about organising the nurses' contribution. In *The Nursing Mirror and Midwives' Journal*, the news of her extension of service was welcomed:

> The retirement of Miss E. H. Becher, RRC from the office of Matron-in-Chief of Queen Alexandra's Imperial Military Nursing Service was to have taken effect next week. But in consequence of the war she will continue in her present appointment ... It is very satisfactory that Miss Becher's experience and knowledge are to be at the disposal of the country during a period when they cannot fail to be of special value.[22]

As a consequence of Ethel Becher's extended term in office, Maud McCarthy, Matron-in-Chief designate, was appointed Principal Matron on the Lines of Communication (LOC), British Expeditionary Force, France and Flanders.

Maud McCarthy was born in Australia, the daughter of a solicitor, and the eldest of eighteen children. She was privately educated at Springfield College, Sydney. By 1891 she was living in England, and at the age of twenty-eight entered the London Hospital to begin general nurse training. Eva Luckes described her as having an 'exceptionally nice disposition and was essentially a lady ... She brought excellent qualities with her for training.' Even so, despite being a model nurse, Eva Luckes had concerns about Maud McCarthy's ability to manage people, stating:

> She needed more force of character; she found it hard to control others, or take firm action when necessary. However, she was too conscientious not to endeavour earnestly to do her duty. Her nature was sweet, and therefore she was easy to help; but she needed more moral courage.[23]

At the outbreak of the war in South Africa, Maud McCarthy, Ethel Becher and four other nurses from the London Hospital were chosen by the Princess of Wales to go to South Africa under the prestigious title of 'Specially Appointed Nurses'. It required strength of character to nurse in the South Africa War, and despite Eva Luckes' concerns about Maud McCarthy's 'moral courage', the concern proved to be misplaced. Throughout the conflict she gained a reputation as a first-class nurse. During Maud McCarthy's time in South Africa, while convalescing after contracting enteric fever, a surgeon who admired her nursing skills sent a stretcher and ambulance party to collect her and bring her to his hospital. His motives were not solely altruistic; he wanted Maud McCarthy to join his hospital staff once she had fully recovered from her illness. After the war she joined the newly formed Queen Alexandra's Imperial Military Nursing Service and went on to become a Matron. In 1910 she became Principal Matron at the War Office, where Ethel Becher was serving as Matron-in-Chief.[24]

On many occasions the lives of the two women crossed at the intersection of nursing practice and administration. However, it was to be their respective wartime roles within the Queen Alexandra's Imperial Military Nursing Service that ultimately defined the relationship and established their reputations.

On 12 August 1914, Maud McCarthy was instructed to report to the Officer in Charge, No. 2 General Hospital at Aldershot, and on the following day she travelled to Southampton with some of the hospital staff. At midnight she, along with the full complement of staff of No. 2 General Hospital, boarded the steamer

Comrie Castle bound for Le Havre. According to her War Diary, at 1 a.m. on 15 August she 'left Southampton on a crowded boat with many Staff Officers on board including Generals Grierson and Haig'. The contingent arrived in Le Havre on the afternoon of 15 August and Maud McCarthy reported to the office of the Deputy Director of Medical Services (DDMS), Surgeon General Woodhouse, only to be informed that he was not available, and she was not expected. It was on the following day she met the DDMS and was instructed to establish her headquarters at Rouen.[25]

Her first duty – to establish suitable accommodation for the nurses arriving from Britain and Ireland – proved to be very problematic. The billeting and transport arrangements for the nursing contingents with the 12 Stationary and 13 General hospitals were deficient and in some cases totally inadequate, particularly the accommodation, bathing and laundry facilities. In carefully chosen words, and understating the problems for the nurses, Maud McCarthy wrote in her War Diary on 26 August:

> After some difficulty billeted all nursing staffs of 4, 6, 9, 11 and 12 [hospitals] in suitable surroundings. 9, 11 and 12 in convents; others in various houses, those in the convents messed there, the others, arrangements were made at the nearest hotels.[26]

The reality of the situation was expressed somewhat differently by some of the nurses. When Sister Kate Haywood (QAIMNSR) landed in France on 18 August, Maud McCarthy met her unit but informed them of the lack of transport available to take them to their accommodation:

> She only had one taxi for the lot of us … we were taken off in sixes … We were billeted in a school for girls … here we found also the staffs of no less than six other hospitals who had landed before us, and had not been allowed to proceed to their destined places.[27]

The Convent School de St Jeanne d'Arc was the main facility used to accommodate the arriving nurses. Sister Jean Todd (QAIMNSR), attached to No. 9 General Hospital, reinforced the problems nurses faced when travelling to France:

> The voyage to France, the best thing that can be said of that is it's over and done with. 'Twas a cattle boat, no accommodation whatever for passengers! A division was erected, Medical Officers, NCOs and orderlies on one side, Matron and her 42 Sisters and Staff Nurses on the other. Our heavy baggage was in a hold so there was no hope of a camp bed or blankets.[28]

When Sister Todd's unit arrived at Le Havre, Maud McCarthy boarded the ship and greeted the nurses with the unwelcome news that no accommodation could be found and they would have to 'stay where they were'. The nurses were eventually billeted in the convent, with eleven of them sharing a schoolroom. On arriving at Le Havre from Dublin, Sister K. E. Luard (QAIMNSR), attached to No. 1 General Hospital and a veteran of the South African War, was more philosophical about the arrangements, and in a letter to her family explained:

We went off in a taxi in batches of five to the Convent de St Jeanne d'Arc. About 130 of us are camping out in a huge very comparatively clean empty convent school. No furniture, no food so we are billeted at a hotel for food. We have not slept on a bed since arriving and live a distinctively simple life separated from our baggage.[29]

In the same unit as Kate Luard was Sister Mary Blair, also QAIMNSR. She eventually found mattresses in the convent but discovered that she was one of four in a bedroom:

We slept on mattresses on the floor, and were only allowed hand luggage and told to hold ourselves in readiness to move at 20 minutes' notice at any time. We were there a fortnight! We had funny experiences trying to keep clean; there were no baths and very little water in the convent.[30]

For Staff Nurse Millicent Bruce Peterkin (QAIMNSR) the long trip from Scotland to France was made worse when, on arrival at Le Havre, her unit was informed there was no transport available to take them to the convent. The nurses spent an extra night on board the ship, and that meant a second night of sleeping on the ship's deck. According to Millicent, it was a very cold night with thick fog, 'the deck of the ship was soaking wet, and everyone was very tired and miserable'. As their entire luggage was packed away, there were few comforts available to make the nurses' situation easier. The following morning her unit disembarked and were driven in an Army Service Corps (ASC) wagon to the convent. With the arrival of so many nursing units and very little suitable accommodation for the women, what was available proved to be less than ideal. The young nurse from Edinburgh was not impressed: 'we were given three rooms, one large and two small, with a small balcony ... two in one small room, twelve in other, seventeen in large room and five on balcony'.[31]

For the nurses, problems with billeting and messing arrangements were aggravated by the lack of information; no one could tell them what was happening, or when and where their Stationary and General Hospitals would be established. When Kate Luard arrived at Le Havre on 20 August her expectations of No. 1 General Hospital being immediately established for the admission of casualties were not realised. Two weeks after her arrival in France she expressed frustration at having no work to do except 'fatigue duty'. The lack of activity led her and many other nurses to wonder where the casualties were that they had been sent out to care for, and when their units would be ready to receive them.

In the early weeks of the War, the medical and nursing arrangements lacked cohesion. On the Lines of Communication (LOC) experienced medical and nursing staff were not being used to full advantage and whole medical units had been stood down since their arrival. At one point there were so many under-utilised medical units in France that the Director of Medical Services, Surgeon General Woodhouse, wrote a letter of complaint to Sir Arthur Sloggett, the Director General at the War Office:

We have more unwieldy units at our disposal than we can use. We may send home, to be kept in reserve, three General and four Stationary Hospitals. We have nowhere to park them out here and the billeting of hundreds of sisters causes a great nuisance.[32]

For the nurses awaiting information on the location and establishment of their hospitals, the frustration was aggravated by unconfirmed reports which suggested that voluntary medical and nursing units had arrived in France and Belgium and were caring for the sick and wounded. Furthermore, these volunteers were apparently working without responsible control or direction from the War Office. Under the terms of the Geneva Convention, voluntary medical units were legally obliged to work with the permission of the Army Council and to come under the orders of the military authorities. Moreover, they were legally required to conform to the constitution, personnel and equipment of army medical units. Also, the volunteers only had jurisdiction if the Commander-in-Chief deemed their incorporation into army medical units necessary, and for whatever purpose he saw fit. This was not the situation at the beginning of the campaigns in France and Flanders.

The official voluntary services – The British Red Cross Society (BRCS) and The Order of St John of Jerusalem (OStJJ) – along with hundreds of unofficial volunteer units, created serious problems for the army administration of the medical and nursing services. The voluntary units were, in effect, going it alone and in the process were breaching international conventions and agreements. The problems for the BRCS were partially brought about by the limitations created by its constitution, for it failed to recognise that, unlike during peace-time activities, in times of war the BRCS had a legal duty to cooperate with the army medical services and other voluntary aid organisations. The stated function of the BRCS in wartime was to offer assistance to the Army Council by way of finance, goods, services and personnel in support of the sick and wounded.[33]

The War Office was not without its share of the blame, for it was culpable in creating the confusion that existed in and between itself and voluntary organisations. In its time-honoured position of intransigence, the War Office had failed to establish what voluntary organisations were capable of contributing and this, embarrassingly, led to duplication of effort. Inevitably, administrative failures between the voluntary organisations and the War Office led to un-coordinated responses in supplying personnel, facilities and goods for the comfort of the troops on the fighting front. Additionally, plans made by voluntary organisations to incorporate volunteer nurses into the care of casualties produced tensions, rivalry and animosity between trained nurses and unskilled volunteers. According to the *Nursing Times*, 50,000 women in London alone were said to have offered their services as 'nurses'.[34]

At the outbreak of war, *The British Journal of Nursing* raised concerns regarding untrained women caring for the sick and wounded and, within weeks, it felt compelled to raise the issue again:

In the grim struggle now proceeding on the battle fields of Europe thousands of brave men must of necessity be stricken down, of whom many will be cared for in hospitals at home or abroad … It is therefore a grave national duty not only that fully trained and experienced nurses should be provided to nurse our sick and wounded troops at home and abroad in sufficient numbers but also that unauthorised nurses should be prevented from proceeding to the seat of war and monopolising places which should be filled by those whose qualifications have been examined and tested.[35]

This was the firm opinion of the irrepressible Ethel Bedford Fenwick, Editor of the *BJN*, a nurse and long-time lobbyist for the State Registration of Trained Nurses. She was also the founder of the Royal British Nurses Association and founder and first President of the International Council of Nurses, and of the National Council of Nurses of Great Britain. Ethel Bedford Fenwick was concerned that, by using untrained nurses, the reputation of trained nurses could be damaged and their political aspirations hampered, and also that the implementation of State Registration could be threatened. Rumours were rife in the national and nursing press regarding the number of untrained nurses from Britain working in Belgian hospitals and voluntary units. One observer claimed, 'All Brussels is truly transformed into one immense ambulance.' It was alleged that in Brussels, 'too many unofficial nurses' had arrived in the city and the work of the authorised and well-equipped organisations was being hindered.[36]

Furthermore, it was claimed the War Office had insufficient numbers of military nurses working at the fighting front and that soldiers were dying for want of care from suitably trained nurses. Also, because of the alleged shortage of trained nurses, there was talk of trained nurses from Australia arriving in France to assist with casualty care. However, the reality of the Australian situation was quite different from the perception. The War Office had commissioned the help of two voluntary hospitals, The Duchess of Westminster's and the Countess of Dudley's, which under the auspices of the BRCS had been organised by committees in England. The facts about the voluntary hospitals and the volunteer nurses were known to Maud McCarthy, for she had personally been requested by Sir Alfred Keogh, Chief Commissioner for the BRCS in France and ex-Director General of the Army Medical Services, to 'choose sheets' for Lady Dudley's hospital.[37]

Eleven trained nurses from Australia, who had volunteered their services to the War Office at the outbreak of the War, staffed that hospital. Resentment against voluntary units was inevitable: while the Director of Medical Services in France was complaining to the Director General at the War Office in London that too many General and Stationary Hospitals had been sent out, and were being stood down through lack of work, the War Office was simultaneously recruiting voluntary hospitals to meet the demand of casualty care. In the opening weeks of the conflict, private ambulances as well as medical and nursing units not attached to any particular service or organisation, left Britain for the fighting front. In the eyes of the civilian nursing leadership, the recruitment, management and deployment of volunteer nurses for employment in overseas and home-based hospitals was in urgent need of appraisal. Where, they wondered, was there a leader within the ranks of the military or civilian nurses who was strong enough to tackle the War Office, and the voluntary organisations, on the contentious issues of voluntary nurses and nurse recruitment?

On the fighting front, at Mons in Belgium on 23 August, the first major engagement between the British Expeditionary Force (BEF) and the German armies took place. The BEF, greatly outnumbered, fought for seven hours before the order to retire was given. The evacuation line established for the casualties of Mons and the ensuing retreat was initially through Amiens and Rouen, but confusion and the quantity of numbers hampered the effectiveness of the plan. Amiens was congested with refugees and also with soldiers of the British, French and Belgian armies who were passing through on troop trains or who were temporarily billeted in the city. Caught up in the chaos of the retreat were Field Ambulances, Clearing Hospitals, Stationary and General Hospitals, Ambulance Trains and voluntary units. Sister Annie Reay, who worked in Lady Dudley's Hospital, claimed there was insufficient equipment and supplies to cope with the casualties from Mons. She also said 'food was in short supply and staff insufficient', and the evacuation of the wounded was impeded by the refugees. The staff from the hospital had 'four days and nights with the minimum of sleep and no water for washing was available'.[38] At the fighting front there was a desperate shortage of appropriate transportation for the removal of the sick and wounded. Sister Mary McLean Loughran (QAIMNS), who was assigned to the evacuation of patients by train, claimed, 'the trains were often cattle trucks. Danger was very great and train lines were likely targets.' On one occasion she was present when a shell destroyed one of the carriages and killed and wounded a number of patients and staff.[39]

The crude nature of the transportation for the sick and wounded was reinforced by Sister Evelyn Killery (QAIMNS), also a regular and working at No. 7 General Hospital, Amiens.

> We were taking in large convoys of wounded from Mons. The lighter cases went straight to the Ports and we only dealt with the more serious ones who were unable to travel so far. At the end of three weeks we were compelled to leave as the Germans were advancing, so we got the only available transport, which was cattle trucks and brought our patients to Havre. Many of them had been very seriously wounded in the chest and head but everyone did their utmost to make the long journey as easy as possible for them.[40]

Such was the speed of the retreat that the staff of No. 7 had to leave all their equipment and personal belongings in the charge of the Mother Superior of the convent where the hospital had been established. Millicent Peterkin, who was working at No. 9 General Hospital, was deployed to nurse the casualties from Mons and saw first hand the results of the rapid retreat:

> About 5 p.m. a train from Amiens passed through bound for Le Havre, loaded with refugees and wounded British soldiers. The latter were laying eight or nine in each truck, and in beside each lot were two sisters from No. 7 General Hospital. They

had to fly from Amiens, abandoning 700 beds, all their tents and equipment, and all personal belongings, having nothing but what they stood in.[41]

At Rouen, on 28 August, Maud McCarthy noted: 'Troops returning from Amiens also many of the staff. Surgeon General Woodhouse spoke to me of the good work done by 7 General Hospital, 16 nursing staff of No. 7 hospital arrived, I went on with some patients to Le Havre.'[42] Within two days of her diary entry all hospitals on the LOC, including Rouen and Le Havre, had been ordered to pack up and were eventually re-established at Le Mans, Nantes, St Nazaire and Angers. Surgeon General Woodhouse probably expressed the sentiments of many of the medical and nursing staff caught up in the retreat: 'Imagine our plight … no preliminary reconnaissance of new bases was possible. Sick and wounded continued to arrive. One general hospital was hurriedly established at Nantes and a stationary and two clearing hospitals were established at Le Mans.'[43]

By 5 September no further hospitals had opened at the new bases, yet the casualties continued to arrive. The Hôtel Trianon Palace at Versailles was established as a receiving hospital for the casualties from Mons. Sister Adelina Walker said the makeshift hospital was:

> Full of terribly wounded men, dying of gas gangrene and tetanus … it was a curious sight, almost unbelievable, the brightly lighted hall, scarlet carpeted stairs, stretcher after stretcher was being carried in with wounded men caked in mud and blood, some of whom had lain out for days before they could be got in. Beautiful bedrooms were filled with hospital beds all full, and in the spaces between the beds were men lying on stretchers, down the corridors, everywhere where there was room. What a night it was.[44]

While hospital units struggled to establish themselves for the arrival of the sick and wounded, the casualty evacuation and transportation system from the fighting front on the LOC was outdated, crude and makeshift. The removal of casualties from the fighting line was carried out by the horse-drawn ambulance wagons of the Field Ambulances (FA). There were no motor ambulances available in the early months of the war. The system was cumbersome and difficult, and traumatic for the casualties and the horses. The ambulance wagons were not designed for the poor terrain they had to travel across, which was extensively damaged from shelling and bad weather. The journey for the casualties was long, uncomfortable and, for the badly wounded, extremely painful; the lack of appropriate suspension in the wagons meant that every jolt and bump was felt in the broken bones and torn flesh of the human cargo. The horses, too, suffered badly for they were worn out and exhausted by continually journeying between aid stations. Many lost their shoes and this caused considerable problems, particularly when they travelled on excessively muddy, rough and rain-drenched roads. Despite the extensive use of horse-drawn ambulance wagons, there were no farriers attached to the FAs and, sadly, much-needed veterinary supplies and equipment for the care and welfare of the horses were lost during the retreat from Mons.[45]

Figure 2.1 A Red Cross horse-drawn ambulance used at the start of the War because motorised ambulances were not available. National Library of Scotland.

From the Battle of Mons in August and the tragedy of the retreat, to the advance on the Marne in September, the reality of the military situation and the deficiencies in the medical arrangements became all too obvious. This was a different type of warfare, for it was being fought with weapons that had undergone extensive scientific and technological developments since the war in South Africa, and those innovations killed and maimed on an industrial scale. In the early months of the war there was very little understanding of the complex wounds the new weaponry inflicted on the human body. The situation presented new and demanding challenges for the medical and nursing services and the army medical administration at the front. If casualties were to survive devastating injuries or chronic illness, an effective system of collection, transportation and evacuation needed to be established. Equally, the plan had to include immediate and ongoing medical intervention and skilled nursing care at appropriate treatment facilities. Furthermore, research facilities to expeditiously investigate traumatic wounding, infections and diseases had to be established in or around hospitals at the front. For all that, *The Lancet* believed casualty care arrangements to be relatively uncomplicated and wrote with all the enthusiasm of blind ignorance:

> British and French armies have made every attempt to send cases from field-dressing
> stations as rapidly as possible to large base hospitals, which have been prepared in,

and among other places, Paris, Rouen and Dieppe. Now base hospitals are arranged presumably in a place out of the sphere of the enemy's activities, and here the arrangements can be made with deliberations and can be thought out beforehand. Although they are of course dependent in a secondary manner on the course of the war, there should not be any reason to alter them from day to day or hour to hour. As long as the lines of communication are preserved the transport of the wounded by train, lorry, or in some cases, water, should proceed systematically; the treatment at the hospital should be scientific and thorough, the nursing and feeding arrangements should be ample, the arrangements for passing the convalescent patients out, so as to make room for new patients, should work well, the horrors of infection should be expected and dealt with.[46]

For those working at the front, their experiences of the transportation and treatment of casualties were not as prescriptive as *The Lancet*'s naive belief. As the war rumbled on, so did the trains, with their makeshift arrangements for casualty evacuation. The train was seen as the quickest and most effective way of removing the sick and wounded on the LOC. In the early months of the War no proper Ambulance Trains were available for the removal of casualties, and the medical services were dependent on the rolling stock of the French railway system. The casualties were transported in carriages, merchandise wagons, luggage vans, covered trucks and horse boxes. However, due to the ingenuity of the officers and men of the Royal Army Medical Corps (RAMC), the wagons and coaches of the French rolling stock were turned into makeshift Ambulance Trains. The wagons were divided, partitioned, scrubbed, disinfected and fitted with iron apparatus known as 'The Brechot Apparatus'. Each set supported three stretchers and there were four sets to each wagon. While the stretcher equipment for Ambulance Trains came from Britain, in France there were problems obtaining from the Army Ordnance Department (AOD) supplies much needed for patient care, comfort and feeding. Sister Reid (QAIMNSR) and fluent French speaker, who, unusually for a woman at that time, and in a war situation, was charged with liaising with the French railway authorities, claimed that 'great difficulty was experienced in obtaining the hundreds of medical articles, blankets, reserve stretchers, pails, jugs, basins, camp stoves, etc., so essential for the requirements of large numbers of patients'. However, the problems were temporarily overcome by purchasing all the equipment locally when a senior officer instructed her to purchase whatever was necessary, where she could, and debit the account to the Government.[47]

While obtaining the necessary equipment was difficult, the makeshift nature of the Ambulance Trains made it almost impossible, even dangerous, to deliver nursing care. In the early Ambulance Trains there was no heating, and only hurricane lanterns and candles provided the light necessary for staff to carry out their work. Furthermore, as there were no interconnecting carriages, in order to render care the army sisters had to make their way along the outside footboards while the train was in motion. According to Sister Phillips (QAIMNS), 'Climbing from coach to coach by way of the footboards was a practice that was absolutely forbidden though, like more than one other rule, it was honoured in the breach than in the observance. Frequently it was an absolute necessity in the interest of one's patients.'[48] Kate Luard reinforced the need to break the rules, and found a way of carrying dressings to the wounded while negotiating the footboards between the carriages: 'got my haversack lined with jaconet and filled with cut dressings, very convenient, as you have both hands free … we get quite expert at clawing along the footboards'.[49]

It was understandable why nurses broke the rules: train journeys could last up to 60 hours and the sick and wounded had to be cared for. One soldier, despite the length of time he had been on the train, wrote to a sister expressing his gratitude for the care he received:

> I was one of 80 badly wounded who arrived in an Army Service Corps wagon at Coulommiers on September 8th, 1914. I did that 60-hour journey in your train and was put on to the *Asturias* [Hospital Ship] at St Nazaire. I had gunshot wound fractures of both my femurs. So I feel I can say nothing less than that I probably have to thank you all for keeping my legs if not my life.[50]

Trying to deliver effective nursing care was not only hampered by rules; quite often the physical restrictions of working in the confined space of a railway wagon or carriage brought their own difficulties. Sister Luard kept a diary and regularly sent pages home to the closest members of her family whom she referred to as 'the inner circle'. In a diary entry written not long after she joined No. 5 Ambulance Train, she described the working conditions:

> Imagine a hospital as big as King's College Hospital all packed into a train, and having to be self-provisioned, watered, sanitised, lit, cleaned, doctored and nursed and staffed and officered, all within its own limits. No outside person can realise the difficulties except those who try to work it.[51]

In the opening months of the War, for the nurses working on Ambulance Trains the problems were numerous, sometimes almost insurmountable. Sister Reid's train carried casualties from the fighting at the River Aisne and, on her part of the line, no hospital had been established in which to deposit the sick and wounded; all that was available was a Medical Aid Post in a repair shed near a railway station. On one occasion the train received orders to unload and return at once to the front. Over 150 stretcher cases required to be carried by hand to the Aid Post, a distance of half a mile, in very inclement weather. The total staff available to transfer and attend to the casualties was three medical officers, six nurses, six orderlies and two cooks. According to Sister Reid, a desperate situation was saved when:

> Out of the blue appeared 250 of the London Scottish, just arrived, who had heard of our difficulties and offered their services. All through the evening and night these men worked for us, and by 7 p.m. we had been able to get the worst 100 cases under shelter, fed, and had begun to dress their wounds … Out of the ranks of the London Scottish stepped Sergeants and Privates, all qualified doctors, also some medical

students and with them their regimental surgeon the gallant Captain McNab ... to the door of our Aid Post came an Officer in Red Cross uniform. He explained to me that he was Dr Braithwaite in charge of the American Ambulance at Neuilly: that, hearing of our difficulty, he had motored out from Paris with 3 other surgeons, instruments, ample dressings etc, that he wished to place himself at our service in every way; and, finally, that he had ordered his fleet of motor ambulances the first I had seen in France to follow him. In them, he would take to Paris Hospitals any of our cases urgently requiring operations.[52]

Many were not so fortunate. Having survived the experience of battle, they had to negotiate the vagaries of the system that was designed to help them survive. The casualties arrived at the Ambulance Trains in whatever was available to transport them, usually carts. It was not unusual for the wounded to arrive with the original field dressings on their wounds and there could be a wait of many hours before they were examined and fresh dressings applied. Furthermore, there was no guarantee that having arrived at the Ambulance Train they would move quickly up the line to the relative comfort of a hospital. Due to the sheer volume of casualties being transported, all too frequently they lay for hours before being loaded onto the trains. In many instances, just when the train was about to depart, the order to proceed was rescinded. The railway line was needed for the transportation of troops and material to the front, and that took precedence over the removal of the sick and wounded. For the casualties, each segment of their journey from the front was an interminable wait for access to medical intervention and nursing care.

By the end of October, Boulogne was the main centre of medical activity and all the large hotels and casinos had been commandeered for use as hospitals. It was described by an army nursing sister as a 'seething mass of ambulances, wounded, doctors and nurses. There seemed to be an unending stream of them ... It gave one a horrid sense of disaster.' In total, three General Hospitals, Nos. 11, 13 and 14, and three Stationary Hospitals, Nos. 7, 13 and 14, were established. The total capacity for the care of the sick and wounded was 2,310 hospital beds. Additionally, hospitals were opened at Rouen, Le Havre, Étretat, Le Touquet, Calais, Le Tréport, St Omer and Abbeville. Furthermore, a large convalescent hospital was opened at St Omer and voluntary and Red Cross hospitals were established at Rouen and Abbeville. During the first Battle of Ypres, the situation at Boulogne became intolerable, with as many as a thousand sick and wounded arriving each day on the Ambulance Trains. Moreover, on arrival the trains could sit for hours before being unloaded. Between 15 October and 23 November, the nine Ambulance Trains in full-time service made 140 trips from the fighting front to Boulogne or other bases, transporting 37,798 casualties.[53]

Many of the hospitals were filled to capacity, and due to the shortage of beds and space, stretchers were placed between occupied beds, in corridors and on balconies. The men were nursed on trestles and on the floor. There was a dearth of mattresses, sheets, blankets, pillows, pyjamas, dressings, antiseptics,

Figure 2.2 Wounded soldiers being unloaded from an Ambulance Train. National Library of Scotland.

bandages, soap, feeding cups, plates, cutlery, and all kinds of medical and domestic stores needed for the care and comfort of the sick and wounded.

Three months into the war, Sister Adelina Walker moved from the Trianon Palace and was assigned as Matron to the sugar sheds on the Gare Maritime, Boulogne, now No. 13 General Hospital. Arriving at the sheds she was overwhelmed by what she witnessed:

> An indescribable scene met us. In the first huge shed there was hundreds of wounded, walking cases, as long as a man could crawl he had to be a walking case. All of them were caked with mud, in torn clothes, hardly any with caps, and with blood stained bandages on arms, hands and legs, many lying on the straw that had been left in the hastily cleaned sheds ... dressings were being done on improvised tables; blood stained clothes, caked in mud that had been cut off were stacked in heaps with rifles and ammunition. Further on, the sheds were being converted into wards; wooden partitions were being run up, bedsteads carried in, and the wounded, meanwhile, lying about on straw or stretchers. These beds were for stretcher cases, and were soon filled with terribly wounded men who just had to be put into the beds clothes and all. As fast as one could get to them, the clothes were off, and the patient washed, and his wounds dressed. Some had both legs off, some their side blown away; all were wounded in dozens of places. Doctors and nurses were hopelessly outnumbered, distractedly trying to meet the demands made on them.[54]

Despite the opening of the various hospitals, there were organisational problems with the deployment of trained nursing staff, as evidenced in an incident at No. 7 Stationary Hospital. On 22 October, Maud McCarthy started an inspection of the hospitals in Boulogne. She arrived to find the place 'crowded with wounded' and at No. 7 found, as well as her own staff, '10 untrained Red Cross nurses who I removed'. According to her diary entry, at the hospital office the Deputy Director Medical Services (DDMS) Staff Officer was 'getting a Red Cross officer to telegraph for Red Cross nurses – was very angry. Said why didn't he telegraph to us – because he thought we knew.'[55]

The problem was caused by insufficient communication between the medical and nursing services at the front, and poor communication between the medical authorities at the front and the War Office. The situation at Boulogne arose because the BRCS headquarters in London received a message from the War Office requesting the urgent dispatch of two Voluntary Aid Detachment (VAD) units to France. According to a BRCS report, the VAD units under the supervision of Commandant Katharine Furse arrived in Paris only to discover their French HQ had moved to Boulogne. The units then travelled to Boulogne but, on arrival, found no one knew why they had been sent for. After two days of enforced inactivity there was a rush of casualties into Boulogne. At the newly opened No. 7 Stationary Hospital there were insufficient numbers of trained nurses to care for the sick and wounded and, although a request for army nurses had been issued, they failed to arrive. An urgent call went out for help and the VADs responded. According to a report written after the emergency, the nurses could do very little but feed and wash the casualties and do whatever was permissible to lessen the suffering of the men. Within forty-eight hours, the trained staff arrived and the VADs were withdrawn. Katharine Furse described the response as 'filling the gap until the plumber came'.[56] However, the following day No. 7 British Red Cross Hospital, also known as the Allied Base Forces Hospital, opened at Boulogne and there great strain was put on the nursing resources. Once again, the VAD units were asked to respond, which they did, staying until additional trained nurses arrived one week later. In Maud McCarthy's diary there is no further mention of VADs doing anything beyond their temporary involvement at No. 7 Stationary Hospital. Her diary entries between 23 and 26 October highlight the strain the army medical and nursing services were under, with notes such as 'nurses urgently required, trains continually arriving, crowded with wounded; hospitals full and not enough beds for everyone; casualties being nursed on mattresses on the floors'. Despite the seriousness of the situation and the shortage of nurses, in a short diary entry on 25 October she states, 'A busy day going round hospitals and trains. Major Myles asked me to go a journey on his train but in consequence of the amount of work and untrained Red Cross wanting to assist, I shall not go until later.'[57]

This was the reality of nursing politics. The volunteers, who were willing and available to bring succour, no matter how small, to the sick and wounded were not to be encouraged. Therefore, by not utilising the VADs' basic skills, many casualties were left waiting, wanting and neglected.

On the home front the reality of the military situation and deficiencies in the medical arrangements were not reflected in the national press, although the nursing press ran anonymous stories and eyewitness accounts of what was happening. Many of the reports were critical of the War Office and its ability to manage the collection, care and distribution of the sick and wounded. One nurse at the front was moved to write:

> All the time men have been dying in the trenches and elsewhere for the want of good nursing, there have been dozens of nurses waiting in Paris for work they might do ... It made one's heart ache to think of it.[58]

Official information regarding the care and number of casualties was practically non-existent. In the House of Commons, Sir William Byles made an impassioned plea to the Government suggesting the need for relaxation of press censorship:

> I do not want to see the War carried on in camera. Its fortunes and misfortunes should not be hidden from us ... I do not want these things to be hidden from public knowledge as far as Whitehall can do it ... Our public are not getting the news of their dear ones, or they are getting it, belated, meagre, and scrappy.[59]

The casualty care problems were rightly attributed to the ongoing lack of cooperation and information-sharing between the War Office in London and the administrative medical officers at the front. As a consequence, there was a disturbingly poor management of services and there were long delays in the supply of much-needed medical supplies and personnel. The situation was further hampered by disputes between the BRCS and the OStJJ regarding their wartime roles and fundraising plans and activities. It took *The Times*' appeals for 'Funds for the Sick and Wounded' to bring the friction that existed between the two voluntary organisations to a head. The BRCS had the support of Lord Northcliffe, the proprietor of *The Times*, who, to help with fundraising, placed his newspaper at the disposal of the Society. This, unfortunately impacted on the planned appeals by the OStJJ as, unmoved by the dilemma, Lord Northcliffe said he would not advertise the appeals by both organisations in his paper. As the two great societies were dependent on public support, Northcliffe's stance would cause a great deal of difficulty for the OStJJ. In order to overcome the problem, the heads of both societies, Arthur Stanley for the BRCS and Sir Henry Perrott for the OStJJ, met to discuss how it might be resolved. After much discussion involving their respective administrative and management committees, the societies amalgamated in a Joint War Committee of twenty-four members, with twelve representatives from each society.[60] However, as the War Office had to sanction the plan if the Joint War Committee was officially to be part of the war effort, the Army Council sent an official notification to the societies, and to the St Andrew's Ambulance Association in Scotland, stating they now formed

part of the Red Cross organisation of Great Britain and were recognised by
the British Government as societies authorised under Article 10 of the Geneva
Convention to assist the medical service in war. In *The Red Cross*, the official
journal of the BRCS, the historic decision was announced:

> It will be a source of unmixed satisfaction both to members of the British Red Cross
> Society and to the general public, to learn that a working arrangement has been
> come to between our Society and St John Ambulance Association ... Those who
> have engaged in the work of directing these two great societies need not be told that
> the formation of this committee means a great deal more than the mere fact itself. It
> would be an affectation to pretend that there has been no difficulty in marking out
> the fields of work for each society.[61]

After covering the events that led up to the formation of the Joint War
Committee, the article concluded: 'We look forward with the utmost pleasure
to a close and harmonious relationship with the St John Ambulance Association,
not only during the continuance of the war but for the entire future.'
    While a satisfactory solution had been found to accommodate the needs of
these two important voluntary organisations, by November the recruitment and
supply of nurses were still contentious issues. At the War Office, Ethel Becher had
overall responsibility for the nursing services and the supply of trained nurses for
war work. Miss Becher worked closely with the heads of other nursing services
and collectively they ensured the challenges of supplying trained nurses for war
service were adequately met. The Territorial Force Nursing Service was represented by its Matron-in-Chief, Miss Sydney Browne. She had joined the Army
Nursing Service in 1883 and, when that was replaced in 1902 by the formation
of the Queen Alexandra Imperial Military Nursing Service, Sydney Browne was
appointed the first Matron-in-Chief. On her retirement from that position, she
became the Matron-in-Chief of the newly formed Territorial Force Nursing
Service and still held the position at the outbreak of the War. In August 1914,
Miss Sarah Swift, a former Matron of Guy's Hospital, known to have exceptional administrative abilities and a well-established reputation in nursing education, offered her service to St John's Ambulance Association and the British
Red Cross. Her offer was accepted by St John's and she was appointed to the
committee that dealt with enquiries from trained nurses wishing to enrol themselves for war work. Following the establishment of the Joint War Committee,
the respective nursing departments amalgamated. The move was designed to
ensure consistency and quality in the selection of trained nurses working for
the British Red Cross at home and overseas. In November, Sarah Swift was
appointed Matron-in-Chief.[62] The volunteer nurses came under the supervision
of Katharine Furse. Unlike trained nurses, the volunteers did not have three
years' training but they did hold first-aid and home-nursing certificates. In 1909,
Katharine Furse had joined the Red Cross Voluntary Aid Detachment and by
1914 she had gained considerable experience, particularly under the tutelage of
Dr James Cantlie. She was considered to be a woman of considerable practical

and administrative capabilities, and was entrusted to set up the first VAD unit in France.[63]

Despite the cooperation that existed between the various services to supply suitably trained nurses for war service, within the nursing profession there was a growing belief that volunteer nurses were being used at the expense of trained nurses. In order to quell the rumours, Arthur Stanley was compelled to write to *The Lancet* refuting allegations made by some doctors that, on the home front, untrained nurses were managing hospitals: 'Only fully trained and certificated nurses are in charge. In the hospitals the services of Voluntary Aid Detachments are utilised as probationers, cooks and in other general ways.'[64] Additionally, there were concerns about the BRCS and the way the Joint War Committee was handling nurse recruitment. The main bones of contention were the length of time it appeared to be taking the BRCS to establish a register of trained nurses available for war service, and the delays in dispatching suitably trained nurses to the front. Moreover, the nursing press wanted clarification on what plans, if any, there were to incorporate volunteer nurses into the care of the sick and wounded.

In an editorial entitled 'Wanted a Woman Kitchener', *The Nursing Times* demanded answers: 'There is much agitation and some bitterness in the nursing world over problems to which it seems impossible to obtain a clear answer.' The editorial concluded with a rallying cry:

> We want for this great national crisis a trained nurse of executive ability, who can hold all the threads of voluntary war nursing in her hands, who, working in touch with the military authorities of all the Allied countries and helped by an expert committee, could send out at an hour's notice emergency units of trained adaptable women for service at any place they are needed. The need is too urgent for any muddling and overlapping, and there is no place for the amateur or Important Person. In fact, we want a woman Kitchener to co-ordinate all the voluntary agencies that supply nurses for the wounded.[65]

On the same day, the editorial of *The British Journal of Nursing* highlighted the growing unrest regarding the use of volunteer nurses, and referred to them as 'war giddy women', carrying out 'spurious and emotional nursing'.[66]

One week after the call for a 'Woman Kitchener', *The Nursing Times* published a joint statement from the BRCS and the OStJJ contesting the allegations made against them. According to the organisations there was no shortage of trained Red Cross nurses or delays in sending them to France. However, omitted from the joint statement was the fact that, despite the availability of trained Red Cross nurses, the Army Nursing Service was reluctant to utilise them. Untrained women were working at the front but not with the BRCS, and the joint statement highlighted the fact and the problems it created. Apparently it was easy for women of influence, social position and funds to establish and equip voluntary hospitals and ambulances which were staffed with enthusiastic amateurs who escaped the War Office rigour of establishing their nursing credentials and capabilities. The joint statement continued: 'These people seem to think that because they have money and influence and the wish to use it, they have the right to insist on becoming part of a highly technical organisation.'[67]

The journalist William Beach Thomas summed up what he believed to be the motivations of those women and awarded them a title that quickly gained currency:

> 'Limelighters' – there are beyond question, women who have forced their way across the Channel for the sake of talking and being talked about and they have not failed their objective. Limelight is not always kind to the complexion of those who seek it.[68]

While debates raged regarding the quality and quantity of nurses for the front, in Parliament questions were raised regarding the whole system of casualty care, including the supply of nurses. The casualty arrangements were of deep concern to Lord Robert Cecil, Independent Conservative for Hitchin, who was not convinced the 'unqualified praise' for the medical arrangements at the front 'was really justified'. Addressing his questions to the Under Secretary of State, he asked for clarification on the length of time it took the wounded to be transported from the front line to Base Hospitals. Were there sufficient numbers of RAMC personnel and nurses to care for the casualties? He also enquired into the use of motor ambulances and trains and asked if they were used for the evacuation of the sick and wounded.[69] Mr Douglas Hall, Conservative MP for the Isle of Wight, was also concerned about the transportation arrangements, and the physical and spiritual care of the sick and wounded. He wished to know from the Under Secretary if 'antiquated horse-drawn ambulances' were still used for the removal of casualties and why men were nursed on straw in Ambulance Trains. Additionally, he wanted to know why casualties were cared for in tents instead of hospital huts. Were there enough army chaplains at clearing hospitals, and why were barges, having been approved by the army authorities for casualty evacuation, not being used?[70] In response, the Under Secretary of State, Mr Harold Tennant, gave a lengthy account of the work of the medical services at the front. Regarding the use and supply of nurses, he responded by saying, 'there is an ample number of nurses in the clearing stations [hospitals] ... Not only is there a sufficient number, but there is a waiting list.' He also claimed that in France there were nurses held in reserve. In response to the question raised by the Hon. Member Mr Douglas Hall, regarding the use of horse-drawn ambulances, the Under Secretary claimed they were in the process of being replaced by motor ambulances. Allegations had been made in the press that the War Office was refusing donations of motor ambulances but the Under Secretary refuted the claim:

> It is not true that we have refused them. All we have said is that we are not ready to accept them just now ... We have told those kindly disposed persons who have been so good as to offer motor ambulances that if they wish to renew their offers in a month or two months' time, we shall be very glad to avail ourselves of them.[71]

No reasons were given for the delay. With regard to the use of straw on Ambulance Trains, the Under Secretary believed the practice was now abandoned, although he had never heard of straw being used. There were also concerns that straw might give rise to tetanus, but the Hon. Member was assured that tetanus was 'extremely rare'. After a lengthy speech to the House, and avoiding some of the questions raised by MPs, the Under Secretary of State concluded, 'I think the members will be glad to know that so far as this phase of the situation [the war] goes, we have been successful.'

The Minister's answers were uninformed, if not misleading. For instance, between mid August and December the most frequently associated condition with gunshot wounds was tetanus. As a result of this type of wounding there were the 273 recorded cases of tetanus, of which 183 proved fatal.[72] However, this was only the recorded cases on the Western Front; the statistics did not take into account the wounded who had hastily been shipped back to Britain and died of tetanus in British and Irish hospitals.

The supply of suitably trained and experienced nurses was a problem; many of the nurses who volunteered for war service were turned down because they did not meet the required training or social status criteria. Once again, information-sharing was in a vacuum and was directly attributable to a lack of communication between the military, the War Office mandarins and the medical administrative services. The supply of nurses, particularly the use of Red Cross nurses, was an ongoing source of concern, if not tension, between Ethel Becher and Maud McCarthy. For example, in a diary entry Maud McCarthy appears to be frustrated by Ethel Becher:

> Replied to Matron-in-Chief's letters in connection with the Red Cross and the employment of nurses, in which I explained the situation very plainly and showed her that no irregularities had been permitted and in all things I had kept the DAMS [Director Army Medical Services] informed of what I was doing and obtained his sanction and approval.[73]

From the early weeks of the War, the supply of nurses was a contentious issue, which was further aggravated when, in October, the Adjutant General, Sir Nevil Macready, wrote to the DAMS suggesting that members of the Army Nursing Service should work at Clearing Hospitals, a practice not yet approved of by the AMS (Army Medical Services) at the War Office. According to Sir Nevil's memorandum, if the Service was unable to accommodate the request, then the BRCS 'might be approached as to their readiness to provide nursing sisters at a rate of 5 per clearing hospital whenever invited to do so'.[74] When Maud McCarthy discovered the request from the Adjutant General, her diary entry suggests the decision to staff Clearing Hospitals with nurses was the responsibility of the DAMS, but privately she was furious. She wrote to the DAMS reminding him that she was responsible for the supply of nurses and any requests should meet with her approval, particularly if the deployment of Red Cross nurses was involved.[75] It was not, however, Red Cross nurses that were posted to the Clearing Hospitals but regulars and reservists. According to Sister Jentie Paterson (QAIMNSR), who, along with four other Sisters was among the first to be deployed to a Clearing Hospital, said, 'We were asked to come here by the Chief Matron and had to say we were going voluntarily and realised the risks in case our home people would gibe.'[76]

Throughout the months of debacle and falling out over the recruitment and suitability of nursing applicants for war service in France, the death of one man temporarily silenced the debate. On 16 November, Sister Luard was still working on No. 5 Ambulance Train. It arrived in Boulogne with 344 casualties from the Clearing Hospitals at Bailleul:

> We loaded up at Bailleul. The Clearing Hospitals were very full and some came off a convoy. One of mine died. One, wounded above the knee, was four days in the open before being picked up; he had six bullets in his leg, two in each arm, and crawled around until found; one of the arm wounds he got doing this ... One said gloomily, 'This isn't war, it's murder; you go there to your doom'.

Almost as a footnote she added, 'Heard the sad news of Lord Robert's.'[77]

Sister Luard was referring to Field Marshal Lord Roberts of Kandahar who, along with his wife, Nora, had been great advocates for the establishment of the Queen Alexandra's Imperial Military Nursing Service. Lord Roberts had also been advisor to and close confidant of Queen Alexandra throughout the development and formation of the Imperial Military Nursing Service. On the same day that Kate Luard made her diary entry, the Prime Minister addressed the House of Commons with the news, 'Both the House and the country learn with the deepest regret of the sudden death of that most illustrious soldier, Earl Roberts.[78]

It was on a visit to France that Lord Roberts became ill. According to one newspaper report, 'Lord Roberts proceeded to France to see the Indian troops at present fighting at the front, of which he was Colonel-in-Chief. He contracted a chill and succumbed, after a short illness, to an attack of pneumonia.'[79]

Just days before his death Lord Roberts had paid a visit to No. 13 Stationary Hospital where, according to the Matron, 'he spoke to every stretcher case in the hospital. The beds were very low, and the men's voices very weak, but he leaned over and spoke to them all; it upset him terribly, to see so much suffering.' Two days later Matron Walker was informed that Lord Roberts was unwell, and she was asked to provide some warm clothing:

> His aide-de-camp motored down for warm things, thinking it was only a chill. So we sent warm clothing with one of Queen Mary's red flannel jackets with a handkerchief in the pocket and a card pinned on 'Good luck from Queen Mary'. The next day we received the sad news that he was dead.[80]

On 17 November, three days after attending to the care of Lord Roberts' body, Maud McCarthy wrote about the funeral arrangements at St Omer:

> Funeral service at Hôtel de Ville. A most impressive procession and service, streets lined, many regiments represented and members of the French Headquarters Staff

present as well as our own. After service remains taken to Boulogne en route to England where another service took place before the embarkation.[81]

As the body of Lord Roberts was received at Boulogne, Matron Walker described the involvement of the nurses and patients in the respectful but low-key funeral arrangements:

> We draped a stand on the platform to receive his coffin and, at the patients' request, I placed a large scarlet cross of geraniums as their offering on the coffin. Men straight from the trenches were his escort; they looked so white and worn. Indians lined the platform and received the coffin on the boat which conveyed it to England.[82]

According to Katharine Furse, due to the intense military action taking place at the front the funeral was anything but a grand affair. Senior figures from the military High Command were noticeable by their absence:

> No grand military escort could be provided to bring his coffin down to Boulogne. Everyone of any importance was at his post and indispensable. The coffin came down with a few dirty Grenadier Guards, straight from action as coffin bearers. The French mounted lancers gave him military honours as his coffin with the smallest cap I have ever seen, and his Field Marshal's baton upon it, lay on the station platform. There was a short service attended by those of us who were sufficiently unimportant to be spared before the little coffin slid on to the daily packet boat, which was to take it across the channel. No destroyer could be spared, even to carry the body of a dead Field Marshal back to England.[83]

Tragically, thousands had made their final journey but, unlike Lord Roberts, they were not returned home. For many, their final resting place was at a makeshift cemetery beside a Clearing Station, Stationary or Base Hospital. Others had the ignominy of being buried in pits or communal graves near or at the front line; for many more, there was no resting place or sacred space.

The first death of a nurse on active service occurred in November. On 18 November Maud McCarthy was informed that thirty-year-old Staff Nurse Ethel Fearnley was 'seriously ill'. On 20 November Maud McCarthy visited Miss Fearnley in hospital and could see her health was deteriorating rapidly. On 23 November, at No. 11 General Hospital, Ethel Fearnley passed away and was laid to rest at Boulogne East Cemetery. Although Ethel Fearnley was the first nurse in QAIMNS to die on active service, Maud McCarthy did not record her death or funeral in her War Diary. However, Ethel Fearnley was not forgotten. For her short but 'gallant and distinguished service in the field', she was Mentioned in Dispatches (MiD).[84]

By the winter of 1914 the war of rapid movement turned to stalemate, and from Belgium to Switzerland the belligerent nations dug in, entrenching their armies along a 475 mile continuous line. The work of the army medical and nursing services increased significantly and the total number of hospital beds available for the sick and wounded on the Western Front reached 20,000, of which 13,731 were occupied.[85] Given the numbers of men needing skilled

medical and nursing intervention, it is not surprising the medical and nursing
services were overwhelmed. Due to the rise in casualties and the expansion of
casualty care facilities there was an increase in the deployment of trained nurses.
From the small cadre of regulars and reserves that arrived in France in the early
weeks of the War, the army nursing establishment increased but it was still
reliant on the support of trained Red Cross nurses. Furthermore, following a
review of the work undertaken at Clearing Hospitals, the decision was made to
appoint five Sisters to each facility. The new directive placed additional pressure
on the already overstretched nursing service. In early November the pressure on
the army nursing service was slightly alleviated by the arrival of a small contingent of trained nurses from the Canadian Army Medical Corps Nursing Service.
In the first week of the War, Canada pledged her support to the Mother Country
and called on 20,000 men to volunteer for war service. Determined to do 'their
bit', in October a contingent of 101 Canadian nurses arrived in Britain. After
a few weeks of waiting in London for their mobilisation orders, a small cadre,
twenty in total, were sent to France. The first group were distributed among
British Stationary and General Hospitals. In December, the first Canadian unit,
No. 2 Canadian Stationary Hospital, opened at Le Touquet with a nursing
complement of thirty-five trained nurses. The hospital had 320 beds but could
accommodate up to 520 patients. The Matron was Ethel Blanche Ridley, who
had served in the 1898–9 Spanish–American War.[86]

While the extra skilled hands from Canada were more than welcome, it
was, however, the considerable effort from the voluntary agencies that helped
alleviate the pressure on the overworked and understaffed medical and nursing
services. The British Red Cross established No. 1 VAD Rest Station at the Gare
Centrale, Boulogne. Under the direction of Katharine Furse, the unit comprised
sixteen VAD members and two trained nurses working for the Red Cross,
Sister Earle and Sister Buxton; Theresa Buxton was a veteran of the Balkan
Wars. Unable to find suitable accommodation, the unit took over three French
rail wagons and two passenger carriages and turned them into a dispensary,
kitchen, Quartermaster's store and billeting quarters. From its establishment
in October and up to December, the unit supplied 38,000 sick and wounded
soldiers with soup, cocoa, bread and butter, ham, cheese, chocolates, apples and
bananas. Additionally, the two Red Cross nursing sisters dealt with 550 medical
and surgical cases. Furthermore, the VAD ambulance transported 660 cases
to and from hospitals in the area. The members of the unit made hundreds of
splints, bandages, sandbags, slings and dressings, and supplied them to hospitals
and Ambulance Trains. In addition to the medical supplies and comforts, they
distributed 80,000 cigarettes among the Ambulance Trains. The unit's most
demanding day was 2 November, when 2,300 men were brought down from
the fighting at Ypres and each man was given food and refreshments, and over
200 wound dressings were carried out by Sisters Earle and Buxton, with RAMC
doctors working with them. According to Katharine Furse, during the Battle of
Ypres, the Ambulance Trains would arrive in Boulogne with very little warning

and with a tragic cargo: 'men with faces blown away; leg wounds, chest wounds, throat wounds sitting up in third class carriages or lying on straw ... They had been three days on the train, many of them, with first field dressings on their wounds.'[87]

The casualty care work was overwhelming; by the end of the year the BEF had sustained 177,433 casualties. Of these, 98,866 were battle casualties which included those classified as missing or held as prisoners of war, those killed, wounded or those who died of wounds. The remaining 78,557 were non-battle casualties whose death, injuries or illness did not result from enemy action.[88]

The continuation of the conflict with its corresponding rise in casualties had become a test of ingenuity for the medical and nursing services. In order to save lives and salvage limbs, the logistical considerations of caring for the sick and wounded required a lot more expertise, planning and cooperation between the services. Furthermore, the War Office needed to be more pro-active and less obstructive. Without the support of the voluntary agencies the army medical and nursing services would not have coped. It is unfortunate, therefore, that within the nursing and voluntary services the conflict had bred conflict. Continuing to complain about the use of volunteers, *The British Journal of Nursing* claimed:

> Hundreds of trained nurses are seething with indignation at the manner in which their skilled work, and their uniform, have been annexed by amateurs, crazy for the excitement of 'going to the front', and the manner in which their livelihood has been economically depreciated by the use of volunteer workers.[89]

Nurses on active service were focused on the outcomes of their labours, and how to survive the physical and emotional demands being made on them. The complaining rhetoric among the services and in the nursing press was an unwelcome distraction from the reality of their lives. One QA Reservist who had gone to France at the start of the conflict and was working and living under canvas at Rouen, said that, despite the back-breaking work and discomfort, she 'liked the life immensely'. With good humour she described the privations of active service:

> The staff have now been provided with bags filled with chaff [grain husks] to sleep on, and we find them warm and most comfortable ... It seems strange that Christmas will soon be here and if we feel a little homesick it cannot be wondered at, what do an armchair, a warm fire, and a hot bath feel like?[90]

NOTES

1. Moorehead, C. (1998), *Dunant's Dream: War, Switzerland and the History of the Red Cross*, London: HarperCollins; Stewart, J. C. (1983), *The Quality of Mercy: The Lives of Sir James and Lady Cantlie*, London: George Allen and Unwin, p. 16.
2. 'Report of Conference of Nursing Officers of the St John Brigade, and St John Ambulance Association, Clerkenwell, London' (1913), Women at Work Collection, Imperial War Museum, British Red Cross Society, pp. 1–10.

3. *The Times*, 5 August 1914.
4. *Daily Mail*, 4 August 1914.
5. *The Times*, 4 August 1914.
6. *Daily News*, 4 August 1914.
7. *The Scotsman*, 4 August 1914.
8. *The Nursing Times*, 8 August 1914.
9. *The British Journal of Nursing*, 8 August 1914.
10. McEwen, Y. T. (2006), *It's a Long Way To Tipperary: British and Irish Nurses in the Great War*, Dunfermline: Cualann.
11. *The Nursing Mirror and Midwives' Journal*, 15 August 1914.
12. Woodham-Smith, C. (1972), *Florence Nightingale*, London: Book Club Association, pp. 323–4.
13. Ibid., p. 324.
14. *Hansard*, House of Commons Debate, 3 June 1913, vol. 53, c. 758.
15. *The Daily Graphic*, 24 July 1919.
16. Royal London Hospital Archives, E. H. Becher Papers, RLHLH/N/1/4.
17. Becher Papers, Letters and References, RLHLH/Z/1.
18. National Archives, WO 399/501, Becher Papers, Nursing Board Minutes, 11 February 1914.
19. National Archives, WO399/501, Becher Papers, L. Gubbins to Nursing Board, 11 February 1914.
20. Ibid.
21. National Archives, WO399/501, Becher Papers, Nursing Board, Petition to Secretary of State for War, 16 February 1914.
22. *The Nursing Mirror and Midwives' Journal*, 19 September 1914.
23. Royal London Hospital Archives, E. M. McCarthy Papers, RLHLH/N/1/1–4: *Australian Dictionary of Biography*, vol. 10, Melbourne University Press, 1986, pp. 218–19.
24. Queen Alexandra's Royal Army Nursing Corps, Unlisted Papers, Private Correspondence between Brigadier H. S. Gillespie, Matron-in-Chief, and S. McCarthy, Army Medical Services Museum, Aldershot.
25. National Archives, WO95/3988-91; McCarthy, E. M., War Diary, 12 August 1914–15 August 1914, Box 10, QARANC Collection, Archives, Army Medical Services Museum.
26. McCarthy, E. M., War Diary, 26 August 1914. QARANC Collection.
27. Spooner, P. K. E., Personal Correspondence to author on K. E. Haywood; Anon., 'Reminiscences, 1914–1919', *Syston Parochial Magazine*, July 1919.
28. Todd, J., Diary, QARANC Archives, 67/1981.
29. Private Papers of Bramston and Luard families, Essex Record Office, D/Dlu55/13/4.
30. Blair, M., Private Papers, QARANC Archives, 1995/10.1.2.
31. Peterkin, M. B., War Diary, Imperial War Museum, Catalogue No. 7058, p. 3.
32. MacPherson, W. G. (1931), *Medical Services General History*, vol. 2, ch. VIII, p. 187, The Naval and Military Press (reprint), HMSO.
33. MacPherson, vol. 1, ch. XI.
34. *The Nursing Times*, 15 August 1914.
35. Editorial, *The British Journal of Nursing*, 29 August 1914.
36. *The Nursing Mirror and Midwives' Journal*, 22 August 1914.

37. MacPherson, vol. 2, ch. XI, p. 241; McCarthy, War Diary, 7 September 1914.
38. Reay, A. V. C., Unlisted Collection, M. McCarthy Papers, Box 10, QARANC Archive.
39. Loughran, M., Ambulance Trains, 'Nurses' Accounts', M. McCarthy Papers, Box 10, QARANC Archive.
40. Killery, E., 'Nurses' Accounts', M. McCarthy Papers, Box 10, QARANC Archive.
41. Peterkin, M. B., War Diary, 29 August 1914, pp. 6–7.
42. McCarthy, M., War Diary, 28 August 1914.
43. MacPherson, vol. 2, ch. X, p. 238.
44. Walker, A. L., 'Nurses' Accounts', M. McCarthy Papers, Box 10, QARANC Archive.
45. MacPherson, vol. 2, ch. XII, p. 245.
46. *The Lancet*, 3 October 1914, p. 855.
47. Reid, B. J. D., *The Story of the British Ambulance Train Service in France from August 1914 to April 1915*, Imperial War Museum, Department of Printed Documents, pp. 89–90.
48. Philips, M., Unlisted Collection, M. McCarthy Papers, Box 10, QARANC Archive.
49. Anon. (1915), *Diary of a Nursing Sister on the Western Front*, Edinburgh: William Blackwood and Sons.
50. Anon., Unlisted Collection, M. McCarthy Papers, Box 10.
51. Anon., *Diary of a Nursing Sister*, p. 35.
52. Reid, B. J. D., *British Ambulance Train Service*, pp. 97–8.
53. MacPherson, vol. 2, ch. XV, p. 331.
54. Walker, A. L., 'Nurses' Accounts', p. 3.
55. McCarthy, M., War Diary, 22 October 1914.
56. Crowdy, R., 'Report of VAD Department France: The Advent of the VADs in France', Imperial War Museum, Women's War Work, British Red Cross Society Archives, 12.2/2, pp. 2–3.
57. McCarthy, M., War Diary, 23–6 October 1914.
58. Anon., *The British Journal of Nursing*, 19 December 1914, p. 486.
59. *Hansard,* House of Commons Debate, 26 November 1914, vol. 68, cc. 1376–7, 1361.
60. Best, S. H. (1938), *The Story of the British Red Cross*, London: Cassell, pp. 114–15.
61. MacPherson, vol. 1, ch. XI, pp. 214–15.
62. *The Red Cross*, 15 November 1914, pp. 358–60.
63. McGann, S. (1992), *The Battle of the Nurses*, London: Scutari Press.
64. Furse, K. (1940), *Hearts and Pomegranates*, London: Peter Davies.
65. *The Lancet*, 24 October 1914, p. 1016.
66. *The Nursing Times*, 7 November 1914, pp. 1387–8.
67. *The British Journal of Nursing*, 7 November 1914, p. 357.
68. *The Nursing Times*, 14 November 1914, p. 1419.
69. *Daily Mail*, 16 July 1915.
70. *Hansard,* House of Commons Debate, 26 November 1914, vol. 68, cc. 1407–9.
71. *Hansard,* House of Commons Debate, 26 November 1914, vol. 68, cc. 1410–13.
72. *Hansard,* House of Commons Debate, 26 November 1914, vol. 68, cc. 1422–4.
73. Mitchell, T. J. (reprint 1997), *Medical Services: Casualties and Medical Statistics*, p. 133.

74. McCarthy, M., War Diary, 18 December 1914.
75. MacCready, N., 27 October 1914, Unlisted Collection, M. McCarthy Papers, Box 10.
76. McCarthy, M., Letter to DAMS, 1 November 1914, Unlisted Collection, Box 10.
77. Paterson, J., Letter 16 November 1914, Imperial War Museum, 90/10/1.
78. Anon., *Diary of a Nursing Sister*, 16 November 1914, p. 107.
79. *Hansard*, House of Commons Debate, 16 November 1914, vol. 68, c. 255.
80. *Kildare Observer*, 21 November 1914.
81. Walker, A. L., 'Nurses' Accounts', p. 2.
82. McCarthy, M., War Diary, 17 November 1914.
83. Walker, A. L., 'Nurses' Accounts', p. 3.
84. John Addington Symonds Family Paper, Katharine Furse Collection, University of Bristol, Archives and Special Collections, DM/1584/12/H.
85. National Archives, WO399/2668; *The London Gazette* (third supplement), 18 June 1915.
86. National Archives, WO222/2134, Report on the Work of the Canadian Army Medical Corps Nursing Service with the British Expeditionary Force in France.
87. Furse Papers, Draft Manuscript, DM1584/10.
88. Mitchell, T. J., p. 121.
89. *The British Journal of Nursing*, 5 December 1914.
90. *The Nursing Mirror and Midwives' Journal*, 19 December 1914, p. 207.

3

Lies, 'Limelighters' and Nursing in the Land of Troy

THE PREDICTIONS WERE WRONG. 'It will be over by Christmas' or 'before the leaves fall' the optimists claimed, but the Secretary of State for War, Field Marshal Lord Kitchener, said the nation should be prepared for a protracted and costly war and that armies of millions of men would be needed. Time would prove his analysis right. On 1 January 1915, after four very demanding months at the front, Millicent Peterkin did not welcome the New Year:

> Never felt so unlike a 'Happy New Year' in my life. Should think last night must have been about the first New Year I have not seen in, but I simply could not raise sufficient enthusiasm to do so this year. Some of the sisters did, and there was a great racket going on over in the Base Camp all night.[1]

Her response was not surprising as these months of the War sorely tested the effectiveness of the army medical and nursing services administrations and, on occasions, they were found wanting. In fairness to their position, it was a war like no other and they, along with the government and the military, were ill prepared for the rapid change in pace and expansion of the conflict. Moreover, the combination of unprecedented professional demands with what at times appeared to be irrational and unreasonable administrative directives from the War Office did little for the morale of the medical and nursing staff. According to Millicent Peterkin, by the end of the year nurses and troops alike were enduring different kinds of miseries:

> Have got a vile dose of rheumatism on me tonight. It has rained incessantly and the mud is too awful for words. Sister D has a bad boil on her forehead and is going about with a very swollen face, and a bandage around her head. On Sunday her eye was so badly swollen up that she had to stay in bed part of the day, applying fomentations to the boil. About 300 sick and wounded, mostly sick, came down from the front yesterday, they were covered with mud from head to foot, and were very dirty and miserable. They say the trenches are awful – mud and water up to their knees, and sometimes higher. One man was practically buried in mud for four days. He was so stiff with cold and rheumatism that he could not help himself, and when others tried to hoist him out the soft soil kept giving way. Eventually he was covered right up to his chin, and nearly went mad, but at least was got out and brought down here. All his joints are swollen, and he cannot move himself at all.[2]

According to Sister Luard, working in No.5 Ambulance Train during the winter months had a detrimental effect on her health. In a letter to her sister she claimed her health had 'gone to pot ... I had some awful nights coughing through a raw, swollen throat with pains all over'. She further explained that 'feeling unwell' had become a regular feature of her life on active service: 'I've had so many colds and headaches on the train, as a matter of fact, I've had so many that whenever I've found myself free of either I've recorded in my Diary how remarkably well I'm feeling.'[3]

In recognition of the hardship the nurses faced, and as a token of appreciation for their 'unstinting dedication', Queen Alexandra sent the QA and Territorial nurses a rather luxurious Christmas gift. According to Sister Margaret Brander (TFNS):

> Miss Sydney Browne crossed the Channel with our presents from Queen Alexandra for the Territorials. I for one got a great surprise. A stout strong holdall bag edged with red, white and blue. The crown on it and inside; such a handsome gift. A grey cloak lined with fur and a fur collar fastening with a scarlet band. A fur lined muff and a hood. A very gracious gift indeed. We are all very proud of them and now a letter of thanks was to be written and all our names signed.[4]

Not everyone was happy with the Queen's generosity. In a letter to her family, Sister Luard was unimpressed that a significant section of the nursing services did not receive the gift: 'Queen Alexandra has sent all the QA Regulars and the Territorials lovely fur lined capes but she missed out the Reserves! Someone ought to advise her better than that.' Obviously aware of the censorship rules, she had to be very careful about what she said, particularly if criticism was suggested of anyone in a senior position or at the War Office. However, in a ditty scribbled alongside her complaining remarks, there was perhaps a clue as to whom she believed was responsible for the neglect of the Reserves:

> Said a Preacher called Henry Ward Becher
> To a hen you elegant creature!
> The hen upon that
> Laid an egg in his hat
> And thus did the hen Reward Becher.[5]

It may of course have been pure coincidence that the Preacher shared the same surname as the Matron-in-Chief at the War Office. It was clear from the earliest days of her war service that when Kate Luard had something to say she would not be deterred by the strict censorship rules and would be determined to get around them. In one instance, she tried to bypass the military censor by sending a letter to her father through the French postal service. The exercise proved to be ineffectual as the correspondence was intercepted but, surprisingly, it was passed with the warning, 'This letter is only passed as a concession. Attempts to evade censorship only defeat their own ends, kindly inform the writer of this. Letters posted by members of the Expeditionary Force in French post offices are liable to be destroyed.'[6]

The censor's letter was understood but only temporarily adhered to. Kate Luard was morally challenged by the imposed censorship, a rule she clearly had difficulty adhering to. Along with many other nurses, she was disturbed by what she witnessed and the testaments of the men she nursed; the press reports, what little there were, did not reflect the truth of the situation and she and other nurses knew it. In a diary entry during the battles for Ypres she wrote, 'The Times and the Daily Mail say the fighting beyond Ypres is severe, but that gives the British public no glimmering of what it really is.'[7]

The BEF, including those charged with the care of the sick and wounded, was struggling with the unrelenting demands of the War and the situation was not accurately reflected in press coverage. Under the terms of the Defence of the Realm Act 1914 (DORA), the government if need be had the power to censor the press, and it did. The press reports were speculative; there were many generalisations and few, if any, facts. If men died due to military or medical incompetence, who was going to tell the public and did the public have a right to know? Kate Luard believed they did; in her opinion the political aspirations were coming at too high a cost to the men who were fighting. After six months of dealing with the human wreckage of warfare she wrote in her diary:

> It is such a vast upheaval when you are in the middle of it, that you sometimes actually wonder if everyone has gone mad, or who has gone mad, that all should be grimly working, toiling, slaving, from the firing line to the base, for more destruction, and for more highly-finished and uninterrupted destruction, in order to get Peace. And the men who pay the cost in intimate personal and individual suffering and in death are not the men who made the war.[8]

Between August and December it had been a steep learning curve for the medical and nursing services. The problems of the AMS, being ill prepared and equipped to meet the trying wartime conditions in which they found themselves, were cyclical and by far the greatest hindrance to the effectiveness of the casualty care arrangements. Driven by the needs of the casualties and the increasing demands being made on them, by December 1914 the AMS had undergone administrative changes. At the front, Surgeon-General Woodhouse was replaced by Sir Arthur Sloggett from the War Office; Woodhouse remained Director General until December, when he became DMS on the LOC. Returning to the War Office, Sir Alfred Keogh left his appointment as a Red Cross Commissioner in France to take up the job of Director General, the position he had previously held between 1905 and 1910. There was a general consensus that, with Keogh back at the War Office, the medical services were in safe and competent hands. Keogh was skilled and experienced in the art of diplomacy, moving with great ease between the military and voluntary services; he was a Member of Council for the BRCS and was a friend of R. B. Haldane, whose army reforms he supported and helped implement, including the formation of the Territorial Forces Nursing Service. The management of the nursing services remained unchanged, with Ethel Becher and Maud McCarthy still in their respective posts. Between

September and December 1914, a variety of eminent medical and surgical specialists arrived in support of the hard-pressed AMS. The first to arrive were Sir Anthony Bowlby and Sir George Makins; Bowlby was appointed Consulting Surgeon for the forward areas and Makins became Consulting Surgeon for the Base Hospitals. The Consulting Physicians covering the forward and base areas were Sir Wilmot Herringham, Sir Bertrand Dawson and Sir J. Rose Bradford. Appointed on special duty to the army for bacteriological investigations into wound care, Sir Almroth Wright arrived in October and established his laboratory at No. 13 General Hospital, Boulogne. Additionally, bacteriology and pathology units were set up for research and development, and dental and ophthalmology services were also established.[9]

However, despite the appointment of sanitation specialists, the control of sanitation became problematic and fears about an outbreak of enteric fever (typhoid or paratyphoid) were soon realised. A memo from the office of the DDMS highlighted the concerns:

> The sanitary condition of the railway station at Abbeville is indescribable. The whole area of the railway line within a quarter of a mile of the station is covered with faeces and filth of every description. The condition of things is principally due to the troops who have passed through the station previous to our arrival. Two sanitary squads have been at work on it since yesterday but have made little impression on it yet. Nothing less than a fatigue party of at least 100 men with the necessary shovels, brushes, picks, etc. will be of any use at the present juncture. They will be required to systematically sweep up and bury or burn faeces and refuse from a square half-mile of ground.[10]

It was well recognised and documented that enteric fever had been the scourge of many military campaigns and contributed significantly to the debility and ineffectiveness of troops. As far back as the Crimea, Dr John Hall had advised on the need to establish adequate hygiene and sanitary arrangements, stating:

> Proper latrines should be dug in the camps, and the soil covered over daily with earth ... It would also be desirable to direct the pioneers to clear round the hospital marquees, and men's huts, daily ... If the present system be allowed to go on, diseases of a graver nature than even those now prevailing amongst the men will make their appearance and carry off thousands.[11]

Following the Crimean War, the British military campaigns between 1884 and 1896 were badly afflicted with outbreaks of enteric fever. In the Sudan, 39 per cent of mortality was due to enteric. In the Chitral campaign it was 28 per cent, and in the Matabele War 32 per cent. The worst attrition rate occurred in the Dongola military action, with 50 per cent mortality among the troops. In the Nile campaign, it amounted to 28 per cent of the army strength. As a result of the reluctance to learn from these campaigns the AMS were vulnerable to criticism during the war in South Africa. When the MP for Westminster, William Burdett-Coutts, was informed that the medical arrangements for the housing and care of the sick and wounded fell well below the expected standards, he travelled to South Africa in order to substantiate the veracity of the claims. On his visits to Bloemfontein and Kroonstad he was appalled by what he witnessed. The prevention, treatment and rehabilitation of enteric cases were nothing short of scandalous. Burdett-Coutts was so outraged by the casualty care arrangements that he submitted a series of highly critical articles to *The Times*, which were subsequently published. On the day of publication of his final article, he addressed the House of Commons and gave the Honourable Members a graphic account of his experiences.[12] Nevertheless, his testimony did not go unchallenged by the government and medical services; yet there was enough compelling evidence to justify the establishment of a Royal Commission led by Lord Justice Romer. However, the report findings became the centre of controversy, with some MPs making accusations of a cover-up.[13]

By 1914, things were different, or so the AMS believed. They had argued that in previous campaigns the medical services lacked executive authority within the military to enforce enteric preventative measures; but by 1914 this certainly was not the situation. It is difficult to understand, therefore, why the medical services were not more pro-active in establishing anti-enteric measures. While the AMS might plead in mitigation that lack of experience was the main reason for their slow response in dealing with the traumatic injuries caused by the new weapons of warfare, they could not say the same where disease was concerned, particularly enteric fever. To some extent the problem was aggravated by enteric inoculation being met with a lack of uptake by troops embarking on foreign service. Arguably, the reluctance could in part be attributed to campaigns waged by anti-inoculation advocates who believed compulsory vaccination to be an assault on the rights of the individual. Conversely, just three weeks into the War, Sir William Osler, Regius Professor of Medicine at Oxford University, wrote a letter to *The Times* advocating compulsory vaccination, claiming that in warfare 'the microbe kills more than the bullet'.[14] Also, Sir Almroth Wright, a pioneer of anti-typhoid vaccine and Head of the Inoculation Department at St Mary's Hospital, London, wrote to *The Times* on 5 and 28 September arguing in most vigorous terms the case for compulsory vaccination. It was Wright's contention that the right of the individual should be subsumed in order to ensure the health of the army.[15] Entering the fray, the eminent Scottish physician and pharmacology expert, Sir Thomas Lauder Brunton, also wrote to *The Times* supporting the views of Osler and Wright.[16] In support of the pro-inoculation lobby, *The British Journal of Nursing* printed an article entitled 'The Religion of Sanitation', citing historical precedents for inoculation and reminding the readership to 'think again of South Africa, with its 57,000 cases of typhoid fever!'.[17]

For the anti-inoculation lobby, the 'doctor knows best' philosophy was unacceptable medical paternalism that interfered with the rights of individuals to make their own health choices. Despite the controversy, within weeks enteric broke out among the troops, with the inevitable consequences. Working on No. 5 Ambulance Train, Kate Luard witnessed the reality of the debates. Her train was temporarily halted at Villeneuve Triage, which she described as the

'Swindon of France; a huge wilderness of railway lines, trains, and enormous hangars now used as camps and hospitals'. She observed that in a railway shed there were 'rows of enterics on stretchers waiting on motor ambulances to take them to Versailles'.[18] One of her enteric patients was desperately ill and in his delirious state revealed some of his personal horrors of the war:

> A Skye man, thinks I'm his mother; told me tonight there was a German spy in his carriage, and that he had 'fifty dead Jocks to bury – and it wasn't the buryin' he didn't like but the feeling of it'. He babbles continually of Germans, ammunition, guns, Jocks and rations.[19]

Working at No. 12 General Hospital, Millicent Peterkin was assigned to nurse enteric cases sent down from the Aisne battlefront: 'Tent I.5 is a special enteric tent, and is very busy, with 4 bad cases, one of whom is just dying.'[20] At Boulogne, in No. 14 Stationary Hospital, enteric wards were established. On an inspection visit, Maud McCarthy commented on the rise of enteric cases and the facilities made available for their care: 'the enterics have increased in number and the whole of the ground floor of this hospital is set apart for them. All arrangements for disinfection, feeding and nursing, are excellent.' Six days later she returned to see 'what arrangements were being made for nursing of Sisters and officers suffering from enteric'.[21] It was, perhaps, too little too late. The first principle in dealing with enteric was prevention. Should an outbreak occur then the source or sources had to be identified swiftly and followed up with containment, isolation, sanitation, disinfection, purification and ventilation, and this was not happening. The appalling sanitary conditions did not go unnoticed by Katharine Furse. Concerned about the spread of enteric at Boulogne station, she informally approached the medical administration to institute preventative measures; due to a lack of response, she was forced to submit a formal report on the lamentable state of affairs:

> Three thousand sick and wounded men lying about all day in the station and only one station-yard latrine. Our Paddington Scout Master, Philip Woolcombe, and a Boy Scout between them fixed up great washing tubs on an unused siding below the platform level and to these the walking wounded carried those who were too wounded to walk themselves.[22]

Her report had the desired effect; fatigue parties were established to remove and destroy the detritus in and around the station. However, there were other problems that were clearly detrimental to the health of the troops, particularly for the sick and injured who lay for hours on the station platform waiting to be moved on. In a further report, Katharine Furse highlighted the lack of care and cleanliness of stretchers and blankets:

> Stretchers would be left from day to day at the station, soaked with blood and with cotton wool sticking to them and covered in flies. We offered to take charge of them and clean them but were immediately informed that the matter was in hand. Blankets would lie on the ground outside the station with the rain driving in on to them so that

they were soaked through and yet, when a man with pneumonia or rheumatic fever was evacuated from an Ambulance Train, his warm, dry blanket would be removed and kept in the train, while the wet blanket would replace them. We offered to set up a drying room, in order to ensure that carefully aired blankets were available, but we were refused permission.[23]

There is no doubt that Katharine Furse was frustrated and angered by the reluctance of the AMS to accept help from the VAD unit and claimed she 'never could forgive' those who would neglect the sick and wounded rather than admit they were not fully able to do all that was necessary. Sharing some of her concerns about the care of the casualties, Colonel Wake, one of the Red Cross Assistant Commissioners in France, made a complaint about the behaviour of the ADMS at Boulogne. The incident involved hospital facilities established for a contingent of Indian troops. In December, the King had paid a visit to France and he expressed a desire to visit some of the British and Indian sick and wounded. According to Katharine Furse, some of the Indian casualties were housed in 'a ruinous building on the outskirts of the town' and when she first visited the hospital a warning notice above the door read, 'Danger dermort'.[24] The Indian contingent had arrived in France in late September and almost immediately was dispatched to the fighting front. Because suitable hospital accommodation was in very short supply, a badly ruined Jesuit College at Boulogne was commandeered for use as a hospital for some of the Indian troops. The medical services' explanation was to downplay the state of affairs: 'there was a delay in getting the ruined buildings prepared for hospital purposes, and temporary accommodation had to be obtained in tents, pending the construction of huts'.[25] Katharine Furse claimed that some of the wounded Indian soldiers were 'housed against orders in tents' and for the sake of 'the prestige of the British Empire no wounded Indians were to be kept under canvas'. In advance of the King's visit, Colonel Wake was contacted by the ADMS at Boulogne and asked to supply Red Cross ambulances to evacuate the Indian sick and wounded to the Hospital Ships. Katharine Furse asserted that complications arose when the ambulances reached the quay and no Hospital Ships were available, and 'the Indians in the ambulances were put into sheds until the official inspection was over'. Colonel Wake, who according to Katharine Furse was notable for his courage and honesty, reported what happened, not to GHQ but to the King's equerry.[26]

As a result of his actions, Colonel Wake fell foul of the AMS and he and his Joint Commissioner, Sir Savile Brinton Crossley, were forced to resign and return to London. However, the scandal was not without its repercussions; within a few weeks the ADMS who issued the fumbled orders was, according to Katharine Furse, 'invalided home with a gastric ulcer though whether the malady was of a physical or diplomatic nature one can only guess'.[27]

The behaviour of the ADMS had placed the medical services in an impossible and highly embarrassing position because accompanying the King on his trip were the Maharajah Sir Pertab Singh and the Maharajah of Bikaner. Furthermore, on the last day of the royal visit the King presented the Victoria Cross to 33-year-old Naik Darwan Sing Negi of the 39th Garhwal Rifles. His citation read:

> For great gallantry on the night of the 23rd–24th November, near Festubert, France when the regiment was engaged in retaking and clearing the enemy out of our trenches, and, although wounded in two places in the head, and also in the arm, being one of the first to push round each successive traverse, in the face of severe fire from bombs and rifles at the closest range.[28]

The consequences could have been unimaginable; an Indian soldier, wounded in an act of valour, awarded the VC, yet questionable medical facilities made available for Indian troops. Thankfully for the AMS a scandal was averted and the embarrassment was temporary. However, in this instance, their handling of the situation could readily be interpreted as a cover-up, and when politically expedient the AMS decided that two wrongs would definitely make it right. The bitterness of Colonel Wake's demise lingered with Katharine Furse. She would later write that a policy of 'appeasement' had been adopted, and 'as the war developed I learnt that this was not an isolated case and my experience of human jealousies and ambitions being allowed to stop useful and altruistic work is one of the factors in my loathing of war'.[29]

After three months in France, Katharine Furse was recalled to London; not because of her vociferous criticism of the AMS but at the invitation of Arthur Stanley, who invited her to take up the position of Commandant-in-Chief of the VADs at the BRCS headquarters. Before agreeing to take up the position she consulted Alfred Keogh, who told her, 'I am quite sure you will be wanted here. The great increase in beds will necessitate calling upon VADs more and more and you should be prepared to watch the thing through.'[30]

By January 1915 Katharine Furse was the new Commandant-in-Chief. Interestingly, sections of the nursing press had referred to Keogh as an 'ardent Red Cross man' and believed that political manoeuvrings at the War Office would see VADs given a more prominent role in the care of the sick and wounded. His statement to Katharine Furse could be interpreted as prophesy or, perhaps, impending policy.

The battles of 1914 had culminated in the brutally contested defence of Ypres. In late 1914 stalemate set in and the war of movement became static. By the turn of the year both sides were entrenched and neither side was spared the misery and hardship of winter. As the sick and wounded flooded into clearing stations, Stationary and General Hospitals, the medical and nursing services found themselves working under the most primitive and trying conditions. The awfulness of delivering care without the necessary equipment and supplies was described by a Red Cross Sister attached to the QAIMNS:

> One recalls a building, a former school, with no lighting or heating arrangements, except in one room where there was a gas jet and a miserable stove, the only means of obtaining hot water. Here urgent operations had to be performed under anything but aseptic conditions, and case after case would be brought in and placed on the floor,

watching and waiting to take their turn on the improvised operating table. The other rooms were full of wounded lying close together on straw. And it was anxious work by the light of a feeble candle, going from one to another watching for haemorrhage or collapse. The food question was also difficult, even milk being hard to get. The sanitary arrangements were practically nil, the only pretence being an open gutter in front of the building ... meantime the wounded were pouring in night and day, to be washed, fed and have their wounds dressed before being sent to England. The wounds were appalling, the odour from gas gangrene cases unbearable, and the mental condition of the patients added to the strain of nursing.[31]

With both sides 'dug in', a temporary lull in wholesale military aggression gave respite to the medical and nursing staff. During the great battles of 1914 they had been primarily absorbed with the care and treatment of the wounds inflicted by the 'new technologies'. The military mantra was to 'preserve the efficiency of the troops' and the medical services now had to refocus their attention on the prevention, early intervention and treatment of conditions and diseases, primarily arising from highly unfavourable environmental and climatic conditions. In one of his dispatches, Sir John French praised the troops for their ability to endure the great hardships of the winter campaign, claiming, 'Frost and snow have alternated with periods of continuous rain. The men have been called upon to stand for many hours together almost up to their waists in bitterly cold water.' The Commander believed that 'every measure which science and medical knowledge could suggest to mitigate these hardships was employed, the sufferings of the men have been very great'.[32]

Sir John was certainly right about the conditions. The first winter of the War was severe and the continual exposure of the troops to cold, wet and damp weather produced illnesses such as bronchitis, pneumonia, rheumatic fever, trench fever and nephritis, as well as trench foot and frostbite. Hospital admissions with frostbite were particularly high – 6,447 during the winter months of 1914.[33]

Attending to the Indian troops at the Meerut Stationary Hospital, Boulogne, the Resident Surgical Officer, Dr Loughnane, RAMC, said that out of 160 casualties admitted to the hospital in one evening, about 120 were cases of frostbite and many of them were stretcher cases:

These were very bad cases in which both feet were affected, and so painful and tender that no walking could be attempted, even with the aid of a stick. This is the largest proportion I have seen admitted to hospital in any one day for over two months, but fortunately, although some were so serious as to be incapacitated completely for the time being, they would for the most part recover, unlike many of those previously admitted, for whom amputation was often necessary.[34]

It was claimed the Indian troops had a predisposition to thermal injuries but this was refuted with counterclaims that anyone exposed to cold and inclement weather could be at risk. Also, Major Charles Miller, RAMC, found it necessary to dispel the ridiculous belief among some that frostbite was psychological in origin or a condition of the 'neurotic'. In an assessment of 376 cases admitted to the British Red Cross Hospital, Netley, Major Miller concluded the primary cause was exposure to harsh conditions and inadequate footwear: 'In all cases the men had been standing in mud or mud and water of a depth varying from eighteen inches to three and a half feet for many hours.' He concluded his findings:

> Certain factors are doubtless of importance. The lower temperature, not necessarily to freezing point, is probably of great importance. But in my opinion the immobility of the feet and legs is even more important. The feet are cramped into boots that are made too tight with the extra socks worn; the legs may be kept stiff by badly applied puttees, and the whole limb is held motionless by the inertia of the mud and water in the trenches.[35]

In Dr Loughnane's opinion men were not neurotic; they were worn out with their experiences in the trenches and, once frostbite developed, their journey to hospital exacerbated their already fragile condition. He claimed the men's 'vitality' was sapped by 'exposure in the trenches and the hardships of transport by train and ambulance. Some of them have been without food for two or three days, and arrived at their journey's end constitutional wrecks, broken down mentally and physically.'[36]

The nursing care of frostbite patients was not prescriptive; many treatments were tried and tested. According to one Sister, the most preferred therapy for chronic cases was bed rest, a nutritious diet and the feet well wrapped to restore circulation. If feet were black, blistered or both, they required frequent dressings. The blistered skin was cut away and the underlying raw tissue dusted with boric, zinc oxide and amylum powder; the toes were separated with strips of gauze between them and the whole foot was then wrapped in gauze and cotton wool. Gentle massage was also employed, but if the foot or feet did not respond to the treatment and became gangrenous, then amputation was carried out. In very bad cases the patients were put on a light four-hourly diet consisting of brandy, egg flips, milk and chicken broth. Pain relief varied according to the severity of the condition; everything from aspirin to morphine was prescribed, although potassium bromide was considered the most effective as it allowed the patient to have a rested sleep.[37]

In the cold weather, the difference between frostbite and 'trench foot' became confused. However, trench foot was characterised by cold, swollen, pale feet, with the men claiming their feet felt numb or like lead weights. The condition could result from long, quick marches to the trenches, where men would arrive with hot and swollen feet, but prolonged exposure to waterlogged conditions was the main contributing factor. Defective or badly fitting footwear and constriction of the circulation by tightly fitting socks or puttees added to the problem. Furthermore, infection and gangrene could set in if the condition was untreated. In January 1915, under Army Routine Order 554, a regime was initiated for the prevention of trench foot. This consisted of a recommended combination of procedures such as wiping army boots inside and out with oil, preferably whale oil; foot hygiene, care of blisters and abrasions, massaging with grease or oil, and regular access to clean, dry socks with no wear or tear in the fabric. Trench foot could be a dreadfully debilitating condition and there was little sympathy for men who suffered from it. There was a general suspicion among the High Command that it was due to carelessness, and that men reporting with it were malingerers. It would have been logical to deduce that if men were left standing in mud and water for days and nights, with little or no chance of drying out their socks and boots, the health and fighting capability of troops would be compromised. But the High Command's powers of reasoning were quite often driven by suspicion, not logic. Was it really malingering when men found themselves unable to walk and had to resort to crawling back from the trenches or be carried on the backs of their comrades because they were crippled with the pain of damaged, deformed feet?

Arguably, the casualty numbers could have been reduced and chronic disability avoided if the army had instituted better relief systems for strained, exhausted and environmentally exposed troops. In an attempt to assist the British and French medical services, J. B. Charcot, a veteran of Antarctic expeditions, with considerable experience of hostile environments, offered advice on how to mitigate the effects of extreme climatic conditions. He produced a pamphlet giving advice on clothing, rewarming and treatments, particularly for frostbite. He modestly claimed that he was trying to 'offer a few suggestions which may not only be the means of preserving men for the national defence', but also to spare those who are fighting for their country 'unnecessary suffering'. Despite his offer, there is no evidence to suggest that his pamphlet was circulated within the BEF or acted upon by the AMS.[38]

The cold winter conditions had a deleterious effect on everyone and the nurses were not exempt. Many of them developed chilblains, a very painful and debilitating condition. Given that nurses were on their feet for twelve hours a day, and quite often longer, it must have been extraordinarily difficult to work with such pain and discomfort. Finding the appropriate footwear too was a problem, and Sister Jean Todd was prepared to be more practical and less conventional:

> Chilblains, both on feet and hands, are a growing complaint. The latest footwear is snow boots, the kind with clasps, and one wears a pair of thin shoes or slippers inside them. Sister C has specially bad chilblains on her feet and has an extraordinary walk, a kind of cross between a duck's waddle and a standstill. One's feet grow bigger daily too, or so it seems ... A Medical Officer offered me a pair of gumboots, too small for him. Accepted them, they certainly are not too small for me. I never seem to know where my feet are and many a tumble over tent ropes I've taken, but two or even three pairs of socks can go on![39]

Sister Peterkin was on night duty when she became unwell with the effects of working in cold conditions and was taken by ambulance to No. 8 General Hospital, where a 'Sick Sisters Ward' had been established. A few hours after her admission she was able to write, 'Am feeling absolutely dead to the world tonight, but at last got warmed through and ceased to shiver. Felt as if I would never be warm again.' The following day she wrote, 'The Home Sister from No. 12 came in today. She has very bad feet, and is going home by the next boat.'[40]

Between January and March, new units and hospitals were opening and the nursing service needed more personnel. However, ill health within the service was a problem not to be ignored, particularly if nurses were sent home with conditions that could be readily managed at the front. Therefore, it was vital that nursing sisters with several months' active service experience were retained; to this end, special hospital accommodation for sick and debilitated nurses was established at Rouen, Boulogne and Étaples. The first convalescent home for nurses was established at Hardelot. The home was a villa, on loan from Princess Louise, Duchess of Argyll; and it became known as the Princess Louise's Convalescent Home for Nursing Sisters. Lady Gifford from the BRCS was appointed Lady Superintendent.

In its first three months, 169 nurses benefited from their stay at the home. The admissions were represented as: 4 Army Matrons; 14 Regulars; 67 Reserves; 26 Territorial; 27 BRCS; 13 St John Ambulance; 12 Australian; 2 Voluntary hospitals; and 4 VAD Members. The nurses came from 24 different hospitals, 2 hospital trains and 1 rest station. The greatest number of the admissions (67) were recovering from debility. Additionally, 38 had influenza; 12 enteritis; 11 conjunctivitis; 8 colds; 7 bronchitis; 6 tonsillitis; 4 septic throat; 4 neuralgia; 4 gastritis; 4 septic finger; 3 quinsy; 3 pleurisy; 2 anaemia; 1 corneal ulcer; 1 ear abscess; 1 synovitis of knee; 1 laryngitis; 1 septic eye; 1 indigestion; 1 embolism of leg; 1 burnt foot; 1 rheumatism.[41]

It is not surprising that the greatest number came from the Reserve and that the highest incidence of illness was debility. With only a small cadre of Regulars, it fell to the Reserve to carry out most of the work. The Regulars were appointed into senior positions and they managed the duties of the Reserve and Territorial nurses. The management structure of the QA was not entirely formulated on professional protocol or ability; quite often it reflected status and preference. It was Maud McCarthy's belief that she was professionally obliged to remove the Regulars from front-line duties and place them in senior administrative positions, claiming, 'In these large units it is important to have Army [Regulars] representatives.' The word 'representatives' was arguably a euphemism for presence and profile; from the first day Maud McCarthy arrived in France she was determined to promote and protect the image of the QAs. She certainly raised her own profile and was described by one General as 'a genius'. In overly effusive terms he commented on her organisational skills: 'she is perfectly splendid, she's wonderful – she's a soldier. If she was made Quartermaster General she would work it, she would run the whole Army and never get flustered or make a mistake ... We couldn't get on without her.' He did, however, commend the work of all the nurses at the front, describing it as 'magnificent', and was particularly impressed with the nurses' 'courage and devotion', not to mention 'their discipline, common sense and organisation'. He further claimed, or rather confessed, that before the War he had been absolutely against the franchise for women: 'If a woman was to ask me now to support that movement I should not be able to find it in my conscience to refuse.'[42] Clearly, it had not taken long for the army nursing service and its most senior representative on the Western Front to establish a positive presence. In one of his spring dispatches, Sir John French was moved to recognise the work of the nursing services and, according to Sister Luard, it was long overdue: 'Yes, Johnny French has mentioned the nurses for the first time for nearly a year of war … So I suppose that someone has got it into his head that we do a little work sometimes.'[43]

The early months of 1915 saw an increase in and the establishment of every type of facility needed for the care of the BEF and Allied forces. Clearing Hospitals, now renamed Casualty Clearing Stations, were increased, as were the number of Sisters working in them. The number of Ambulance Trains expanded, and temporary Ambulance Trains were staffed and equipped at periods of high demand. The First Ambulance Flotilla was established, consisting of three Hospital Barges that journeyed from Versailles to Rouen. Sister Kate Read was appointed Acting Matron to the Flotilla. As a member of the Reserve she had been serving in France since the outbreak of the War. Additionally, a Sister and Staff Nurse were _allocated to each barge. Due to outbreaks of infectious diseases, Isolation

Figure 3.1 QAIMNSR Sisters on board one of the many Hospital Barges which could not be used when the canals were frozen. National Library of Scotland.

Hospitals became a permanent feature of the casualty care arrangements. In order to deal with the enteric problem affecting the civilian and refugee population in and around the British sector at Ypres, an Isolation Hospital was established in a convent at Mallassise. The hospital was primarily staffed by British nurses and comprised a Matron, Miss Helena Hartigan, a Regular, and two Sisters from the Reserve, Sisters Elston and Davey; all three were fluent in French. Additionally, thirty BRCS-trained nurses and twelve BRCS VADs were deployed. In addition to the British nursing staff, three Belgian bilingual nurses worked at the hospital. The medical staff was drawn from the RAMC and the BRCS, and Lieutenant Colonel Guise-Moores was appointed CO. According to Maud McCarthy, 'this was the first occasion on which VAD Members were employed in a Military Hospital in France'.[44]

The VAD 'question' had not gone away and trained nurses on the home front were still lobbying about the use of untrained personnel for war work. The National Council of Trained Nurses of Great Britain and Ireland sent a report to the Director General of the Army Medical Services voicing their concerns about the use of VADs for nursing duties in military hospitals. The BRCS also came under pressure from trained nurses and the nursing press, and was urged to set up a working group to advise on the use of volunteer nurses. The pressure from lobbyists and the shortage of nurses for war work combined to bring the

Figure 3.2 Ward accommodation on a Hospital Barge. QARANC Collection.

BRCS and the medical military authorities to the negotiating table, where issues and concerns regarding the use of VADs could be addressed. At a meeting held at the BRCS HQ on 27 January, the Joint Executive War Committee heard a proposal from Lady Ampthill that a 'Special Standing Committee on Voluntary Aid Detachments' should be established; the proposal was accepted, and the Hon. Arthur Stanley MP was appointed Chairman. By February the Committee could report:

> The Army Council have approved of the control of all VADs being vested for the duration of the war in a Committee consisting of representatives of the Territorial Forces Association, The British Red Cross Society and the Order of St John. The said Committee will be known as the Joint VAD Committee.[45]

Twelve representatives were appointed: three from the Territorial Forces Associations; three from the British Red Cross; three from the Order of St John; and the War Office was represented by Surgeon General Sir Launcelotte Gubbins, the Matron-in-Chief, Ethel Becher, and a senior civil servant. In response to the developments, *The British Journal of Nursing* saw the move as positive, and hoped that in a spirit of consensus, 'the formation of this Committee is in earnest of better things'.[46]

Not everyone welcomed the news; the 'Limelighters' were now part of the system, but in the eyes of many trained nurses the decision was unwise and problematic. In an Editorial entitled 'Are Nurses Jealous?', *The Nursing Times* cautioned against the use of 'ignorant amateurs' and claimed that if trained nurses were jealous, it was with justification. 'What was the root of the discontent?' the Editorial asked. Since the outbreak of the War it had been stated many times in nursing journals and newspaper articles that trained nurses were concerned about the professional reputation of nursing being damaged should VADs get a foothold in casualty care. Moreover, they did not want 'Limelighters playing at nursing' and wanted assurances that when the War was over VADs would not be able to 'pose as a nurse on the strength of a short experience in a military hospital'. Furthermore, trained nurses were fearful that volunteer nurses could replace trained nurses in the labour market, a concern they had raised on many occasions but which had been greeted with little reassurance:

> There is a very real danger that these women, whatever you may call them now, will when the war is over claim that they have nursed in military hospitals for a definite period, and there is no doubt that some of them will attempt to take up private or other forms of nursing on the strength of it.[47]

Despite the protests, the deal was done and, in military parlance, there was to be no retreat; the VADs were officially recognised by the War Office as contributors to the casualty care system. By the end of February the British were preparing for a March offensive and for the military and the nursing profession the period of stasis was over.

On 9 March, the Commander of the First Army, Sir Douglas Haig, issued a special order informing the troops they were about to engage with the enemy but under very auspicious conditions: 'At no time in the War has there been a more favourable moment for us, and I feel confident of the success. The extent of that success must depend on the rapidity and determination with which we advance.' Haig was referring to the battle for Aubers Ridge, scheduled to start on 10 March. To reach Aubers, the village of Neuve Chapelle, which in the early months of the War changed hands several times before being secured by the Germans in November 1914, had first to be retaken. At approximately 7 a.m. on the morning of 10 March, men stood knee deep in mud and waterlogged trenches waiting for the order to advance, and when the whistle blew the advance was swift. The battle was a murderous encounter in which every known weapon of modern warfare was deployed. The BEF successfully broke the German-held line at Neuve Chapelle but, once this objective had been achieved, problems with supplies and coordination seriously hampered attempts to advance towards Aubers Ridge. The army could advance no further and the offensive turned out to be costly, particularly in casualties. The vulnerability of the human mind and body pitted against machine guns, bombs and howitzers ensured the Regimental Aid Posts (RAP), Advanced Dressing Stations (ADS), Field Ambulances (FA), Ambulance Trains (AT) and Casualty Clearing Stations (CCS) were packed with physical and psychological wrecks. According to Sister Luard, the hospitals in Rouen had to be cleared for the new intake of casualties, and the Ambulance Trains were being rushed up the lines: 'We are now on our way up again; shortest time we've ever waited – one hour after the last patient is off. ATs have been tearing up empty and back full all day.'[48]

The medical arrangements for the immediate care and evacuation of the battle casualties consisted of four British, one Canadian and two Indian CCSs, three motor ambulance convoys, one British and one Indian advance depots of medical stores, a mobile bacteriological laboratory, and twelve ATs. Additionally, each division had its own FAs. The DMS estimated the casualty rate to be approximately 3,000 per day.[49]

According to Adelina Walker, the Matron at No. 13 Stationary Hospital, 'the battle of Neuve Chapelle was one of our most terrible times, gas gangrene and tetanus were rampant and the wounded streamed in day and night'. She had been at No. 13 since October 1914, when it changed from its pre-war use as a sugar storage shed to a fully functioning hospital. Since then, the medical and nursing staff had perfected a system of triage whereby the procedures for receiving and distributing casualties had improved significantly. Despite not being a regular hospital, Matron Walker believed the sheds were practical when it came to dealing with heavy intakes of casualties:

> One advantage of these sheds was that by one door we received the wounded, and by
> the opposite door they were passed to the boats … In the casualty ward, where the

men walked in, as many as 3,000 were dressed and fed in the day and passed onto boats. We were well fitted up by this time, NCOs met the patients as they arrived, and drafted the walking cases to different benches according to degrees of wounds. They were immediately seen by the doctors who prescribed for them – the treatment being written down by a Sister, and a band of nurses followed carrying out the treatments. Then the men were sent to long comfortable tables, where a hot meal was served with a mug of tea. From there they were passed out at the far side of the ward, decorated with 'Blighty tickets', and so onto the waiting boats.[50]

Sister Margaret Brander was in charge of the night duty staff at No. 14 General Hospital when the flood of casualties started arriving from Neuve Chapelle; many were in an appalling state, with injuries almost beyond description:

There has been some dreadful fighting; we have been so very busy every night, the wounded pouring in. The wounds are ghastly, some of the men are frightfully mangled … Fractured femurs, many of the men having face wounds, fractures of the arms, etc. One man I may give as an example. His nose was broken, his humerus compound fracture, femur compound fracture, penis shattered, and not a grumble from him only gratitude. Another in the corner, compound fracture of femur and bullet wound of anus, bullet probably lodged in pelvis. Another both eyes shot out and part of brain bulging out from forehead. Yet another with one huge wound extending shoulder to shoulder. A little boy of 19 years has wound of right shoulder, hip and leg and compound fracture of arm and wound of hand. Bullet also in his abdomen. Tonight he has all the symptoms of peritonitis. The head cases are innumerable. One has died tonight, he only came this afternoon never has been conscious. Many more are dying. There are many bad chest cases. Trephining and amputations are continuous. Words can never describe this scene.[51]

The following night the intake of critical casualties did not abate, and despite the best efforts and hard work of the medical and nursing staff, many of the previous day's admissions did not survive. The casualty care demands were relentless and Sister Brander and her staff had to cope with the vast increase in hospital beds:

Another rush of ambulances, and dying all around you … there were 29 funerals today 26 yesterday. I have just been giving advice to two sisters, hope they will be the better of it … I hear our beds number 1,000 now and another 1,000 being got ready. The men's stories are dreadful. Nothing but murder they say … we scarcely have a minute to hear their terrible stories. Bad mouth cases and a lot of head cases, some bad legs also, and the smells almost suffocating.[52]

According to Sister Brander, two days after the final rush of casualties into No. 14 General Hospital, the Matron asked her, 'If I should care to go daffodil picking with Major Knox. I laughingly replied that the night sister could not afford herself such a luxury. He'll have difficulty I should think in getting company.'

It would be difficult to know what was more surreal, the almost Dantesque vision of nurses diligently working to preserve lives and limbs from the obscene effects of weaponry or what appeared to be the Matron's detachment from the reality of the situation. Perhaps what appeared to be an incongruous question belied the personal trauma behind it or, as a good Matron, she was simply attempting to bring some normality into the life of a hard-working Sister. The psychological state of Neuve Chapelle casualties was observed by Sister Blair: 'the poor boys were dreadfully done up by the time they reached us. It was days before they could speak or take an interest in anything.' When the soldiers eventually spoke to her they were unanimous in their description of the battle: 'it's hell up there Sister'.[53]

The mental healthcare of the troops was not of paramount importance to the military and medical authorities, despite cases of nervousness, mutism and 'madness' being identified in the 1914 engagements, particularly during the Ypres offensive. In November 1914, *The British Journal of Nursing* alluded to men suffering from 'nerve concussion' and claimed there was much to learn about treatments and prognosis. In the same month, Sister Luard noted that on board her AT was a young boy with no wounds but who 'was suffering from shock of shell bursts'.[54] By March 1915 there was a rise in the reported cases of psychological breakdown.

It was the considered opinion of Dr Aldren Turner, Physician to King's College Hospital and the National Hospital for the Paralysed and Epileptic at Queen's Square, London, appointed Temporary Lieutenant Colonel to the RAMC, that 'One of the features of the early fighting was the heavy shelling to which our troops were subjected, and which to a large extent accounted for the prevalence of nervous shock at the time.'[55] In other words, the men appeared to be suffering from 'shell shock'.

Even so, injuries of the mind did not occupy the minds of the AMS hierarchy; there were greater concerns with the management of physical trauma. A Sister working at No. 4 General Hospital described the different types of wound trauma the nurses were dealing with: 'We get a great variety of wounds, the cleanest cases being the simple wounds caused by bullets. Shrapnel wounds are mostly very dirty, but perhaps the worst are those of a ricochet bullet, which lacerates terribly.' The Sister warned of potential complications, particularly cautioning against ignoring the signs of tetanus:

> As it develops sometimes after a patient has come into hospital it is as well that nurses should be on the watch for any signs – general restlessness; violent headache, frequent yawning, and possibly some feeling of giddiness, with darting pains in different parts of the body.[56]

The Sister also suggested the need for vigilance in the early detection of gas gangrene, particularly casualties with shell wounds of the arms and legs: 'The patient has severe pain in the early stages and the wound is most offensive with a characteristic odour, so that after dealing with one case of gas gangrene another would be easily recognised.' The reference to the malodorous smell from gangrenous wounds is omnipresent in nurses' testaments and was described by one very experienced nurse as 'hardly bearable'.

In addition to the smell of rotting flesh, nurses dealt with offensive smells from discharging wounds; stale blood and sweat; vomit; and clothes and linen soiled with urine or faeces or both. Many of the casualties admitted into hospitals were in uniforms and underclothing they had worn for weeks without change, and the smell of their clothing ranged from stale to sour. According to Sister Paterson, men could arrive with 'clothing moulded to their limbs, generally been on 5, 6, 7 weeks'. The men were deeply embarrassed by the filthy, lice-ridden state of their bodies and garments but regardless, Sister Paterson claimed, 'I still love the British Tommie even at his grubbiest ... poor souls, we assure them not to worry, they've done their share of the work and now it's our turn.'[57]

Yet it was not the smell of unwashed, stale uniforms that exercised the doctors serving on the Western Front, it was the pathology behind malodorous wounds. In the early part of 1915 the RAMC instituted a Medical Society at Rouen; doctors and specialists met to discuss the conditions they were dealing with and how advancements could be made in research, treatments and rehabilitation therapies. At the February meeting, Sir Almroth Wright opened up a discussion on bacteriology and the treatment of traumatic wounds, particularly those associated with tetanus and gas gangrene, claiming that 'practically every wound in the present war is infected'. He also asserted the established wound-management regime of daily irrigation with antiseptic solutions to be ineffective against infected, suppurating wounds and that there was little evidence to support the procedure having any value. He concluded his presentation by suggesting there needed to be a willingness to think differently about wound management and that, in order to save lives and limbs and to reduce disability, new prophylactic and therapeutic measures were urgently needed.[58]

While the specialists concentrated on reducing the effects of traumatic wounding, by April the War had moved into a more sinister and deadly phase. On Thursday 22 April, at Langemarck in the Ypres Salient, the Germans mounted a gas attack against the British, Canadian, Indian, North African and French forces. The use of poisonous gas was proscribed at the 1899 Hague conference when, on 29 July, the 'Declaration on the use of Projectiles the Object of which is the Diffusion of Asphyxiating or Deleterious Gases' was signed.[59] Germany was a signatory to the Declaration but demonstrated a wilful disregard for it when a loophole was found in the agreement by which lethal gas could be dispersed. The Germans were not the first to use chemicals. In the first month of the War the French used tear-gas xylyl bromide grenades. In October 1914, the Germans, in their attempt to capture Neuve Chapelle, fired shells at the French which contained a chemical designed to irritate the nasal passages and induce violent fits of sneezing. By January 1915, they unsuccessfully deployed tear-gas on the Eastern Front, but two months later they used an enhanced version of lachrymal gas against the French. However, the gas discharged at Langemarck was designed to asphyxiate but not before it produced severe irritation of the eyes and worked its toxic effect through the respiratory system. As it settled in the lungs it produced a lethal build-up of fluid and caused corrosion of the tissues; eventually this would lead to men coughing up and vomiting blood. In the final throes of their agonising death, men felt severe constriction of their chest, followed by frantic struggles for breath. It was a harrowing, frightening and traumatic way to die.

The awfulness of watching men struggle for breath was described by a medical officer working at No. 2 CCS, where many of the gassed casualties were taken for treatment:

> To see those men tearing at their throats, rending their tunics, screaming to us in hoarse rattling voices to put them out of their misery. Many were in a semi-comatose state and as fast as we laid them down on their stretchers in the great ward here on the ground floor with all the windows open to let in the air, they slipped down from the pillows propping them up and began to struggle. It took us all our time to go from stretcher to stretcher to prop them up again.[60]

The use of chlorine gas took the army medical and nursing services by complete surprise, despite the military having anticipated several months earlier a chemical deployment against its troops. The British had, allegedly, considered the use of chemical warfare. Moreover, according to Haig's recollection of a conversation in March 1915, Lord Dundonald had 'hopes of being able to apply an invention of his grandfather for driving a garrison out of a fort by using sulphur fumes'.[61] Even so, the illicit use of gas at Langemarck opened the door for further unspeakable horrors in the development and use of chemical warfare.

Sister Phillips first became aware of the gas attack when a Belgian civilian 'came staggering in' to her CCS. She said her first impression led her to believe the man was in an advanced stage of pneumonia, but it was difficult to make a diagnosis because 'he only spoke Flemish of which none of us understood a word'. It soon became apparent what the problem was when ambulances arrived at her CCS carrying women, children and troops. According to Sister Phillips, it did not take long before the CCS was filled with civilian and military personnel suffering from gas exposure and the staff were 'filled with astonishment at this fiendish mode of warfare which certainly never entered into our calculation'. Due to the unexpected nature of the condition, Sister Phillips claimed 'every conceivable remedy was tried … but being the first we had ever seen or even thought of made them seem much more difficult to tackle'.[62] On 23 April, GHQ in France sent a telegram to the War Office claiming:

German used powerful asphyxiating gases very extensively in attack on French yesterday with serious effects (stop) Apparently these gases are either chlorine or bromine (stop) Will send further details later but meanwhile strongly urge that immediate steps be taken to supply similar means of most effective kind for use by our troops (stop) Also essential that our troops should be immediately provided with means of counteracting effects of enemy gases which should be suitable for use when on the move (stop) As a temporary measure am arranging for troops in trenches to be supplied with solution of bicarbonate of soda in which to soak handkerchiefs (stop)[63]

British doctors tending gas victims observed that the presence of violent coughing spasms and irritation of the eyes, and the fact that men's tunic buttons turned green and their bayonets black, confirmed their suspicions that chlorine gas had been discharged at Langemarck. Within twenty-four hours of the attack, Dr John Scott Haldane travelled to France to investigate the type of gas deployed by the Germans. It was on Lord Kitchener's instruction that Haldane was sent to France because the War Office needed the best specialist it could garner. For years John Haldane had been investigating the causes of deaths in colliery and mine explosions, and authored works on the physiology of respiration and air analysis. He was a graduate of medicine from the University of Edinburgh and received an MA from Oxford. When Haldane arrived in France he travelled to No. 2 CCS at Bailleul, where he met with Consultant Physician to the BEF, Sir Wilmot Herringham. The two specialists carried out a joint consultation, examining several soldiers from Canadian battalions who were suffering from the effects of the gas. Haldane believed they were dealing with the effects of chlorine gas poisoning and, shortly after he and Sir Wilmot arrived at the CCS, one of the soldiers succumbed to the gassing. In order to establish the cause of death and confirm their suspicions, a post-mortem (PM) was carried out conducted by J. W. McNee, RAMC Officer Commanding (OC) Mobile Laboratory No. 3 attached to the Second Army and Assistant to the Professor of Pathology and Bacteriology at Glasgow University. In the PM narrative, Lieutenant McNee described the admission to hospital and subsequent death of the soldier:

This man was poisoned two days before death. When this man was brought in he showed marked cyanosis and a pulse rate of 130. His chest showed signs of acute catarrh. He showed more and more 'air hunger' and finally died with that as the chief symptom. The body showed definite discolouration of the face, neck and hands. There were no external marks or injury.[64]

Following the PM, Lieutenant McNee concluded that the cause of death was asphyxia caused by irritant gas. On the same day a second death followed at No. 2 CCS and, again, Lieutenant McNee carried out the PM. The results were similar; fluid build-up in the lungs due to irritant gas, causing slow asphyxiation. A deposition was taken from a Captain in the Canadian Expeditionary Force (CEF) who was also at No. 2 CCS suffering from the effects of the gas and a wound. The Captain's narrative described the experience that he and his men were subjected to. He spoke of a greenish cloud, drifting along the ground until it reached the Canadian trenches. He claimed 'men in the trenches were obliged to leave, and a number of them were killed by the effects of the gas'. He spoke of a counter-attack made by the Canadians just fifteen minutes after the gas came over their trenches, and saw twenty-four men lying dead from the effects of the gas on a small stretch of road leading from the advance trenches to the support trenches. Drawing on further witness statements and PM results led the specialists to conclude they were in no doubt at all that chlorine or bromine had been discharged by the Germans for the purpose of asphyxiation.

When Haldane announced his findings, *The Times* responded by describing the use of poisonous gas as an 'atrocious method of warfare'. The AMS initial advice to all troops was, in the event of further gas attacks, immediately to dip a handkerchief or whatever cloth was available into a bucket of sodium bicarbonate and then cover the mouth and nose. If no buckets of the fluid were available, which in the trenches was generally the case, it was suggested that soldiers should urinate onto a rag or pad and place it against their faces to give some relief from the effects of the gas. According to Stanley Casson, serving in the Lancashire Fusiliers, within a few days of the initial gas attacks:

> The men had already shown signs of nervousness of gas, a nervousness based only on the wild stories that runners had brought. Even so, senior officers were alarmed at the developments and they waited for guidance and support. The support came in packages marked 'Gas Mask Type 1'. The mask consisted of a small square of blue flannel, large enough to cover the mouth, with a tape on each side to tie round behind the head. Whatever benign personage contrived these amiable death traps I do not know. But anything more futile could never have been devised by the simplicity of man.[65]

Conversely, Haldane liaised with his colleague Professor Lorrain Smith, a pathologist at the University of Edinburgh, on the physiology issues, and consulted with T. F. Winmill, Chief Chemist, Doncaster Mine Owners' Research Laboratory, on the development of an effective respirator.

Between 2 and 7 May the gas attacks continued and 685 gas cases were admitted to No. 8 CCS, Bailleul. The soldiers arrived at 1.30 a.m., having been gassed at 7.30 the previous evening. They were transported by motor ambulance convoys from the Field Ambulances, a distance of 10 miles between the Field Ambulances and the CCS. According to one RAMC medical officer working at No. 8, it was 'difficult to convey the mental impression produced when the first batch were unloaded'. The doctor explained the distressed state of the soldiers as they struggled for breath:

> One soldier died before he was removed from the ambulance ... most of the others were in a choking condition, making agonizing efforts to breathe, clutching at their

throats ... At one moment they propped themselves up to gasp, at another they fell back exhausted by their struggles.[66]

Some of the men, particularly the older ones, were in a state of collapse; the majority of these cases did not survive. The PM results showed the cause of the deaths to be asphyxia due to fluid congestion of the lungs; the results supported the earlier findings of Lieutenant McNee. The treatments for gassed casualties were based on trial and error, but very quickly a general rule-of-thumb regime was established that proved to have some beneficial effects. In the first instance, a 10 ounce dose of salt-and-water emetic was given, followed by a large drink of lukewarm water; vomiting was immediately induced by touching the back of the throat with a soft brush or by the soldier using his finger, and the casualty would then vomit yellowish frothy fluid. This procedure, it was claimed, brought great relief. Additionally, stimulating expectorants were administered three-hourly, usually of ammonium carbonate with vinum ipecacuanhae added. Moreover, patients with severe breathing difficulties were given oxygen therapy, and in restless cases, particularly those caused by anxiety, opium was the drug of choice. When there were concerns about heart failure developing, pituitary extract and brandy were administered. Chronic breathing problems and respiratory arrest were treated by the Schafer's method of artificial respiration. The most serious cases generally stayed at the CCS for five days before being moved on to Base Hospitals, or some were shipped back to Britain.[67]

Caring for gas casualties had an emotionally distressing effect on the nursing staff, and *The Nursing Mirror and Midwives' Journal* wasted no time in sympathising with their situation: 'few have to undergo such a trying experience as the nurses to whose lot it has fallen to look after the victims of poisonous fumes'. The commentary further stated that a nurse working with gas patients had described the experience as 'the most terrible of all the terrible war experiences'.

Everywhere there were 'terrible' nightmare visions of suffering, and the situation at No. 2 Stationary Hospital represented what had become commonplace. On a routine visit, Maud McCarthy observed that the hospital was 'full of patients, every one of them seem to have either lost a leg or an arm, it was dreadful'. In a heartfelt and despondent diary entry, Sister Jean Todd, who was working at No. 2, summed up the situation: 'There is a war, an abominable war, how can I put on paper the scenes of suffering and tragedy that goes on day and night in this small hospital, and is just what is going on, even more so, in other big hospitals.'[68]

By April, the nurses probably believed the situation could not get any worse, but with the introduction of poisonous gas the expansion of lethal weapons had widened, and so had the war; in the same month, a new front opened up in the Mediterranean and British, French, Indian, Australian and New Zealand troops were on their way to the Land of Troy.

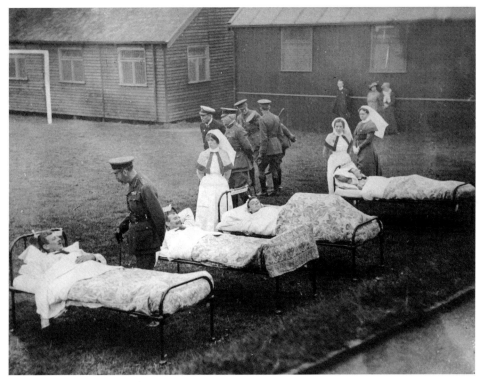

Figure 3.3 A Royal visit by King George V to the Western Front. QARANC Collection.

IN THE FOOTSTEPS OF AGAMEDE

The Gallipoli Expedition was, as many believed, the unwanted child of a hastily arranged marriage. In October 1914, Turkey entered the War and allied with Germany; in the same month the Ottoman Turks attacked the Russians in the Caucasus Mountains. The British and French were concerned that, with Turkey's entry into the War, the position on the Eastern Front would be weakened, and if the Russians were defeated then a large number of German troops could be deployed to the Western Front. It was the considered view of Winston Churchill, First Lord of the Admiralty, that Russia had to be supported, but this would involve opening up a new fighting front. He convinced Lord Kitchener that military action was needed and could best be achieved by gaining control over the Dardanelles Straits in north-western Turkey, which separated Europe and Asia. The straits were of strategic maritime importance and had been since the Trojan War was fought near the Aegean entrance. The planned objective was to seize or destroy the Turkish forts on the Gallipoli Peninsula, thereby securing an unobstructed water corridor; this would enable Allied ships to deliver vital supplies to the hard-pressed Russians fighting on the Eastern Front. Also, having gained control of the straits, an Allied advance would be made on Constantinople, the capital of the Ottoman Empire. It was an audacious plan which failed to take into account the geography of the Gallipoli Peninsula and underestimated the determination of the Ottoman defenders.[69]

Initially, the campaign was planned as a naval engagement with the fleet bombarding the forts, but within weeks of the first attacks it was deemed necessary to deploy troops for a joint assault. On 12 March, General Sir Ian Hamilton was appointed Commander of the Mediterranean Force. Along with his General Staff, he left Britain on 13 March and arrived at Mudros on the island of Lemnos on 17 March. Logistically, Mudros was ideal because it was 60 miles from the Gallipoli Peninsula and had a suitable deep-water bay. Even so, it had major drawbacks in that there was insufficient water to meet the required needs and standards and, after consultation between the military, medical specialists and the High Command, it was agreed that Mudros was unsuitable and a new base was established at Alexandria, the city founded by Alexander the Great, and once the epicentre of development in the sciences and humanities.[70] The piston, cylinder and valve were pioneered at Alexandria, along with an important piece of medical apparatus – the syringe.

The seizure of the Gallipoli Peninsula was problematic for a variety of reasons. An amphibious landing was necessary, which meant disembarking troops were exposed to gun and artillery fire as they landed on the narrow exposed beaches. Also, the terrain was irregular and extreme, the beaches were narrow strips of sand below overhanging cliffs, and the composition of the land varied; there were hills, peaks and ridges, gullies and ravines, as well as open rugged ground covered in thick scrub or prickly bush. Moreover, the climatic conditions ranged from bitter cold in the winter to excessive heat in the summer, and the peninsula was prone to sudden strong winds. In addition, the nearest base at the opening of the campaign was Alexandria, 700 miles from Gallipoli, and it was also the nearest hospital centre for casualties evacuated from the peninsula.[71]

Despite the hazards and obstacles, the first British and French landings took place on 25 April around the tip of Cape Helles, while the Australian and New Zealand forces were concentrated on the Aegean coast at a small inlet they named Anzac Cove. The medical arrangements for the landings were predicated upon the success and advance of the landing forces. It was anticipated that three Stationary Hospitals, Nos. 15 and 16 and No. 2 Australian, would be immediately established on the shores and they would retain the wounded for two or three days until they were assessed and classified for transportation. That was the plan. But it was impossible to establish the hospitals due to murderous shelling and firing on the disembarking troops and, instead, makeshift casualty care facilities were hurriedly put in place wherever protection could be found. Unlike the casualty care and evacuation chain on the Western Front, the medical logistics on the Gallipoli Peninsula did not involve Ambulance Trains or Base Hospitals, nor any of the nursing services. The planned casualty evacuation chain consisted of Regimental Aid Posts (RAP), Advanced Dressing Stations (ADS), Casualty Clearing Stations (CCS) and Stationary Hospitals (SH). Serious casualties would be evacuated from the peninsula and that involved transporting them by lighters to the awaiting Hospital Ships, where the sick and injured had their first encounter with nurses.[72]

Thousands of years earlier, in this same part of the world, the wounded at Troy were carried off the battlefield and taken to makeshift hospitals on the beaches or tended to in berthed ships. In Homer's *Iliad*, the wounded Eurypylus asks Patroclus to 'save me and take me to your ship; cut out the arrow from my thigh; wash the black blood from it with warm water and lay upon it those gracious herbs'. Despite the passage of time and some advances in wound management, the evacuation plans were not dissimilar. The testaments of nurses working on the Hospital Ships may not be in the Homeric style, but their narratives highlight the tragedy of an equally brutal campaign.

On the first day of the landings, there were only two Hospital Ships present, the *Gascon* and the *Sicilia*. Sister Ella Tucker from the Australian Army Nursing Service (AANS) was working on the *Gascon*, staffed by the Indian Medical Service and British and Australian nurses. She described 25 April as a 'red letter day … shells bursting all round, we're off to Gaba Tepe'. She was, of course, referring to the position the Australian and New Zealand Force held on the peninsula. According to Sister Tucker, the first casualties:

> Commenced to come on board at 9 a.m. and poured into the ship's wards from barges and boats. The majority still had on their field dressings and a number of these were soaked through. Two orderlies cut off the patients' clothes and I started immediately with dressings. There were 76 patients in my ward and I did not finish until 2 a.m.[73]

Also working on the ship was Sister Peters (AANS), who described the state of the casualties as 'pitiable' and said the first batch of casualties to reach the *Gascon* were 'severely wounded'. She further claimed the ship was 'over-filled and proceeded to Alexandria in dangerous waters'. Stationed on the *Sicilia*, on 25 April, Sister Lydia King (AANS) was professionally and personally challenged by the limitations of the care she could render to the wounded:

> I shall never forget the feeling of hopelessness on night duty. It was dreadful. I had two wards downstairs, each over 100 patients, and then a small ward upstairs – altogether about 250 patients to look after, and one orderly and one Indian sweeper. Shall not describe their wounds, they were too awful. One loses sight of all honour and the glory in the work we are doing.[74]

For those nurses who kept diaries of the Gallipoli Campaign, their descriptions of the first day's landings are brief, sometimes no more than a few words or a couple of sentences. No doubt time pressure, the enormity of what they witnessed and the challenge of trying to deliver effective nursing care under trying and dangerous conditions made it almost impossible to record and describe their experiences and feelings. Just as the nurses on the Western Front had experienced earlier, the nurses at Gallipoli very quickly came to realise there was no equivalent in civilian nursing that could have prepared them for the traumas of military engagements.

On the eve of the landings, Sister Anna Cameron (QAIMNSR) was assigned for duty on the Hospital Ship *Delta*. The ship was staffed with four medical officers, a Matron, three Sisters and six orderlies, Captain and crew. The *Delta* was instructed to sail to the island of Lemnos and await further instructions. When the 'proceed' to Gallipoli order was issued it took four hours' sailing time to reach the peninsula. On arrival, the ship took up a holding position and awaited instructions to join the casualty evacuation queue. The Hospital Ships were in vulnerable, exposed positions and were not immune from the effects of shelling, a point reinforced by Sister Cameron: 'shells from the Turks were dropping round our ship. We were actually in the firing line.' After hours of laying in wait, the *Delta* was ordered to Cape Helles and took up a position from which the ship's crew, medical and nursing staff could observe the activity on the shore. The sights were deeply disturbing: with the use of field glasses the staff on board the *Delta* could witness the intimacy of the killings. Sister Cameron claimed they saw RAMC men being shot as they tried to rescue the wounded, and a padre killed by sniper fire as he ministered to casualties on the beach.[75]

The evacuation of the wounded from the peninsula beaches to the Hospital Ships involved the use of lighters, small flat-bottomed boats usually capable of carrying twelve stretcher cases per trip. It was a perilous journey and the already vulnerable casualties were exposed to secondary injuries from sniper fire as they lay on the beach waiting to be evacuated or as they were loaded into the lighters during the shore-to-ship transportation phase. According to Sister Cameron, the medical and nursing staff were shocked when they found 'some were shot further in the boats that took them to us. The gangway ran with blood.' The *Delta* took on board over five hundred casualties from the third day of the Gallipoli landings.

One of the first Australian nurses to work on the Hospital Ships was Sister Elsie Maud Gibson. She was stationed on the *Gascon* and described in detail the evacuation plan:

> The removal of the wounded was difficult and subject to loss and caused great pain endured with maximum fortitude. The wounded were sought and found by the medical stretcher bearers, given first aid and taken from the battlefield by stretcher bearers in relays, taken to the First Aid Post beyond the lines and then carried by relays of stretcher bearers over miles of sand dunes to the shore ... When arrived at the shore and awaiting their turn for attention, the wounded were placed, as convenient, in a box, conveyed to the ship standing out from the shore by barges or pontoons. The box containing the patient was then hauled up the side of the ship by the stretcher bearers. Medical Orderlies awaiting, lifted out the stretchers, carried them to a lift ascending the deck. The wounded met at the lift by Orderlies who took the stretcher to a swinging bed, one side being let down like the side of a cot. The stretcher also has a drop side. Three Orderlies lift out the patient and carefully place him on the bed. The Medical Orderlies who were very good were Indians mostly.[76]

At the beginning of the campaign the main hospital base was Alexandria and the Hospital Ships spent several days at sea before arriving in Egypt. Unfortunately there were no local bases established for the care of the sick and wounded, which proved to be even more problematic because there were not enough hospitals in Alexandria to cope with the volume of casualties arriving from Gallipoli. However, as well as having insufficient hospitals, there were not enough ships or staff to cope with the demands of rapid evacuation from the peninsula; troop transporters were hastily converted into makeshift Hospital Ships but they were in a miserable state. They became known as the 'Black Ships' because, unlike the Hospital Ships, they were not painted in the officially recognisable colours and, because they were converted troop transporters, under the Geneva Convention they were not subject to the same protection as properly constituted Hospital Ships. Moreover, they were euphemistically labelled 'Black Ships' because their human cargo suffered great privations. Aboard these improvised 'Hospital Ships' or 'ambulance carriers' the conditions were appalling; even the basic comforts needed for casualty care did not exist. As the ships were so overcrowded, the sick and wounded lay on the decks and floors of the transporters. There were no basic items such as pillows and blankets and in some cases lifejackets were used as pillows. There was a serious lack of food and drinking water. The sanitary arrangements were scandalous, with some ships having no conveniences at all, and newspaper being used as a receptacle for defecation and for cleansing. In one ship not even paper was obtainable, and only four bedpans stolen from another ship were available for 800 casualties. Many of the men had to perform their natural functions on the decks where they lay. Given that many of the evacuated casualties were suffering from enteric or dysentery, and there appeared not to be even the pretence of any kind of isolation policy, the non-infected casualties had little chance of avoiding also succumbing to infection.

The deplorable situation was described by Major Fred Waite, New Zealand Force, who witnessed the transportation fate of the sick when the Hospital Ships were full: 'The cry would be "Ship full" and the next load would be taken to an ordinary transport, dirty, full of vermin and entirely unsuited for handling the wounded.' Not only were the ships inappropriate for the needs of the casualties but there was a lack of doctors to care for the sick and wounded. According to Major Waite, some of the doctors tending to the casualties on the troop transporters came from the 'overworked and understaffed field ambulances ashore and laboured like galley slaves against the inrush of broken men'. The situation was so chronic that naval surgeons and dressers were commandeered from battleships to assist with the wounded. Major Waite claimed the serious deficiencies were met with desperate measures: 'On one ship, the only man with any knowledge of medicine was the veterinary officer who, assisted by clerks and grooms of the waiting Echelon B, saved dozens of lives by prompt and careful attention.'[77]

The testament of Dr Cane, RAMC, reinforced the depressingly unsatisfactory evacuation and transportation arrangements:

Within three weeks nearly twenty thousand wounded were brought back to the base at Alexandria, and hundreds still arrive daily. Many of these were shot long before they reached the Turkish shore: some of the boats were sunk and others turned back full of wounded, with scarcely an uninjured man left on board to land. From the beginning the hospital ships have been quite insufficient to deal with such thousands of wounded, and have had to be supplemented by the transports in which the troops went out ... Several medical officers from the field ambulances or other units were put on board each transport, with what orderlies could be spared. They worked night and day during the return voyage, but in spite of all exertions, found it often quite impossible to render more than the most urgent first aid treatment. Several transports returned with over 800 wounded, one with nearly 1,100 and one with 1,618, and in each only three over-worked medical officers, a few orderlies and no nurses to do the entire work of an improvised floating hospital.[78]

The mortality rate on some of the Black Ships was deplorable but only to be expected when there was such a paucity of basic facilities needed to care for the sick and wounded. For the casualties delivered to the relative comfort of a Hospital Ship, all immediate life- and limb-saving interventions were carried out on the floating equivalent of the CCS. As was the practice on the Western Front, the time of the medical staff was primarily spent operating on the wounded; it therefore fell to the Sisters to prioritise the casualties most in need of urgent attention and, if possible, to stabilise them until surgery was carried out. By having to make those decisions, usually very quickly, the Sisters were placed in a trying and professionally and legally unusual situation. Traditionally the role of the nurse was to carry out unquestioningly the doctor's orders, and her professional opinion was seldom solicited. The new responsibilities were not lost on Sister Cameron: 'casualties came pouring in and oh the wild rushes stopping haemorrhage, treating shock and collapse'. The exigencies of war brought unthinkable challenges and opportunities for trained nurses, for never before had they exercised such autonomy in the management and delivery of patient care. As Sister Cameron attested, the new dispensation carried an understandable degree of angst, if not risk, particularly when in her own experience one of the doctors told her to 'give morphia at my own discretion and to do as I like. Oh dear that few hours. I had such scares.' The nurses on the *Delta* made the most of the authority they were given and quickly set about prioritising the care needs of the casualties. According to Sister Cameron, sleep and rest became one of the main priorities of care even if, initially, the casualties were left unwashed and without a change of clothing:

Some of the men as soon as they dropped asleep woke screaming through shock, none were undressed – at least very few by that time. They were so deadbeat we wrapped them in blankets in their filthy clothes poor fellows, and let them rest, faces shot away, arms, legs, lungs, shots everywhere. One man had a shattered hand, a broken arm, a smashed wrist, shrapnel through the top of his head, his lips shot, and his right knee, and all he said was 'Thank God we have the Sisters'.[79]

The policy made sense; nurses learned very quickly that mud and dirt were less life-threatening than haemorrhage, shock, undressed wounds, uncontrolled pain, and physical and mental exhaustion. The latter was the most insidious because nurses identified physical and psychological exhaustion as a silent killer; without encouragement, some casualties would give up hope. Also, nurses understood that it was important for casualties to believe in or hold on to some ideal that would assist them towards recovery; the thought of loved ones, home, religious or spiritual beliefs did not always suffice.

It was not unusual for nurses to be the non-sexual but heroic object of that ideal. Idealisation brought its own therapeutic rewards. One casualty lying among the wounded on the deck of a Hospital Ship was inspired by watching a Sister at work: 'A Sister was moving from man to man, performing wonders in an incredibly short space of time. I watched her wonderingly; her fingers were so skilled and so swift.' According to the casualty, he was so taken with the way the Sister carried out her demanding tasks that he enquired if she ever got downhearted; her response was more practical than despairing: 'Yes, but only over one thing. I want twelve hands instead of two, and a relief brain when my overworked article becomes deadly tired.' On board the same ship a night duty Sister used humour to allay the concern of some patients who worried about so few overworked nurses looking after too many patients. She told them 'nearly two thousand men in charge of three night Sisters' was the real problem – they loved her. It was the Sister's light-hearted attempt to address their anxieties but also to confront the reality of the situation. In appreciation of the nurses, one of the casualties spoke for many when he told the disembarkation officer, 'while we have been lying here, we chaps have realised that the hardest work is not done in the trenches'.[80] Remaining focused and stoic was the unwritten rule among nurses and there can be little doubt they worked under the weighty responsibility of high expectations – not only of doctors and casualties, but particularly their own.

The management of the medical services at Gallipoli was dysfunctional; as with the military, they suffered from inadequate planning and poor communication, although to a large extent the medical services blamed the military for the havoc. Even so, the medical services appeared to operate on a Plan A policy, with little evidence that Plan B contingencies were established or a 'What if?' school of critical thinking was ever considered. Ultimately, the medical and nursing staff were caught up in the maelstrom and casualty care was compromised. When the *Delta* arrived in Alexandria with a large cargo of sick and wounded there was huge relief because the voyage had entailed great hardship for the casualties and back-breaking work for the doctors, nurses and orderlies. However, the staff were shocked to discover that no hospital accommodation was available. Laid alongside the *Delta* and suffering the same fate was a transport ship which had been converted into a makeshift Hospital Ship; nine hundred wounded were on board. Due to the shortage of hospital accommodation the casualties languished on the decks and passageways of the transporter, awaiting medical and nursing intervention. For six days their wound dressings remained unchanged and many of the wounded still had on their original field dressing. The situation arose because there were no nurses on the transporter and only three doctors and four orderlies, overworked and exhausted. Furthermore, there were not sufficient medical and nursing staff in Alexandria to care for the influx of casualties. The situation was described by Sister Elsie Cook (AANS), who went on duty 'in an empty ward' which, within twenty-four hours, was working to full capacity:

> Boots, packs, bandages, blood stained tunics etc, greeted the eye, everywhere the poor old patients looked miserable and dirty and as if they hadn't slept a wink. Terrible short of staff in the hospital we have got 700 badly wounded men and six Sisters and Matron! Wounded still arriving in hundreds, tents being put up in the grounds to make extra room … dressings from early morning till late at night, without a stop.[81]

On 10 May, when Miss Elizabeth Oram, the newly appointed Matron-in-Chief of the Mediterranean Expeditionary Force, arrived in Egypt, she found a small number of very overworked nurses and doctors. In a report, she claimed:

> There were no more than a handful of nurses at the Base in Egypt and these were already fully employed … No fewer than 16,000 cases were landed and distributed among the hospitals ashore in the first ten days … The extreme difficulty however of coping with the demands made upon the nursing staff cannot well be overrated.[82]

It was claimed that the Australian Sisters working at No.1 Australian General Hospital at Heliopolis and No. 2 at Mena were so hard-worked that 'those of the wounded who knew them previously were shocked at the change which the strain had produced in them'. The situation only served to reinforce the tragic lack of strategic planning between the military and medical authorities for transporting, treating and receiving the casualties from Gallipoli. The Matron-in-Chief had her work cut out, but she took comfort from the fact that, to relieve the situation, Ethel Becher was urgently deploying Reservists and Territorial nurses from Britain to the Mediterranean.

In her report, Miss Oram claimed nursing staff were urgently needed for the 'hastily improvised hospitals in Egypt, the ships bringing the wounded from the seat of war, and the hospital trains transporting so many of them to Cairo and elsewhere'. The hospitals in Alexandria were established at the 'Abbassis Schools' and the Victoria College, as well as at the Deaconesses, a German hospital, and at Raps-el-Tin barracks. Until the much-needed reinforcements arrived from Britain, Miss Oram was forced to call upon locally trained and semi-trained nurses and volunteers for help.[83]

There were of course the Australian General Hospitals established in Cairo and Mena. Despite having the additional support, the logistical problems of moving casualties from Alexandria to the alternative hospitals were further hindered by a lack of suitable ground transportation. Voicing concerns at the appalling state of affairs, *The Nursing Mirror and Midwives' Journal* wasted no time in calling into question the judgement of those at the War Office responsible for the situation. Furthermore, the journal expressed outrage after a letter was sent to the Editor highlighting serious problems with the care of the sick and wounded at Alexandria: 'It is inevitable that there should be difficulties in pioneering work, but according to a private letter just received from Alexandria the defects in the nursing arrangements there amount to an open scandal.'

The information received by the journal referred to the alleged deplorable conditions at the Victoria College, requisitioned by the military for use as No. 17 General Hospital. The writer of the letter claimed the situation at the hospital was intolerable:

> Here chaos and confusion reigned everywhere. Most of the wounds were fearfully septic, and the dirt, heat and flies added to the terrible pain bravely borne by the wounded men, some of whom were British and some Australian. Spinal cases with bad bedsores, were lying, bathed in perspiration, on mackintoshes, owing to a shortage of sheets.[84]

The letter also alluded to a shortage of dressings, and not enough staff – only five Sisters for day duty and no night-duty cover. Also, it was claimed, the doctors' valuable time was taken up with paperwork and administration, leaving them little time for patient care. Following publication of the damning revelations, the journal reported it was awaiting 'communication from the authorities responsible for such a state of affairs'.

Moreover, in relation to the shortage of trained nurses, the journal highlighted that through its own inquiries to the War Office, it had been officially informed that there were no vacancies for new members of the Queen Alexandra's Imperial Nursing Service. Evidently, however, the shortage had now made itself felt, for on the morning of 7 July, the War Office announced in the daily press that fully trained nurses wishing to be employed in the new war hospitals should apply without delay to the Matron-in-Chief, QAIMNS.[85]

The shortage of hospitals and staff led to offers of independent, privately funded hospitals being established in Egypt. The situation was raised in the House of Commons by Sir Arthur Markham, who asked the Under Secretary of State for War, Mr Harold Tennant:

> Whether the Secretary of State for War refused to give his consent to private persons sending out to Egypt private hospitals at their own expense; and whether as a consequence, when the wounded from the Dardanelles arrived at Alexandria they were sent to the German hospital to be nursed by German nurses?[86]

The Under Secretary responded by stating: 'private hospitals were not and are not required in Egypt … the arrangements for the reception of the wounded at Alexandria were adequate in all respects'. Regarding the use of the German hospital, he said, 'The General Officer Commanding in Egypt exercised a wise judgement in making use of the German hospital.' Furthermore, he asserted there would have been 'adverse criticism, in this House and outside, if all suitable accommodation in Alexandria was not made use of'.[87] Surprisingly, *The British Journal of Nursing* took an unusually low-key diplomatic response to the controversy: 'There is no doubt that with a little foresight nursing arrangements at Malta and in Egypt might have been more complete and efficient in time for the wounded returned from the Dardanelles.'[88]

According to government figures, the number of casualties sustained by the naval and military forces between 25 April and 31 May was: Officers – killed 496, wounded 1,134, missing 92, total 1,722; Other ranks – killed 6,927, wounded 23,542, missing 6,445, total 36,914. From the first landings, the combined total of naval and military losses amounted to 38,636.[89] The casualties were increasing, and by the end of May the DMS, Surgeon General Birrell (MEF), agreed that Base Hospitals should be established nearer to the fighting front. Within weeks, hospitals were created at Mudros and Imbros and the garrison hospitals at Malta and Gibraltar were expanded. Interestingly, despite Mudros previously being considered 'unsuitable' as a base, British, Australian and Canadian Stationary Hospitals were established as well as Indian and British Field Ambulances for the care of Indian troops. Additionally, the facilities were supported by medical stores and a convalescent facility.

The medical management of the campaign was reflected in administrative changes; Surgeon General Babtie was brought from India to act as Principal Director of Medical Services in the Mediterranean. However, his casualty evacuation and transportation plans differed markedly from Surgeon General Birrell's and were generally not well received. Furthermore, his new scheme led to friction and differences of opinion between the naval and military commands. In order to reach a consensus on the evacuation plan, the Quartermaster General held a conference in London with the Director Generals of the AMS and the Royal Navy. The outcome was almost predictable; yet another reorganisation of the hospital transportation service, with Surgeon General James Porter from the Royal Navy appointed as Hospital Transport Officer (MEF). The appointment was not popular and his casualty evacuation scheme met with resistance from the medical services.[90] While the navy and AMS tried to resolve the impasse on the chain of evacuation, the first support contingent of British nurses arrived in Egypt on 27 July, three months after the start of the Gallipoli campaign and more than two months after Miss Oram's request to the War Office for immediate help.

The cadre comprised approximately fifty nurses: four Sisters and forty-four staff nurses from the Reserve, and two Sisters from the Territorial Service. Between the end of July and the beginning of August, further contingents arrived bringing a total of 200 additional nurses for duty in Stationary and General Hospitals, Hospital Ships and Ambulance Trains. Despite the additions, serious deficiencies still existed, in part due to health issues among the nursing staff. For some, the effects of an excessive workload and exposure to diseases eventually led to a physical or psychological breakdown.

In the same month the War Office finally responded to the issues raised in the *Nursing Mirror and Midwives' Journal* regarding the casualty care and nursing arrangements in Alexandria. Predictably, it refuted the allegations, but the journal was wise enough to obtain corroborating evidence. A second letter was produced, written by another correspondent, unknown to the first one, who claimed a hospital 'official' had written to her relatives in England stating the published comments on the state of the hospital were 'a perfectly true account of the whole concern'.[91]

In defence of its decision to publish the information, the journal claimed, 'our one objective is to arrive at the facts, and to provide as far as possible that every hospital receiving wounded sailors and soldiers shall attain the maximum of efficiency everywhere'.[92] Despite being subject to DORA regulations, the nursing press was bold and, clearly, was not going to be silenced by official censorship. However, the journals were dependent on unofficial dispatches coming from nurses working at the different fighting fronts. Although many of the narratives are laced with patriotism and stirring deeds, between the lines the politics and horror of the war was evidenced. It is to their credit that some nurses were prepared to break the rules and send what little information they could, because three months into the Gallipoli campaign the casualty situation had become even more intolerable. In addition to the management of traumatic wounds, the medical and nursing staff were challenged with containing and treating conditions and diseases such as diarrhoea, dysentery, enteric fever, jaundice and rheumatic fever.

Over the summer there had been a marked increase in fly- and dust-borne diseases. The low rainfall accompanied by high temperatures and an affluence of dust and flies made the peninsula an ideal breeding ground for diseases. On the instruction of Surgeon General Babtie, field laboratories were set up on Mudros and the peninsula to investigate the outbreak of the different types of dysenteries and diarrhoeas, malaria, relapsing fevers, infective jaundice, typhoid and paratyphoid fevers.[93] The Sisters working on the Hospital Ships noted the higher incidence of dysentery and enteric among the troops. Caring for infected patients involved intensive nursing, and in isolation facilities on the Hospital Ships it was impossible. According to Sister Mary Fitzgibbon (QAIMNSR):

> The wounded were easy enough to deal with, but the sick! They were in a terrible state, all suffering from dysentery and enteric. Their insides had simply turned to water, and all they had been able to do for them was to tie their trousers tight round their legs with pieces of string. We had to rip their trousers off with scissors, and then we washed the boys as best we could. We couldn't do very much for them because we only had them for a few hours – just the length of time it would take to get them back to Mudros. Of course, they were all running high temperatures and they wanted drink, drink, drink … We had wounded as well, of course, because there were many wounded – but it's the sick I remember, I'll never forget them. Just pouring with dysentery – sick, miserable, dehydrated and in terrible pain.[94]

It was not surprising that dysentery became the leading cause of sickness among the troops because the sanitary arrangements were atrocious. The problem was caused by a dearth of suitable materials to build fly-proof latrines, insufficient local water supplies for a large force and unsuitable ground for the construction of deep pits for waste products. It was three months before affirmative action was taken to address the sanitation problems and by that time intestinal diseases were rife. Furthermore, the access to water was a constant source of concern and supplies had to be transported from Egypt. It was estimated that, per day, 80 tons of water were needed. The men were living on a pint of water per day, and in the heat of the summer their vitality was sapped by dehydration. The amalgam of problems conspired to cause highly debilitating conditions, particularly dysentery. A New Zealand soldier, ill with dysentery, claimed, 'I was running all the time. I couldn't enjoy my food. We were down to skin and bone. Dysentery just ate away our intestines.' A sergeant from the Newfoundland Regiment described the fatal effects of the disease: 'There was slow death everywhere. The body was slowly dying from the inside … A man would pass me holding his stomach, groaning in agony. I would take him off the latrine, dead. The bullets did not take a big toll. It was death from germs.'[95]

In the House of Commons on 28 July, again, Mr Joynson-Hicks pressed the Under Secretary of State for War to supply the House with information of the health of the troops at Gallipoli. The Under Secretary responded, 'There is a certain amount of enteric and dysentery.' Was the Under Secretary badly briefed or, worse, lied to by his military and medical advisor, or was he being economical with the facts? The records of the time, subsequently published as official figures, showed dysentery and diseases of the digestive system accounted for 50 per cent of the hospital admissions for sickness among the British troops in the Dardanelles campaign.[96] According to the *Daily Telegraph*, 'The peculiar conditions of warfare in the Dardanelles and the special hardships endured by our gallant fighting men are by this time fairly well known to the general public', but not, apparently, to the Under Secretary for War.[97]

In order to ameliorate the discomfort of the sick and wounded and the troops, 'comfort funds' were set up. One of the earliest schemes was established in Athens by Lady Montgomery-Cuninghame, wife of the Military Attaché, and Mrs Kerr, wife of Admiral Kerr, Head of the Naval Mission to Greece. Additionally, Sir Ian Hamilton's wife established the Lady Hamilton's Dardanelles Fund, and his sister-in-law, Mrs Moncrieff, set up a fund particularly focused on supplying the Bell Stretcher Tents which combined to make a portable bed, stretcher and mosquito net. The initiative was endorsed by Sir Alfred Keogh as being 'exactly what is required to protect our wounded from flies and dust, sun, wind and rain'.[98] Furthermore, appeals were made in newspapers by members of the general public, such as, 'Appeals for funds to provide mosquito nets and fly swatters etc. for hospitals in the Dardanelles where the plague of flies is so terrible.'[99] Sadly, it was more than 'comfort funds' that the money was needed for. In a note to her family, Sister Cameron refers to the medical supplies sent out to her: 'The splints and bandages have been a Godsend.' In another letter she alludes to donated funds which allowed the theatre sister on the *Delta* to obtain 'a special appliance the army won't give and which lessens her strenuous work'. Sister Gibson was still serving on the *Gascon* and said, 'An appeal was made from the Sisters of the Hospital Ship for medical dressings and pyjamas, and the Red Cross generously supplied the articles for the patients' comfort.' Because of a great shortage of hospital equipment and casualty care supplies, the BRCS raised millions of pounds through public subscription to help equip every type of care facility needed for the sick and wounded on the home and fighting fronts. As the War escalated, more equipment and supplies were needed, and emotive public appeals were launched to 'help their loved ones'. The fate that befell the troops on the Gallipoli Peninsula at the beginning of August ensured the need for plentiful medical supplies.

On 6 August, the military launched a second landing but, like the first attempt, it met with a tenacious Turkish defence. After days of vicious fighting, the tragic human consequences of the engagement were disturbingly described by Sister Cameron:

> The *Delta* was one mass of suffering humanity. How to cope with over 1,240 when we are inadequately staffed for 536. The ship's crew helped to a man, especially feeding the deck cases. The worst cases were in the wards and my ward was a perfect hell. It was so awful I can't bear to think of it yet – sixty terrible cases. Several burnt from head to foot. Eight of my cases died ... Some begged to be finished off with morphia and those who were in agony were kept under till they died.[100]

Serving on the Hospital Ship *Gloucester Castle*, Sister Mary Webster nursed the casualties of the August landings:

> Every day that passes, shows more plainly that the great attack has failed ... We are up at 6 a.m. and very seldom in bed before midnight. On our arrival, operating went on for 36 hours without a pause. Fortunately the weather is fine and the poor maimed, suffering boys, the majority are nothing more in years, lie in rows on the deck of the ship outside the operating theatre, just as they are taken from the lighter, awaiting their turn ... We have a good many medical officers among the patients as well as chaplains.[101]

In just one line, Sister Webster probably summed up everyone's sentiments about the ill-fated second landings: 'August 1915 will not soon be forgotten by any who spent it at the Dardanelles.'

Within weeks of the failed attempt of the second landing, there were rumours of a withdrawal from the peninsula and Sister Cameron could not contain her anger: 'It is sad about the Dardanelles – not nearly forced yet. When I hear any possibility of abandoning it how it makes me savage when so much blood has been spilt on it ... When we see how the men come in hundreds each week – thousands rather – from the beaches, wounded and ill, we wonder how their places are filled.'[102]

Lieutenant Sorley Brown was relieved the campaign was over but decided discretion was the better part of valour when discussing the plans to evacuate. However, he did have something to say about the non-participants of the campaign:

> Of the tragedy of the Gallipoli Peninsula I will say nothing, and in point of fact would not be so indiscreet as to say anything in the meantime, excepting to point out that there can be no question as to the wisdom of the policy of evacuation. The fine people who wanted us to hold on to what we had gained at so terrible a cost ought to have been there to form a properly considered opinion. I say they ought to have been there; I say no more.[103]

But Sister Cameron was there and, with first-hand experience on a daily basis, she saw the level of suffering endured by the troops. However, military decisions are made on the best outcomes for a campaign and, in warfare, logistical considerations and moral choices are usually not compatible. Sister Cameron felt that withdrawal from the peninsula could only add insult to injury – thousands of injuries. On 5 October, two months after the traumatic second landings, it could be argued that the War Office insulted the medical officers and nursing sisters working on the Hospital Ships and ambulance carriers when it circulated a memorandum suggesting they should not be unduly influenced by the testaments of the sick and wounded in their care:

> It has been brought to the attention of Sir Ian Hamilton that, here and there, on Ambulance Ships and Ambulance Carriers, Medical Officers and Nurses have allowed themselves to become too seriously impressed by the stories of young officers and men who have come on board sick and wounded. It is natural, under the conditions, that these tales should be over-coloured; it is natural also that contact with so much suffering should incline the listeners to sympathy; but it is certain also that, whether from the standpoint of the individual sick or of the military operations as a whole, such enervating influences should be resisted. All grades and degrees of the medical staff must make it a point of professional honour to maintain a hearty tone of optimism calculated to raise rather than lower the confidence and courage of the fighting men who have been temporarily committed to their charge. 'Canst thou not minister to a mind disease'd?' Thus Macbeth enquires of the physician who, too diffident, replies, 'Therein the patient must minister to himself.' But our hospitals at Mudros have proved to us that those who minister to the body diseased are best qualified at the same time to 'Raze out the written troubles of the brain.' Let Medical Officers and Nurses on Hospital Ships and Ambulance Carriers see to it then that, under all trials, they surround their sick and wounded with an atmosphere of enthusiasm and of invincible hope.[104]

By issuing the memo, the War Office failed to appreciate that for seven months the medical and nursing staff had been working in an 'atmosphere' of dedicated 'enthusiasm', and 'hope' was probably their greatest motivator. Furthermore, the content of the memo highlighted the professional and moral chasm that existed between the policy-makers in London and the practitioners at the fighting fronts.

There are few redeeming words that can be said about the Gallipoli Campaign. However, the witness accounts make tangible the fortitude and tenacity of the troops and the humanity and compassion of those who cared for them. When the decision was finally taken to evacuate the peninsula, Sister Cameron wrote to her family:

> By the time this reaches you the evacuation of Suvla and Anzac will be quite old news. We were there for the landings, that dreadful time in August when we carried 1,250 wounded on the *Delta* and we were there for the absolute finish. [105]

In the House of Commons, just two days before Christmas, Joynson-Hicks MP wanted to know the total casualty figures for the Dardanelles Expedition. In a response from the government, Harold Tennant claimed that between 25 April and 11 December, the sick admitted to hospitals numbered 96,683; the killed, wounded or missing, in all ranks, including the army and navy, amounted to 112,921. Total combined casualties were 209,604.[106]

In the Land of Troy, the Dardanelles Campaign became another epic legend. In the *Iliad*, Agamemnon laments,

> Beside the ruins of Troy they lie buried,
> those men so beautiful; there they have their
> burial-place, hidden in an enemy's land

Three thousand years later, it was a fitting epitaph for the fallen at Gallipoli.

In one of her last letters home, Sister Cameron illustrates that, despite living and working through the traumas of war, she and the other Sisters on the *Delta* were keen to normalise Christmas for their patients and themselves:

> We were at our wits' end what to do as the ship had been rushed off so quickly and we had no stock in for extras for Christmas. Many were convalescent, and they decorated the wards beautifully with mottos, etc. put on red handkerchief neck-ties in cotton wool letters and everyone raked up everything. The captain gave out about forty flags and the result was marvellous. One sister wore with great fortitude an atrocious artificial flower, presented by a sick man; another had a scrap of very dirty crochet lace wrapped in grubby newspaper stuffed into her hand ... a gentleman ranker in the next bed said, 'This ship has caught a wonderful spirit of kindness, to some of us it's a revelation.'[107]

But it wasn't just the spirit of Christmas that existed on board the *Delta*; indomitable spirit existed in all those who took part in the Gallipoli Campaign. Just before Christmas, Sister Cameron claimed, 'there is a curious fever flying round the ships. Doctors, Sisters and Orderlies go down with it in turn. I only hope I shall escape.' Unfortunately she did not, and despite her strong spirit and stoicism Sister Cameron became a casualty of the conflict. She was hospitalised for five months and was medically discharged from the QAIMNS in 1916.[108]

On 25 December, *The British Journal of Nursing* ran an editorial entitled 'Principal Events in the Nursing World in 1915', but it was not about 'principal events'; it was a polemic about the use of untrained women caring for the casualties of the War, with the journal reminding everyone:

> The National Council of Trained Nurses constitutionally approached the War Office on this subject and on December 31st, 1914, the President, Mrs Bedford Fenwick, sent to the Secretary of State for War a Resolution, passed by the Council, recording its unqualified disapproval of the present organization of the nursing of the sick and wounded soldiers in military auxiliary hospitals at home and abroad.[109]

It was, of course, referring to the use of volunteer nurses. One year later the journal was still complaining about the deployment of untrained nurses, but who else could support the hard-pressed QAIMNS and TFNS? It had become all too obvious in 1915 that there were not enough trained nurses available to work in military units, and the Gallipoli Campaign exemplified the problem. Perhaps, in the 'Principal Events' editorial, *The British Journal of Nursing* could have been mindful of and listed the thrity-nine nurses who lost their lives while on active service: among them, the first known suicide to take place within the QAIMNS; ten deaths in a contingent of thirty-six New Zealand army nurses who were on board the troop transporter *Marquette* when it was struck by an enemy torpedo, 30 miles south of Salonika; three Sisters lost in an explosion aboard the *Natal* on the Cromarty Firth; and a Sister drowned in the sinking of the Hospital Ship *Anglia*. The remaining deaths occurred due to sickness or disease, contracted on active service.

Only one nurse's death made the headlines and created public outrage and revulsion. Edith Cavell was a British nurse working as a Matron in Dr Depage's School for Certified Nurses in Brussels' Barkendalle Medical Institute. She was accused of helping Allied soldiers escape across the frontier but, despite diplomatic representation and pleas for clemency, she was executed by a German firing squad on 12 October. Although not attached to the military nursing services, in the eyes of the public she became the 'nurse heroine' and, cynically, the government exploited her death for propaganda purposes. The die was cast; traumatic deaths within the ranks of the nursing services caused by enemy action were shamelessly used to gain support for the war effort and to encourage recruitment. Not a word, however, about those nurses who died in far-off remote places, who were suffering with and dying from the effects of environmental conditions and dreadful communicable diseases. Alas, the pity and hypocrisy of war.

NOTES

1. Peterkin, M. B., War Diary, 1 January 1915.
2. Peterkin, M. B., War Diary, 16 December 1915.
3. Luard Papers, Letter to Sister, 2 February 1915, D/DLu/55/13/4.

4. Brander Diary, Unpublished, Private Papers, Imperial War Museum, Documents 13190.

5. Luard Papers, Undated Note to Sister, D/DLu/55/13/4.

6. Luard, K. E., Undated Note, Captain, Chief Censor, D/DLu/55/13/4.

7. Luard, K, E., Diary, 28 October 1914, p. 96.

8. Luard, K. E., Diary, 22 February 1915, p. 199.

9. MacPherson, W. G. (1931), *Medical Services General History*, vol. 1, pp. 335–6.

10. National Archives, WO95/3982, Report on Sanitary Conditions, 1914.

11. Shepherd, J. (1991), *The Crimean Doctors: A History of the British Medical Services in the Crimean War*, vol. 1, Liverpool: Liverpool University Press, p. 313.

12. *Hansard,* House of Commons Debate, 29 June 1900, vol. 85, cc. 89–184.

13. *Hansard,* House of Commons Debate, 19 March 1901, vol. 91, cc. 517–56.

14. *The Times*, 29 August 1914.

15. *The Times*, 5 and 28 September 1914.

16. *The Times*, 2 September 1914.

17. *The British Journal of Nursing*, 26 September 1914, p. 239.

18. Luard, K. E., Diary, 10 October 1914, p. 33.

19. Luard, K. E., Diary, 18 October 1914, p. 65.

20. Peterkin, M. B., War Diary, 21 October 1914, p. 21.

21. McCarthy, M., War Diary, 1 and 6 December 1914.

22. Furse Papers, DM1584/10.

23. Furse, K., Draft Manuscript, *Hearts and Pomegranates*, DM1584/10, p. 13.

24. Ibid., p. 12.

25. MacPherson, W. G., vol. 2, pp. 129–30.

26. Furse, K., Draft Manuscript, DM1584/12/H, p. 12.

27. Ibid., p. 9.

28. Mumby, F. (1915), *The Great World War*, vol. II, London: Gresham Publishing Company, p. 21; *The London Gazette*, 4 December 1914, No. 28999, p. 10425.

29. Furse, K., *Hearts and Pomegranates*, pp. 322–3.

30. Ibid., p. 325.

31. Swift, S., *The War Work of the British Red Cross Nursing Service*, Guy's Hospital Reports, vol. LXX, King's College Archives, GB0100G/Reports, 1856–1985.

32. Mumby, F., p. 233.

33. Mitchell, J. and Smith, G. M. (1931), *Casualties and Medical Statistics of The Great War*, London: HMSO, p. 132.

34. *The Lancet*, 17 April 1915, pp. 803–6.

35. *The Lancet*, 17 April 1915, pp. 801–3.

36. *The Lancet*, 17 April 1915, p. 805.

37. *The British Journal of Nursing*, 13 February 1915, p. 132.

38. Charcot, J. B., 'Protection Against Cold: Practical Advice Regarding Protection of Soldiers in a Winter Campaign', *Journal of the Royal Army Medical Corps,* vol. XXIV, 1915, p. 95.

39. Todd, J., Diary, Box 7, QARANC Archives, 67/1981, p. 11.

40. Peterkin, M. B., War Diary, 30 January to 1 February 1915, p. 40.

41. *The British Journal of Nursing*, 15 May 1915, p. 415.

42. *The Nursing Times*, 17 April 1915, p. 468.

43. Luard Papers, Letter to Family, 2 May 1915, D/DLu/55/13/5.

44. McCarthy Papers, 'Summary of Annual Report', 1915, Box 10, p. 9.
45. Joint VAD Committee, 23 February 1915, Women at Work Collection, Imperial War Museum, BRCS, 11.1/40.
46. *The British Journal of Nursing*, 13 February 1915, p. 135.
47. *The Nursing Times*, 10 April 1915, p. 427.
48. Luard, K. E., Diary, 13 March 1915, p. 199.
49. MacPherson, W. G., vol. 2, ch. XVII, p. 369.
50. Walker, A., Papers, p. 4.
51. Brander, M., Diary, 13 March 1915.
52. Ibid.
53. Blair, M., Diary, nd, pp. 9–10.
54. *The British Journal of Nursing*, 14 November 1914, p. 380.
55. Aldren, T., 'Cases of Mental Shock Observed in Base Hospitals in France', *Royal Army Medical Corps Journal*, 1915, vol. XXIV, pp. 343–6.
56. *British Journal of Nursing*, 13 February 1915, pp. 131–2.
57. Paterson, J., Letter, 16 November 1914.
58. Rouen Medical Society, Meeting, 27 February 1915, *Royal Army Medical Corps Journal*, pp. 262–6.
59. The Hague, Convention (II) with Respect to the Laws and Customs of War on Land and its annex: Regulations concerning the Laws and Customs of War on Land. Article 23, 29 July 1899.
60. Haldane Papers, National Library of Scotland, MS 20233, Folio No. 178.
61. Terraine, J. (1982), *White Heat: The New Warfare, 1914–1918*, London: Sidgwick and Jackson, p. 161.
62. Phillips, Unpublished Manuscript. QARANC Archives.
63. NA, WO142/24, Gas Telegram, 23 April 1915.
64. BMJ, Gassing, June 1915, p. 774.
65. Chapman, G. (ed.) (1937), *Vain Glory*, London: Cassell, p. 142.
66. Black, J. E., Glenny, E. T. and McNee, J. W., 'Royal Observation of Six hundred and Eighty-Five Cases of Poisoning by Noxious Gases Used By The Enemy', *Royal Army Medical Corps Journal*, vol. WW1V, pp. 509–18.
67. Ibid.
68. Todd, J., Diary, p. 11.
69. Moorehead, A. (1956), *Gallipoli*, London: Hamish Hamilton.
70. MacPherson, W. G., vol. 4, ch. 1.
71. Ibid.
72. Ibid.
73. Bassett, J. (1997), *Guns and Brooches*, Oxford: Oxford University Press, p. 44.
74. 'Australian Army Nursing Service in the Great War', Reports and Biographies, Imperial War Museum, Documents 10603.
75. Cameron, A., Women's War Work, Imperial War Museum, BRCS 25.4/3.
76. Gibson E. M., Imperial War Museum, Australian Nurses' Memoirs.
77. Waite, F. (1919), *The New Zealanders at Gallipoli*, Christchurch, NZ: Whitcombe and Tombs Ltd, pp. 100–1.
78. *The British Journal of Nursing*, 14 August 1915, p. 133.
79. Cameron, A., Women's War Work, Imperial War Museum, BRCS 25.4/3.
80. *The Nursing Times*, 29 May 1915, p. 421.

81. Cook, E., Diary, 30 April 1915, Australian War Memorial.
82. Oram, E., Nursing in Egypt and Palestine, Nurses' Accounts, QARANC.
83. Ibid.
84. *The Nursing Mirror and Midwives' Journal*, 26 June 1915.
85. *The Nursing Mirror and Midwives' Journal*, 3 July 1915.
86. *Hansard*, House of Commons Debate, 8 July 1915, vol. 73, c. 526.
87. Ibid.
88. *The British Journal of Nursing*, 17 July 1915, p. 50.
89. *Hansard*, House of Commons Debate, 1 July 1915, vol. 72, c. 1930.
90. MacPherson, W. G., vol. 4, ch. 1, pp. 37–9.
91. *The Nursing Mirror and Midwives' Journal*, 14 August 1915, p. 375.
92. Ibid.
93. Mitchell and Smith, p. 207.
94. MacDonald, L. (1980), *The Roses of No Man's Land*, London: Papermac, p. 116.
95. Purdom, C. B. (1930), *Everyman at War: Sixty Personal Narratives of the War*, London: Dent and Sons.
96. *Hansard*, House of Commons Debate, 28 July 1915, vol. 73, c. 2263.
97. *The Daily Telegraph*, 21 September 1915.
98. *The Tatler*, 24 September 1915.
99. *The Daily Express*, 20 August 1915.
100. Cameron, A., BRCS, 25.4/4.
101. Webster, M. E., QARANC Archives.
102. Cameron, A., BRCS, 25.4/7.
103. Sorley Brown, W., *My War Diary 1914–1919. Recollections of Gallopoli, Lemnos, Egypt and Palestine*, Galashiels: John McQueen and Son, pp. 109–11.
104. Wellcome, Memorandum (MES), RAMC 523/14.
105. Cameron, A., BRCS, 25.4/13.
106. *Hansard*, House of Commons Debate, 23 December 1915, vol. 77, cc. 605–6.
107. Cameron, A., BRCS 25.4/13.
108. Cameron, A., National Archives, WO399/1260.
109. *The British Journal of Nursing*, 25 December 1915.

4

The Scandal of Battles and a Battle with Scandals

1915 HAD BEEN A pivotal year for the War; the belligerents no longer confined their fighting to Europe and it was now a global conflict. In addition
to the Dardanelles Campaign, British and Indian troops were deployed to
Mesopotamia. Britain had oil interests in the Persian Gulf and they had to be
protected. In the initial phase of the Mesopotamia Campaign, the army, led by
an Indian Army Officer, General Charles Townshend, successfully occupied
Basra and Kurna and established a presence in the Tigris Delta. By September
1915 the troops had taken the town of Kut-al-Amara, 120 miles south of the
main objective, Baghdad. Unfortunately, when the army engaged with the Turks
at the Battle of Ctesiphon, their success was not assured and the engagement
cost the joint force over 4,000 casualties. As it fell back to Kut-al-Amara, the
army lacked adequate transport, sufficient medical supplies and staff. Generally,
the medical arrangements for the campaign were ill conceived, if not negligent.
General Townshend was advised by the Government to retire further down the
Tigris but he decided to stay at Kut; this was astonishingly bad judgement on
his part and the British and Indian troops were under siege for 147 days.[1] The
conditions within the besieged garrison quickly deteriorated and the troops were
near starvation rations; the medical situation was appalling and there was little
or no equipment or supplies to care for the sick and wounded. The garrison
finally surrendered on 29 April 1916. Approximately 13,309 men gave themselves up; of those, 3,248 were Indian non-combatants, and the sick or wounded
numbered 1,456. The fate that befell the garrison ended in a terrible human
tragedy. Weakened by the effects of the siege, the captured British and Indian
troops were in no fit condition to march to the Turkish prisoner of war camps
in Anatolia. Of the men that left Kut on 6 May, 4,250 died either on their way
to captivity or in the camps.[2] This was yet another scandalous campaign for the
Government to explain.

In Europe, Italy entered the War on the Allied side; conversely, Bulgaria
joined the Central Powers. With Bulgaria now in the War there was a threat of
further instability in the Balkans, and British and Allied forces were dispatched
to Salonika in October 1915.

In late 1914, British troops had been sent to German East Africa to neutral-
ise the threat to shipping lanes posed by Germany's African colonies and to

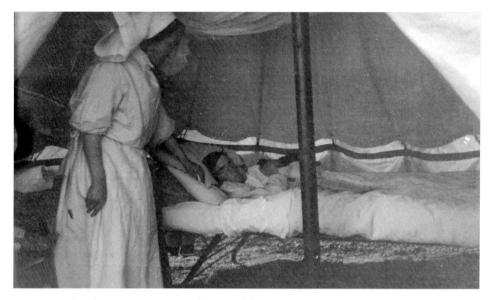

Figure 4.1 A QAIMNS nurse caring for a diphtheria patient in Mesopotamia. QARANC Collection.

protect Britain's considerable interests. After military success in Togoland and the Cameroons, there was very little military engagement up to the beginning of 1916.

On the Western Front, the last great offensive of 1915 took place. On 25 September, the British First Army's six divisions engaged with their French allies to launch the Artois–Loos offensive. The engagement cost the BEF 50,000 casualties, half of them sustained by the 15th Scottish Division.[3] Working at an advanced unit specialising in abdominal injuries, Sister Jean Birrell (TFNS) described the outcome of the battle in just a few words: 'nothing but tartan and gore all round'.[4] At St Omer, Sister Mary Blair worked in No. 20 CCS, a boarding school converted by the military into a clearing station. The classrooms and dormitories were used as wards and the first intake of casualties came from the Loos offensive. According to Sister Blair, the team at the CCS 'worked at high pressure for three or four days until all were operated on, then evacuated to Base in France'. One feature of the Loos Campaign she observed was the psychological effects of the battle, noting 'a considerable number of cases who had lost the power of speech from shock'. According to Sister Blair, 'a specialist from London came over to see these patients and in many cases was able to restore the power of speech, but eventually all were sent home'. She also said that No. 20 'received a considerable number of mentally deranged patients, their case was most pathetic. They only came to us for evacuation.'[5] It would appear there was a corresponding rise in the number of psychological casualties with the aggressive use of artillery. The army, wishing to mitigate 'inefficiency' and 'wastage' in the troops, appointed Dr Charles Myres, a Cambridge psychologist, to investigate and deal with the increase in psychological trauma. Prior to his army commission, Myres worked briefly at the Duchess of Westminster's Hospital in Le Touquet, where he observed memory loss in some casualties and, in others, a loss of vision, smell or taste. His novel findings were published in *The Lancet* and, initially, his theories set the standard for understanding psychological war trauma and dealing with its manifestations.[6]

By the end of 1915, the casualty care facilities in France and Flanders expanded: twenty additional British and Allied hospitals were established; Ambulance Trains increased from twelve to twenty-three; Ambulance Flotillas increased to four, whereby sixteen barges were transporting the most serious cases by the inland waterways. The AMS and ANS were supported by contingents from Canada, Australia and America. Despite bitter protests and criticism from representatives of trained nurses, the VADs established their presence in military hospitals.[7]

From the various theatres of military operations, there were lessons to be learned about casualty care arrangements or, more accurately, the lack of them. The time had come for a reappraisal, a point made in the House of Commons by Lord Henry Cavendish Bentinck, Conservative MP for Nottingham South. He expressed his disgust at the inadequate planning for the care of the sick and wounded in the Dardanelles and Mesopotamian campaigns:

> There is, I am sorry to say, an unfortunate similarity between the Gallipoli and the Mesopotamia Expedition … what I wish specially to register a protest against tonight is the treatment of the wounded. When on the top of this terrible waste of human life we are faced with the fact that the wounded are disgracefully neglected, I confess it is impossible to conceal one's anger and disgust. The treatment of the wounded in the Dardanelles Expedition was absolutely disgraceful. I am not speaking of the later days of that Expedition, when the hospital arrangements were about as good as they possibly could be. I was in a hospital myself, and I speak from experience. During the early days the hospital arrangements were absolutely disgraceful. The wretched men did not have their wounds attended to from the time they left the front to the time they reached the hospitals in Egypt, some four or five days later. I think it is really lamentable to see the experience of Gallipoli being repeated in the Mesopotamia Expedition. We hear of a shortage of hospitals, and we hear of a shortage of nurses, doctors, medical dressings, anaesthetics and antiseptics. We hear of men being shipped down the Tigris with only one blanket for three men in these bitter cold nights. It is not in the least bit surprising that these wretched men suffer from sepsis in their wounds, and even from gangrene. Nothing surprises me more than the way in which the people of this country have treated these lapses from efficiency and these lapses from humanity on the part of the Government.[8]

Lord Henry was not alone in his concerns; Mr Ronald McNeil MP raised serious issues about the administration of the Army Medical Services, of which he was deeply scathing. He wanted to know why at the outbreak of the War the AMS 'scrapped' the work of their Advisory Board, leaving one person, Sir Arthur Sloggett, to have 'complete control over the Army Medical Service'.

The decision inevitably had serious repercussions for the AMS but the Army
Nursing Service was equally affected because the Advisory Board was the ultimate arbiter over decisions made by the Nursing Board. The MP was so outraged over the failures of the AMS to ensure effective casualty care arrangements
that he levelled both professional and personal attacks on senior medical officers
at the War Office. Referring to Arthur Sloggett, he reminded the House that
when war broke out, 'within a week he took sick leave from the War Office'.
The MP asked the House to consider:

> Just imagine the one man who had scrapped the Governing body of the Army Medical
> Service, and was therefore responsible for everything and for seeing that the service
> was properly administered, went on sick leave for nine weeks ... Was advantage
> taken of this gentleman's disappearance ... Not at all. That is not the way with the
> War Office, and they appointed in his place a stop-gap deputy, Surgeon General
> MacPherson.

After highlighting Surgeon General MacPherson's academic achievements
and personal qualities, he launched into a bitter attack, describing him as 'utterly
unfit' to manage the medical services:

> At the end of nine weeks he left the War Office, under what circumstances I am not
> certain ... He went on as Surgeon General to the First Army in France, and in that
> position he was responsible for a most terrible breakdown of the medical arrange-
> ments at the battle of Festubert.

However, McNeil did not stop with one example; he went on to cite
MacPherson's administrative directives at the Battle of Loos:

> He was removed from the First Army in France to another Army, where, a year later
> he was responsible for the still greater failure at Loos ... so far as I know, he still occu-
> pies a responsible post at the head of our Army Medical arrangements at Salonika.

It was with the greatest concern for the health of the troops in Mesopotamia
and Salonika that McNeil concluded the first part of his speech to the House:
'After all this long experience of present fighting, we should still be maintaining
a system based upon South African experience is only proof of the utterly stupid
conservatism amongst those who are managing the service.' The MP then cited a
litany of casualty care blunders that took place under MacPherson's directorship
and they were nothing short of scandalous.[9]

On the Mediterranean Front, the British, Australian and Canadian hospitals
established at Mudros on the island of Lemnos were closed and dispatched to
the other fields of military operations in Mesopotamia, Macedonia, German
East Africa and on the Western Front.

For seven months, the nurses stationed on Mudros had faced a great many
challenges and privations. Apart from the professional and emotional demands
that arose from nursing the casualties from the Gallipoli Campaign, the environment was hostile, the weather extreme and resources scarce, particularly water,
which had to be shipped to the island, prepared by filtration and rationed. At

the beginning of the campaign, Mudros was proposed as a base for the High Command (MEF) but military advisors deemed it unsuitable for habitation. However, despite the initial recommendation and the environmental and logistical problems, the military then decided it was suitable for military hospitals. Between May and September 1915, British, Australian and Canadian Stationary and General hospitals were established at Mudros. Also, medical facilities for the care and treatment of Indian troops as well as convalescent facilities and rest camps were created. Four months after the construction of the hospital settlements, the Matron-in-Chief, Miss Oram, sailed from Port Said to Lemnos on the Hospital Ship *Delta*. The purpose of her trip was to carry out an inspection of the hospitals and the nurses' accommodation and messing facilities. In a report she wrote:

> The weather unfortunately was extremely bad when the ship arrived. It was so difficult to land in the first place and then get from point to point. The cold was intense and the wind overpowering, but all this enabled me to realise how hard the conditions were, and the discomforts that both sick and well had to suffer during the winter months ... I managed to visit all the units but it was very difficult to form an opinion under such weather conditions as prevailed during my stay of four days.[10]

No doubt Miss Oram had the best of intentions for the welfare of the patients and the nursing staff. But her visit to Mudros, no matter how brief, must have alerted her to the fact that supply problems and environmental issues could seriously impede the recovery of casualties already weakened by disease or injury. Also, the unfavourable conditions had the potential to impact on the health and effectiveness of the staff. For whatever reason, Miss Oram's report did not record the dearth of medical supplies, nor that food for casualties, particularly the dysentery cases, was unsuitable, and that for the other patients and staff the diet was totally inadequate. The shortage of water caused major problems. Each person was allowed two pints of water per day, the ration to cover personal hygiene and drinking water. Sister Kate Wilson, Canadian Army Nursing Corps (CANC), serving with No. 3 Canadian Stationary Hospital, highlighted the challenge of making a small allocation of water go a long way, particularly in hot weather:

> Not realizing how quickly a quart of water can disappear, I drained my jug bone dry in the morning. My face and hands were still to be washed and my teeth needed brushing. And I needed a drink of water, as I never had before.[11]

Additionally, the tented accommodation and clothing were inappropriate for inclement weather, and fuel was scarce. Furthermore, there was no electricity and the lighting for hospitals and billets was supplied by hurricane lamps; the operating theatres relied on battery-powered electricity. In order to keep warm, the nursing staff wore sheepskin coats, sou'westers, gum boots and riding breeches. They also wore men's underclothing and large woollen socks.[12] An appeal was made to the BRCS for assistance with clothing and supplies and they were duly dispatched; eventually a small Red Cross depot was established on the island. Interestingly, after her visit Miss Oram was of the opinion that 'the patients were happy and contented and considered themselves in clover after their experiences on the Beaches [Gallipoli Peninsula]'.[13] It is impossible to know the accuracy of her statement. However, there is evidence to suggest that, despite the lack of effective intervention by the responsible authorities to improve conditions for the patients and staff, a 'Mudros Spirit' existed among and between carers and casualties.

The inadequate provision of water and accommodation was a recurring issue of concern. After spending five months working at No. 18 Stationary Hospital, Sister Eva Lea (QAIMNSR) claimed, because of the water shortage, the water in hot-water bottles had to be reused, and the tented wards did not stand up to the demands of the inclement weather:

> It is a job keeping the patients warm in the tents. One hot water bottle full of water has to be used over and over again because water is so precious. The tents too are always being blown to bits.[14]

Sister Wilson commented on the makeshift hospital arrangements that were in place when she arrived on the island:

> It was a sorry looking hospital ward I entered that morning. The marquee had been pitched on the first slope of quite a steep hill. There was no covering, as yet, to protect our feet from the many small stones that covered the whole place. As I went from cot to cot where most of the patients were suffering from amoebic dysentery or malarial fever, I rolled the large stones under the bed with my feet. Since water was such a problem, only hands and faces could be washed, once a day. Millions of flies infested the place. With forty-eight patients, it was almost impossible to keep the pests from the sickest of them and they were all sick. Mosquito netting was pressed into use until the supply ran out, and it took one to two weeks to bring a new supply from Egypt.[15]

It is inconceivable that a policy of water rationing should be applied to those casualties suffering from fevers and intestinal complaints. However, despite their earlier reservations, the High Command deemed the island 'suitable' for hospitals, even with its limitations, particularly the shortage of water. But it was not the men of the High Command who languished in primitive 'make-do' facilities; it was men who had spent months on the Gallipoli Peninsula, living and fighting under intolerable conditions. When they became sick or were wounded, the military and medical High Command offered them more of the same.

The water shortage presented serious problems for patients and staff alike. Apart from the obvious issues of personal hygiene, hydration was a very important therapeutic factor; if casualties became chronically dehydrated the consequences could be fatal. Furthermore, water was needed for sanitary arrangements and hospital hygiene. Water was not a luxury, it was a necessity, and without an adequate supply it could lead to outbreaks of dysentery, and it did. Within weeks of establishing hospitals at Mudros, members of the medical and nursing staff and ward orderlies became ill with dysentery. Thankfully, sickness among the nursing staff did not present too serious a problem. But, sadly, Sister Mary Frances Munro and Matron Jessie Jaggard of the Canadian nursing service succumbed to dysentery; Sister Munro, age 49, died on 7 September, and 44-year-old Sister Jaggard died on 25 September; they had been on the island for less than two months.[16]

The sanitary arrangements on Lemnos were described as being 'imperfectly enforced' and there had been 'much fouling of unoccupied ground, and anti-fly measures were not taken seriously'. After an investigation into the water supply by the Medical Advisory Committee and the Entomological Commission, the Committee concluded the fly was responsible for the outbreak. The doctors and medical orderlies were badly afflicted by the condition; at No. 3 Australian General Hospital, 60 per cent of all male staff became infected. Because dysentery was not as prevalent in the nursing staff, an investigation took place which concluded the disparity was due to the Sisters taking much greater care of domestic cleanliness and hygiene, and further investigations highlighted that staff in British and Canadian hospitals on the island shared similar experiences. Following the Medical Advisory Committee's recommendations, considerable improvements were made to try to control the infection, particularly the introduction of fly-proof latrines. However, despite the best efforts of sanitary squads, it was reported that 'sanitary discipline was never enforced at Lemnos with the relentless determination due to an enemy with such grave potentialities'.[17]

Life on the island was difficult, and a great deal was asked of its temporary residents. When it came time for each hospital to step down and move on, there were mixed feelings of sadness and relief. Sister Wilson spoke of the camaraderie among the British, Canadian and Australian units: 'The very fact of the many trials and hardships we had endured together had woven a network of friendship never to be forgotten.'[18] Sister Cameron remembered nurses from No. 3 (CSH) being transported to Lemnos on her ship, the *Delta*. In a letter home she wrote:

> You may remember we took 50 Canadian Sisters out here to a hospital on the Island. We have seen some of them this time. The Matron and one Sister died of dysentery, and the Colonel nearly died of it. Two Sisters went mental and the rest seemed somewhat depressed.[19]

The perceptions and contradictions of the respective writers are interesting and illuminating.

In early 1916, when the Hospital Ships were steaming away from Mudros and MPs in the House of Commons were on their feet calling for investigations into the management of the Gallipoli and Mesopotamia Campaigns, a news item appeared that ensured further problems for the Government and the military authorities. On this occasion, however, it was the soldiers stationed at home or on leave who were involved, not the troops on the fighting fronts.

On 4 February *The Scotsman* reported that in England two individuals were charged with giving cocaine to soldiers. According to the report, the Public

Prosecutor was taking up the case and the drugs were being analysed. The prisoners were allowed bail but on their own security of £25 each, and one other security of £25.[20]

One week later, *The Times* carried the headline 'Drugs for Soldiers'. It reported that, on 10 February at Marlborough Street Police Court, the New Bond Street chemists Savory and Moore Ltd were summoned for selling morphine and cocaine to private individuals without going through the proper procedures. The regulations stipulated that in order to obtain the drugs the purchaser had to supply a formal letter of introduction, written by a person of good standing, and they were required to enter their name and address into a register held by the chemist. Acting for the prosecution, Mr Glyn Jones said the defendants had placed an advertisement in *The Times* recommending a 'useful present for friends at the front' – a small pocket case of thin sheets, 'lamels' impregnated with different types of drugs. In mitigation, it was claimed the advertisement did not invite people to apply for any particular type of drug. One gentleman who did respond to the advert obtained a case of lamels, two of which were morphine and cocaine. The solicitor acting for the defendants claimed the offence was due to a 'slip' on the part of an 'assistant' who acted in 'direct contradiction to instructions'. After legal deliberations, the chemists were acquitted of any serious wrongdoing but were fined.[21] On the same day, at Folkestone, a male and female were sentenced to six months' imprisonment with hard labour for selling cocaine on three different occasions to Canadian soldiers. In the course of evidence it was revealed there were '40 cases of the drug habit in one camp' but the name of the camp was withheld.[22] In response to *The Times* article, in a letter to the Editor one gentleman felt compelled to share his experience:

> The recent prosecution at Folkestone for the sale of cocaine to Colonial troops prompts me to suggest the danger of sending small quantities of morphia to men at the front. I have recently been shown what appear to be small silver matchboxes, which can be obtained from well known jewellers and silversmiths in the West-end. In reality these matchboxes are provided with a chain for suspension around the neck, containing three tubes filled with tablets of morphine hydrochloride. The idea is that when the wearer is wounded he can place a tablet on his tongue and so obtain relief from pain.[23]

The writer then went on to say he had no doubt the scheme was 'well intentioned' on the part of the 'jewellers and friends' but it may lead to instances of drug abuse. He also stated he was informed by medical officers that 'the numbers of cases of morphia habit that have arisen from this practice is becoming serious'. On 11 March *The British Journal of Nursing*, in its 'Prize Competition' feature, posed the question: 'Why has the cocaine habit such ruinous results for health?'[24] Nurses were asked to submit an essay in response to the question. The Editor, Ethel Bedford Fenwick, was known to have a wide and informative network of news-gatherers but the speed of reference to the ills of cocaine was remarkably swift even for her. Arguably, she was encouraging nurses to think about addiction problems and the role nurses could play in prevention, care and rehabilitation. Conversely, it may have been fortuitous rather than insightful. Regardless, it raised a level of awareness that could only enhance practice and patient care. However, it was not the sale of cocaine that dominated the parliamentary debates or the headlines of national newspapers; it was the ongoing scandal of the inadequacy of the medical arrangements in Mesopotamia.

On 25 March *The British Journal of Nursing* wrote, 'The country owes Mr Ronald McNeil a debt of gratitude for his powerful speech in the House of Commons on Army hospital administration; and also to Mr Ian Malcolm for his courageous letter in *The Times*.'[25] The *BJN* was referring to Sir Ian Malcolm, a Scottish Conservative MP and Red Cross Officer (Foreign Affairs). In his letter, Sir Ian described the appalling state of the sick and wounded in the Mesopotamia Campaign, which he claimed was due to neglect, confusion and administrative problems between the War Office and the Indian Government:

> The news that is now beginning to come to hand from distant theatres of war is little short of ghastly. We hear of lack of hospital accommodation, shortage of medicines, anaesthetics, dressings, bandages – in fact, all hospital equipment to an extent it is positively alarming. One letter from the spot tells me three medical officers in charge of 1,000 badly wounded men with practically no dressings or bandages, and have to do their surgery without anaesthetics. Another correspondent writes that a single nurse was in charge of 500 cases, mostly amputations, with only coolies to help.[26]

The letter was truly shocking and Sir Ian blamed the War Office for the tragic situation. The War Office, however, claimed the management of the medical arrangements came under the purview of the Indian Government but Sir Ian reminded the readership: 'After all, it is the War Office that sent fathers and brothers and sons to fight on the Tigris; it is not fair, when they are wounded or dying, that the War Office should wash their hands of them.' In his summary he asserted that the British Government had to take responsibility for the care of casualties. However, in the final lines of his letter, he clearly believed that nurses would be the salvation of the sick and wounded: 'more nurses should be sent there; the sex that has faced the brutalities of the Germans at Mons ... will face the dangers from the Turk and Arab with equal fortitude'.[27]

At the beginning of January 1916 there were only six nursing Sisters assigned to the Mesopotamia Campaign and they came from the Queen Alexandra's Imperial Nursing Service for India (QAIMNSI). They were attached to No. 3 British General Hospital established at Basra in November 1915. The hospital comprised 200 beds.

On 29 March the first support contingent of twenty-six nurses and a Matron, Miss Hodgins (QAIMNS), departed from Suez with No. 32 General Hospital and arrived at Basra on 9 April. According to Miss Hodgins, No. 32 GH was established at Makina near Basra, but the 'hospital' was actually a liquorice factory and consisted of corrugated-iron sheds. Soon after their arrival, the small cadre was split up and eleven Sisters were dispatched for duty on Hospital Ships and eight were sent to No. 3 BGH. The Matron and remaining Sisters were stationed at Rawal Pindi Hospital, Amara. The two main hospital centres were at Amara and Basra.

After the fall of Kut there were prisoner exchanges and Miss Hodgins said that men arriving at her hospital were in a 'pitiable state', which was not surprising because it took weeks for the men to be transported from Kut to Basra or Amara and they received very little, if any, medical attention.[28] The men when they arrived were half-starved, infection-ridden and emotionally disturbed. The nurses arrived just as the rainy season broke and were duly supplied with gum boots and pith helmets which became part of their daily attire. In addition to the rain, it was extremely hot and no one escaped the daily battle with fleas. The corrugated sheds converted into No. 32 GH were insufferable and clearly unsuited for casualty care and effective nursing. Generally there was a scarcity of suitable tentage, rations and medical supplies, and drinking water. Due to the unfavourable conditions, some nurses were sent home within weeks of arrival suffering from exhaustion and general debility. The situation for the Sisters was described by Miss Hodgins as 'very trying'.

Conversely, in the AMS there was a high sickness attrition rate and morale was low.[29] One officer was scathing about the casualty arrangements: 'the accommodation here for getting sick men to hospital is shockingly bad; in fact hopeless'. The doctor claimed that Field Ambulances were acting as hospitals, looking after 500 patients instead of a maximum of 120, and kept the sick and wounded for up to three weeks instead of a few days. The staff of the FA were also succumbing to sickness, which made the situation worse. He also complained about the inadequacies and deficiencies of the transport arrangements. The medical officer said the whole system of casualty care 'makes us fairly boil with righteous indignation'. The doctor's experience was supported by a letter published in *The Times*, with the writer claiming that from the very outset of the Mesopotamia Campaign there were problems with the casualty arrangements:

> Even at the very beginning the supply of dressings and bandages gave out at once, and yet but two months ago the medical staff at Amara had no bandages and had practically run out of antiseptics and anaesthetics, the wounded often had no chance of dressings for four or five days, there were not nearly sufficient blankets. For 2,000 wounded preparations had been made for 200 and so on. Surely after 15 months' campaign something must be very wrong for such a state of things to be possible.[30]

It required a collective gargantuan effort by the Government, War Office, the Director of the AMS and the Matron-in Chief QAIMNS to rectify the appalling situation and to raise the standard of facilities required for humane and effective casualty care. The War Office promised more nurses for Mesopotamia, and Miss Becher duly dispatched the Matron of the Cambridge Military Hospital, Miss Beatrice Jones, QAIMNS, who was accompanied by a contingent of 250 trained nurses and VADs.

On the home front the sale of cocaine became an issue again, with *The Times* carrying the headline: 'Cocaine Hawking in the West End'. The newspaper claimed 'the use of cocaine is now largely on the increase amongst prostitutes and some soldiers', and advocated for 'special legislation to be introduced to cope with what has become a serious social evil'.[31] The Government had been slow to respond to the cocaine problem but, fearing yet another scandal, issued a notice stating that the following order had been made by the Army Council under the Defence of the Realm (Consolidation) Regulations 1914:

> No person shall sell or supply any article specified in the Schedule to this Order to or for any member of His Majesty's Forces unless ordered for him by a registered medical practitioner on a written prescription, dated and signed by the practitioner with his full name and qualifications, and marked with the words 'Not to be repeated' and unless the person so selling or supplying shall mark the prescription with his name and address and the date on which it is dispensed.[32]

The notice appeared in *The Times* on the same day the paper was calling for regulation of the drug. While the Government was slow to respond over the sale of cocaine, MPs were decidedly silent on the matter, although *The Times* reported that Colonel Norton Griffiths planned to raise 'the abuse of cocaine by soldiers' in the House of Commons. The paper went on to state, 'In spite of the publicity given to reports of a number of cases recently, the evil has not been stamped out and the habit is claiming new victims.'[33] The report was accurate: Colonel Griffiths did raise the issue in the House of Commons. He asked the Home Secretary what steps the Government was taking to control the sale of cocaine throughout the country; the response from the Home Secretary was disappointing, for he merely referred to the Army Council under Regulation 40 of DORA. However, he did say, 'I am considering what further action should be taken.'[34] From the first mutterings about the abuse of cocaine by soldiers, *The Times* had followed the developments. If its reports on an increase in the illicit sale of cocaine, particularly to soldiers, were accurate, then what damage had been done to individuals and to how many? Furthermore, did it have an impact on the war effort on the home and fighting fronts?

While the Government battled with controversies, a battle was brewing among trained nurses and, for once, it did not involve the VADs. In December 1915, the Honourable Arthur Stanley MP, Chairman of the BRCS, and Sarah Swift, Matron-in-Chief of the BRCS, jointly compiled a letter in which they advocated the establishment of a College of Nursing. This was sent out to the Matrons and Chairmen of the Committees of Management of the principal hospitals and infirmaries in the United Kingdom. Stanley and Swift felt a unified voice was important for the success of the proposed new college.

Their approach was bold, controversial and, as some believed, badly timed, and was bound to have serious repercussions within the Nurse Registration movement, particularly with the Society for the State Registration of Trained

Nurses. The move towards state registration had a long and chequered history, and had been fraught with division and self-interest. Between 1895 and 1904, the British Medical Association examined the arguments for the state registration of nurses and finally adopted a resolution 'supporting in principle' the registration of nurses. For the next five years there were serious problems in obtaining a consensus among nurses and doctors on what exactly the Nurse Registration Bill should include. After several meetings between representatives from a variety of interested parties from Britain and Ireland, a final Bill was drafted for the purpose of promoting the passage of the Bill through Parliament. In 1910, the Nurses' Registration Bill was introduced in the House of Commons by Mr Munro Ferguson, and at every subsequent session of the House thereafter until 1914. As the Bill was consistently blocked and the Government did not allot time for its consideration, it did not reach a second reading. On 3 March 1914, the Bill was introduced by Dr Chapple under the ten minutes rule. Upon a division, 311 voted for the Bill and 82 against. The further passage of the Bill was suspended for the duration of the War. At the outbreak of the War, the Prime Minister debarred the introduction by private members of contested Bills into the House of Commons on subjects unconnected with the War. It was absurd; there was never a time when the work of nurses was more important and prominent. Between January and April, the proposers of the College of Nursing held four meetings with a variety of interested parties, the purpose being to establish a dialogue, build consensus and create a framework for the aims and objectives of the new College of Nursing. According to the college advocates, its primary aims were educational and professional, which included a uniform training curriculum, and central examinations and qualifications. Furthermore, the college would strive for 'state recognition' of trained nurses, not 'state registration'. These proposals did not sit well with the pro-registration lobby and fell far short of their professional and political aspirations. Moreover, there were concerns about the respective roles and links between Sarah Swift and Arthur Stanley and the BRCS, and whether VADs would be included in the new proposals. In his vision for the college, Arthur Stanley believed there was room for different types of nurses, trained and partially trained. However, in the eyes of his critics and opponents of the college, the VAD Home Nursing and First Aid Certificates did not suffice for any level of entry to the college.[35] Despite representation from a variety of nursing associations, leagues and unions, doctors and hospital governors, one group was excluded: male nurses – they were even more ostracised than VADs.

The Army and Navy Male Nurses Cooperation was founded in 1907 by Miss Ethel Rosalie Ferrier McCaul, RRC, a nurse, pioneer and true visionary. Ethel McCaul served in the Boer War. During the Russo-Japanese War of 1904–5 she went to Japan under the auspices of the Japanese Government and with the approval of Queen Alexandra; she was to inspect and report on the Japanese military nursing methods in Field and Base Hospitals. She also examined the work of the Japanese Red Cross Society in the field. On her return to

Britain she made a special report for the British military authorities, including the nursing service, although there is no evidence to support that her findings were acted upon by the AMS and ANS. She founded the Union Jack Club for NCOs and other ranks, as it was her firm belief that if officers could have their own clubs then other members of the forces should have the same entitlement. Furthermore, she was a Member of Council of the BRCS and held a seat on the Society's War Executive Committee.[36]

The purpose of the Army and Navy Male Nurses Cooperation was to find employment for men of the Royal Army Medical Corps and Sick Berth Staff of the Royal Navy who, after leaving their respective services, found it difficult to procure civilian employment as nurses. To qualify for enrolment in the Cooperation, the nurses had to possess a certificate of three years' training in military hospitals, or be retired members of Sick Berth Staff of the Royal Navy. The men were well trained and the selection sub-committee of the Cooperation ensured men of good character and exceptional ability. Only long-service men were accepted for enrolment in the scheme. The Cooperation had strong patronage: the Queen was Patroness, and support came from the First Lord of the Admiralty, the Secretary of State for War and Presidents of the Royal Colleges of Physicians and Surgeons.[37] It was strange, therefore, that such a well-regulated and well-supported organisation was not invited to join the proposed new College of Nursing. It would appear the male nurses were being discriminated against, and the exclusion also involved male nurses working in asylums and prisons. Perhaps nurses were concerned about the security of their employment, which hitherto had been dominated by women, and they wanted the *status quo* to prevail, or maybe it was the fear of a potential power struggle between the sexes for control of the profession. Furthermore, there were concerns about VADs taking over their work once the War was over and, as they saw it, they did not need the further threat of male nurses. Moreover, it was bad enough that women were in dispute with each other over the future of the profession, but if male nurses entered the debacle this could further complicate an already sensitive situation. Whatever the reasons, the male nurses were excluded from the dialogue.

Despite all the political machinations, Arthur Stanley hoped that 'one of the permanent memorials of the war would be the creation of a College of Nursing in a central position in London'. The statement did not augur well for relationships with Scotland and Ireland; it was too London-centric and the countries were looking for more devolved power-sharing. It was an inauspicious beginning for what was supposed to be a unifying aspiration. Between June and July, further meetings were held to discuss the way forward for the new College of Nursing but behind the facade of an alleged common cause divisions began to appear.[38]

On the Western Front there were rumours of a new Anglo-French offensive. On 21 February, the Germans mounted an assault on Verdun and by 26 February the French losses amounted to 25,000 men. To secure Verdun

the French were compelled to deploy 259 out of 330 infantry regiments. The
German Chief of Staff, General von Falkenhayn, deduced that, because of the
heavy losses sustained by the French in the 1915 engagements, they would be
unable to mount a robust defence of Verdun. He was wrong, very wrong, and
the blood-letting on both sides was calamitous.[39]

By the summer of 1916 the British Army had a new Commander-in-Chief,
Douglas Haig, and he was persuaded by the French to open up a new offensive in the Somme region. After months of fighting at Verdun, the French were
exhausted but they were still defending the fortress. The French Commander,
Joffre, calculated that if French casualty rates continued at the February and
March levels, then by the end of May the French army would cease to exist;
therefore, they required Allied support to relieve the pressure on the much-
depleted, worn-down French forces. In order to achieve this objective, the BEF
would have to deflect the German attacks on Verdun by drawing them into a
new offensive. It was agreed the BEF and Allied troops would engage with the
Germans in the Picardy region of northern France. The offensive would begin
on the Somme.[40]

It became obvious to Maud McCarthy there was something of great signifi-
cance being planned. Between February and April there was an urgent demand
for an increase in the nursing establishment; nearly 300 trained nurses and

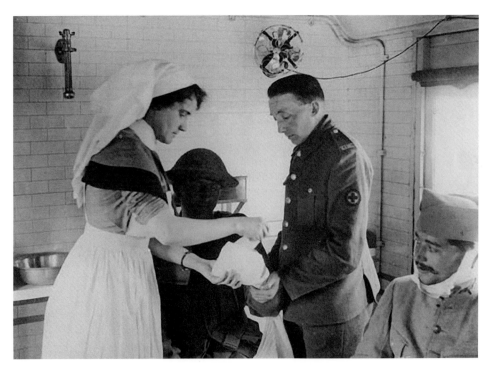

Figure 4.2 French and British soldiers having their wounds dressed by a Nursing Sister on
an Ambulance Train in France with an orderly in attendance. National Library of Scotland.

250 VADs were requested. Additionally, there was an expansion of hospital beds on the LOC, and this included 'crisis beds' for emergency use only. Due to the increase in bed capacity, a further 376 trained nurses were requisitioned from the Matron-in-Chief at the War Office. Unfortunately, by June there were serious deficiencies in the required quota for trained nurses. At the end of June, Maud McCarthy received notification from the War Office stating that '200 trained nurses would be sent at the earliest opportunity and the remainder of the requirements would be completed by VADs'.[41] The situation was contentious and was bound to have repercussions, particularly with the anti-VAD lobbyists. However, the VADs could not be held responsible for the shortage of trained nurses; that, for the most part, was a War Office recruitment problem. In addition to the supply of nurses, Maud McCarthy was pressed to find suitably trained nurses for the new units dealing with 'mental problems'. In April, a large facility for the care of shell-shocked men was opened at No. 8 Stationary Hospital, Wimereaux, where Charles Myers was the Consulting Medical Officer. According to Maud McCarthy, for several weeks he asked her to find a suitably qualified nurse to manage his new specialist centre. It would appear Myers lost patience and went direct to the DMS for help. Maud's War Diary entry states:

> Asked to supply mental trained nurses to look after certain cases in the areas. Colonel Myers, Nerve Specialist, had been to see the DMS on the subject. He is applying officially and in the meantime I am looking up in our register to see how many nurses we have in the country with mental experience.[42]

The new appointment was taken up by Elizabeth Lusk MacAuley (QAIMNSR), a nurse with considerable psychiatric experience. Until the War she was the Matron of Craig House, a branch of the Royal Edinburgh Mental Hospital. She spent most of her career working in psychiatric institutions and obtained a certificate from the Medico-Psychological Association. In civilian practice she gained an excellent reputation and when she left Craig House for war service, the Medical Superintendent, Dr Robertson, claimed it was a 'terrible blow to the hospital but we understood'. Elizabeth MacAuley was well qualified to run the new pioneering unit and she came from the 'common sense' school of thought on the humane care of psychologically disturbed patients. She was a well-read, educated woman and was familiar with the historical management of psychological trauma.[43]

After weeks of secrecy and speculation, on 1 July the Allies launched their Somme offensive. For a week before the attack, the British artillery carried out a relentless bombardment on the German front line in the belief that their trenches and fortifications would be destroyed. The British High Command was of the view that by destroying dug-outs, gun emplacements and barbed-wire entanglements, the troops would meet with little resistance when they 'went over the top'. The reality was brutally different. The German defences were almost impregnable and their fortifications, despite days of bombardment, were not destroyed. What was destroyed *en masse* were the lives of 20,000 British and Allied soldiers. For their bold endeavours, they lay tangled or hanging on uncut wire, riddled with bullets or shrapnel, or mangled or vaporised by high-explosive shells. In the first twenty-four hours of the battle, 26,675 wounded were removed from the battleground, their fate and the fate of those who were missing telling another gruesome story of the obscenity of warfare. According to Maud McCarthy, by 3 July the wounded were 'being received everywhere in large numbers'. According to Miss D. Field, a VAD working at No. 10 General Hospital, Rouen, at 4 a.m. a convoy arrived with 170 casualties 'just as we were going off-duty'. She said the evacuation trains were going up and down the line, and 'the ambulances and trains were full of sitting cases'. The nearest place to the Somme battlefront was Abbeville and it was overwhelmed. Sister Birrell was sent to No. 2 Stationary Hospital at Abbeville, which she said 'was turned into a Clearing Station':

> We were very short of staff there, sometimes I was on duty receiving patients till 12 mid-night. It was a case of opening up new marquees all the time. Patients were waiting in their ambulances to come in before we evacuated our old ones.[44]

The Sisters were sent to wherever their skills were needed most. Some of them were sent to railway stations to help with the influx of men arriving straight from the front on the Temporary Ambulance Trains (TAT). Also, at Le Havre and Rouen, the work was excessive with hospitals receiving more patients than they were equipped to handle; some hospitals admitted as many as 2,000 casualties. For several days after the first offensive the hospitals were receiving two

Figure 4.3 Ambulance convoy at Abbeville. QARANC Collection.

trains a day packed with the wounded. In a report on the nursing activities on the first days of the Somme battles, Maud McCarthy said the intake of casualties was so overwhelming that 'some of the nurses had been on duty for 48 hours at a stretch'. She also noted that 'in addition to our own wounded, there were a large number of German prisoners, many of them very seriously wounded'.[45] From Abbeville, Sister Birrell was then sent to No. 13 CCS on the Somme, where she nursed Allied and German prisoners: 'We had any amount of German wounded but they gave us no trouble and were most grateful for everything that was done for them. Some of them looked on the verge of starvation. We had such an amount of our own poor boys sent in badly gassed.'[46]

The CCS was the beating heart of all life- and limb-saving interventions. If casualties stood a chance of survival, this is where they needed to be. Since the beginning of the War the work and character of the CCS had changed considerably. In the early days they were called Clearing Hospitals and Sisters were debarred from working in them; after the 1914 engagements, the name changed and so did the policy towards the presence of nurses. Each Casualty Clearing Station now had a complement of five Sisters.

By 1916, the CCS system had reached an enhanced level of efficiency but it had taken the tragedy of so much suffering before the hard-learned lessons were translated into effective practice. The staff became adept at many things; when an offensive was imminent they quickly set about organising the CCS even before they received official notification. Sister Luard described the process of preparing the CCS for the reception of the wounded and the increase in staff:

> Extra wards were put up, enormous stocks of dressings, splints, medical and Red Cross stores were got ready; pyjamas, shirts and socks in thousands instead of hundreds were ordered. The theatre would be arranged for 6, 8 or 10 operating tables – with separate outfits of everything necessary for each table or pair of tables. The mortuary would be enlarged, convalescent patients would be detailed for special duties and the rest sent down to the Base. Extra mess tents and sleeping tents would appear in officers, Sisters and orderlies quarters. Batches of 50 extra stretcher-bearers, theatre teams of 4 consisting of surgeon, anaesthetist, Sister and orderly would arrive, with relays of other Sisters and medical officers till the personnel had trebled or quadrupled itself.[47]

After the initial bombardment and countdown to zero hour, within two hours the first casualties would start to arrive at the CCS in all manner of vehicles. The walking wounded arrived by buses, lorries, charabancs and open box carts, and in supply wagons on broad- and narrow-gauge railways. Unfortunately, due to the makeshift but effective use of the railway lines, there was no covering on the wagons and casualties were exposed to the elements. The seriously wounded and lying-down cases were brought in by the motor ambulance transport of the Field Ambulances. At the beginning of the Somme offensive the Indian troops went to an Indian cavalry Field Ambulance at Vecquemont but it was soon replaced by a section of the Lucknow CCS.[48]

Not only did casualties arrive in all manner of vehicles, they were afflicted with all manner of trauma and often in an obscene state of tissue decay. Captain Laurence Gameson served at a Field Ambulance with the 15th Division and could not comprehend how some managed to cling to life:

> I saw more human tissue than one would have thought possible in so short a time. There was hardly a part of the body I did not see cut or exposed. Maggot invasion was common. An unconscious man who arrived with part of his frontal lobe protruding through a hole in his skull. The protruding portion of the brain was moving with maggots. When men had been left out for a while their shoulders, buttocks or whole back were invaded by the creatures in the areas of skin compressed by the weight of their immobilised bodies. One man I saw lying out because both his legs were wounded. Prolonged pressure had produced necrosis of the skin over his buttocks and the superficial portions of muscle beneath it. Maggots had invaded the deeper tissues. I had to pick them out with long forceps. The man was unaware of his condition. Maggot invasion was also accompanied by a foul smell, since it flourished in tissue undergoing decomposition.[49]

By the time many of the wounded arrived at the CCS from the field hospitals they had already been 'cleaned up'. However, they were still in a deplorable state and in order to save their lives rapid surgical intervention was necessary. The amputation of limbs became the rule not the exception.

The writer, and later *Manchester Guardian* journalist, Frederick Voigt, volunteered for war service. Both his parents were German but he was born in Britain. In his memoirs he wrote about the experience of working as an orderly in a CCS on the Somme. With a writer's eye for detail, he described the operating theatre after an influx of casualties:

> The operating theatre looked like a butcher's shop. There were big pools and splashes of blood on the floor. Bits of flesh and skin and bone were littered everywhere. The gowns of the orderlies were stained and bespattered with blood and picric acid. Each bucket was full of blood-sodden towels, splints and bandages, with a foot, or a hand, or a severed knee joint overhanging the rim.[50]

Voigt remembers one occasion when the CCS was under threat from aerial bombing; he was working in the operating theatre and was amazed at the various reactions of the surgical team, particularly the Sister. He said a soldier was brought into the operating theatre with a badly shattered knee and an immediate operation was necessary. In the course of the operation the CCS came under fire with shells whistling overhead. There was an anaesthetist, the Sister, the surgeon and an orderly who some months earlier had won the Military Medal for bravery in an air raid. According to Voigt, bombs were dropping nearby and the sound of explosions was unnerving:

> The orderly who had held his hands in front of his face, now gave way to fear. He darted madly to and fro and then scuttled beneath the table. The Sister who remained quite calm, said in an amused voice, 'Pull yourself together, it's all over now' ... The Sister was the only one of us who showed no fear at all.[51]

According to Sister Luard, it was not unusual for the staff at CCS to work with 'the lively accompaniment of the whistling of enemy shells over the hospital and sometimes an ugly crash alongside or right in'.[52]

Thankfully there were now facilities for those whose 'nerves have given out' under the pressure of battle or who were picking up the pieces of the war's traumatic effects. However, rank and class divisions deemed that different types of hospital arrangements were put in place. Not only were there differences in the treatment facilities, there were different names for the psychological trauma suffered: the officers were suffering from neurasthenia, while other ranks were classed as being shell-shocked, hysterical, neurotic, insane, simple-minded or 'scrimshankers'.

Whatever class- and rank-driven name the military authorities cared to give psychological trauma, it was a very real condition and a big problem for the military. The ferocity of the Somme battles guaranteed an increase in the numbers suffering psychological breakdown and therefore in hospital admissions. The issue of 'Nerve Strain' was the subject of an Editorial in *The British Journal of Nursing*, which claimed that 'Hundreds of soldiers return from the front on a few weeks' leave, with nerves jangled by the terrible experience of exposure in the firing line to imminent death, to the roar of the guns, and the strain of bombardment.' The Editorial suggested:

> When these lads return home on leave, for the rest they have so well earned, we have our opportunity. Let us help them to forget. During the brief weeks they spend at home let us so far as in our power surround them with an atmosphere of rest, let us make their lives easy and pleasant where we can ... There are many men uncomplaining, reserved, who are not hospital cases who yet need all the warmth with which friendship can surround them, and the strength which faith can give them to rest their souls and fortify their nerves.[53]

In the autumn of 1916, Sister Catherine Black (QAIMNSR) was assigned to a ward for shell-shocked officers. It was her first experience of the condition, which she said was 'one of the saddest of modern warfare'. The main problem for Sister Black and her nursing colleagues was that there was no precedent for the treatment of the condition and, as she noted, 'no two cases were ever the same'. Many of her patients had lost the power of speech and it was therefore impossible for them to articulate their fears or concerns. In order to help the men regain their speech, she and her nursing colleagues had to 'teach them simple words, spelling them out, explaining them as one would do to a child'. She said some men were so disturbed they would have 'one sentence imprinted on their brains and keep repeating it over and over under any stress of emotion'. Sister Black claimed the worst time for the shell-shocked cases was during the night, 'where a cheerful ward became a place of torment, with the occupant of every bed tossing and turning and moaning in a hell of memories let loose'. The treatment of the condition for the officer class was prolonged rest away from the front line.[54] Catherine Black maintained it was necessary in the initial stages of care:

Rest was the one thing that all of them most needed, and so for the first week or ten days we gave them opiates and tried to build up their general health. After that we could study each individual case and deal with it as best we could. It was work that demanded endless patience, for results were slow, and you could only go a step at a time and hope for the best.[55]

It was suggested by some liberal-minded doctors that what was needed was an 'atmosphere of cure' before curative therapy began. There was merit in this argument because it was observed that hysterical manifestations disappeared when the Sister of the ward had considerable experience in dealing with hysteria-based conditions. The definition of 'dealing with' was probably empathy and compassion. However, this was not standard treatment for NCOs and other ranks; in the new pioneering unit hypnosis and psychoanalysis were favoured. As the referral numbers rose and more specialist units opened, 'nerve specialists' were employed by the army. The more enthusiastic therapist favoured faradic stimulation and re-education, which translated meant electric shocks and bullying. The worst excesses of this therapy were carried out by Lewis Yealland and Edgar Adrian. Like many doctors at that time, they 'dabbled' in conditions and diseases of the mind. Their work with shell-shocked soldiers was experimental, with no reference to any scientific or ethical precedent. Probably one of the worst examples of their 'treatment' involved a young soldier who volunteered for military service at the outbreak of the War. In 1915, when he was attached to the British Salonika Force, he collapsed with what appeared to be heat stroke. For five hours he was unresponsive and when he regained consciousness he was unable to speak and developed an exaggerated tremor. Nine months after the episode and following various treatments, the young soldier was still afflicted. He was referred to Yealland and underwent what can only be described as 'excessive therapy'. For four hours the soldier was subjected to electric shocks to the back of the throat, the side of the neck, his arms and legs. Although the voltage was low, it was still traumatic. According to Yealland the soldier eventually managed to speak – probably to plead for respite.[56] However, Yealland and Adrian believed that non-compliant patients who tried to resist 'treatment' should be disciplined, and this meant having a higher voltage applied. Arguably, this was their way of exerting authority over fearful, vulnerable and traumatised patients. Even so, there developed an almost obscene voyeuristic interest in shell shock by neurologists, pathologists, psychologists and psychoanalysts, and even general medicine specialists engaged with the discourse on causation and treatment. By the end of 1916, the theories on shell shock were like the Somme battlefields – numerous and peppered with holes.

The Somme battles exacted a heavy toll on everyone, including the nurses. Despite the propaganda posters suggesting a great strength of mission and purpose in their ministrations, nurses were not immune to sickness, disease or injury. In 1916 there was an elevation in diagnosed cases of neurasthenia among the nursing staff. Additionally there were a number of nurses classified under the NYD – not yet diagnosed – category; this usually referred to psychological problems.[57]

By the autumn of 1916 there were serious concerns about the shortage of nurses, and ill health alone was not the problem; the shortages were omnipresent from the outset of the War. A global war was being waged which required a global presence of trained and volunteer nurses but, in the laws of supply and demand, there were just not enough. The situation became chronic and the Government responded by establishing a committee to examine the supply of nurses; it was suitably, if not predictably, titled The Supply of Nurses Committee. On 15 September a communiqué was sent out from the War Office announcing its establishment:

> A committee has been appointed by the Secretary of State for War to consider the existing system for obtaining Nurses for the Hospitals for sick and wounded soldiers at Home and Abroad, and to make such recommendations as they may consider necessary for augmenting the supply.[58]

The committee comprised six men and one woman: Katharine Furse, the Commander-in-Chief of the VADs from the BRCS, who was not a trained nurse. No sooner had the ink dried on the official notice than letters of complaint started to arrive at the War Office, the dissenting voices of trained nurses demanding to know why there were no nurses on the committee. The College of Nursing, still dealing with its own divisions, wrote to the Secretary of State for War expressing concern about the unsatisfactory state of affairs. The college representatives laid out in detail the case for suspending any action by the committee. On 20 September, the War Office issued a notice stating, 'some misunderstanding seems to have arisen as to the functions of the Committee recently appointed by the Secretary of State for War to consider the supply of nurses'. The notice continued with language that only civil servants or lawyers would understand but, in essence, the War Office backpedalled on the issue and concluded the statement by announcing: "The Secretary of State for War has therefore decided to add to the Committee certain representatives of those interests. The names will be announced in the Press as soon as selection has been made and the invitations accepted.'[59] In response to the unfolding debacle, *The British Journal of Nursing* could not resist reminding its readership, 'In 1914 we suggested to the War Office that an expert committee should be appointed.' However, the Executive Committee of the Society for State Registration of Trained Nurses (SSRTN) issued a statement saying it was deplorable that the nursing profession should learn through the press what was happening with The Supply of Nurses Committee and commented particularly on the new additions which represented the 'Army Nursing Boards and some of the large general hospitals'. Furthermore, it suggested that, as the SSRTN represented '10,000 certificated nurses, they may be accorded representation on The Supply of Nurses Committee'.[60] As a result of the protests, the War Office wrote to the great and the good of the nursing establishment and invited them to join the Supply Committee; they were Ethel Becher,

QAIMNS; Sidney Brown, TFNS; the Countess of Airlie; Miss McIntosh, Matron of St Bartholomew's Hospital, London; Miss Lloyd Still, Matron of St Thomas's Hospital, London; Miss Haughton, Matron of Guy's Hospital, London; Miss Gill, Matron, Royal Infirmary of Edinburgh; and Miss Barton, Matron, Poor Law Infirmary, Chelsea. Interestingly, most if not all were involved with the College of Nursing or were on the QAIMNS Advisory Board. However, the SSRTN was denied representation on the committee; it would appear that those on the committee were an elite cabal determined to get their own way and protect their interests. Furthermore, the committee was not representative of the national picture and the relationship with Ireland. On 7 October, the Irish Nurses' Association wrote to the Secretary of State for War complaining that, 'No representative for Ireland has been appointed to serve on the Committee. We presume this is an oversight which will be rectified at an early date!' On 18 October, the Irish Nurses' Association secured a seat on the Advisory Board but they had to request it.[61]

The War Office was probably just breathing a sigh of relief when another request arrived: the Secretary of the Joint VAD Committee for Ireland wrote suggesting that a VAD representative should be invited to join the Committee. The War Office response was swift and no doubt disappointing:

> ... in response to an appeal from the Irish Nurses' Association they invited that association to select a representative to serve on the committee. Your committee will thus see that representation from Ireland is already provided for. I am to add that Mrs Furse, the Commandant in Chief of the Joint Women's VAD Department, is already a member of the Committee.[62]

The Irish could take heart from the knowledge that out of a now very expanded Committee, Ireland and Scotland each had one representative. Since the supply of nurses from Ireland and Scotland was considerable, it would have been reasonable to assume there would have been parity of representation on the Committee. Conversely, as far as can be ascertained, no representative from Wales was invited to serve, or indeed from anywhere in England other than London. In October, the newly reconstituted Supply of Nurses Committee met for its first sitting. The terms of reference had been altered and the Committee was now to 'ascertain the resources of the country in trained and women partially trained in nursing so as to enable it to suggest the most economical method of utilising their services for civil and military purposes'.[63]

While the supply of nurses was a very serious matter, the prosecution of the War had become a source of concern to the public and politicians alike. In the House of Commons on 18 October, Sir Charles Trevelyan asked the Government 'what the British casualties have been for July, August, and September last?' Interjecting, Colonel Griffiths said, 'Before this question is answered, may I ask whether it is advisable to put a question like this?' David Lloyd George, on behalf of the Government, responding to Trevelyan, said, 'I would refer my Honourable Friend to the answer which was given to the Honourable Member for North Somerset on the 21st August.'[64] On that date, Joseph King, Member for North Somerset, had asked the Secretary of State for War:

> Whether he will allow Members of Parliament, on personal application, to receive confidentially information concerning the casualties suffered by our forces on the various fronts; and whether public announcements can be made from which the nation may gather a more complete estimate of the military position?

In a written response, Henry Forster, Financial Secretary to the War Office, claimed:

> As the Prime Minister has stated, there is no objection to any Member being shown privately and confidentially from time to time the total casualties for all theatres of war. I am not clear to what my Honourable Friend refers in the latter part of the question, but I can assure him that every effort is made to publish as full information as possible, subject to military expediency, of the progress of the British operations in the various theatres.[65]

As the Somme offensive drew to a close, it was claimed the military operations in Picardy had cost the BEF 1,295,583 casualties, represented as battle and non-battle casualties; the figure also included the 6,698 gas casualties for 1916.[66] However, given that the Government was reluctant to release casualty figures, there is no way of knowing if this is the true figure and it should therefore be treated with caution. There were of course the thousands that had been shipped back to Britain and Ireland whose lives and fate were dependent on the quality of care and rehabilitation which the overstretched military and civilian hospitals could give them. But complete details of the numbers who were discharged from the service as invalids during the War are not available. There are, however, statistical samples drawn from the theatres of war in 1914–15, with the exception of East and South West Africa, and samples from 1916 onwards. The second source of statistical information comes from sample cases from the Ministry of Pension files.

1916 had been a difficult year for the Government and the military authorities. First, there was an outcry over the Gallipoli Campaign, quickly followed by the Mesopotamia scandal. The public and politicians alike wanted answers and, in fact, demanded them. Sir Edward Carson's question to the Prime Minister in the House of Commons on 12 July succinctly summed up the concerns:

> May I ask the right hon. Gentleman is this House and the country never to get, from time to time, any kind of reports of what is going on in Mesopotamia? May I ask the right hon. Gentleman if these reports are being purposely kept back? May I also ask him whether he does not know that there is amongst a considerable portion of people, who have had communications from that country, and from gentlemen like my hon. Friend who asked the question, the very gravest anxiety as to the negligence that has taken place in reference to the whole of the operations in Mesopotamia?[67]

Due to ongoing public concerns and recurrent questions raised in the House of Commons about the military and medical management of the Dardanelles and Mesopotamia Campaigns, the Government capitulated and finally agreed to hold enquiries. In July 1916, the Special Commissions (Dardanelles and Mesopotamia) Bill was approved.[68]

The cocaine problem continued to be covered in the press, with particular geographical areas highlighted as being 'problematic' but not of great concern. Also, there were unconfirmed reports of the sale of hypodermic syringes to officers. The latter could be true, but not for sinister reasons; on more than one occasion medical officers complained about the shortage of needles and syringes. During the Battle of the Somme, Dr Gameson was attached to a Field Ambulance at Fricourt and complained about the needle problem, particularly for anti-tetanus serum:

> One of our problems was the shortage of serum needles. It was impossible to keep sharp what we had. To shove a large, blunt needle into a man already tired beyond endurance was no nice task, but it had to be done. It was then that orders came from a distance forbidding all MOs to inject serum. The orders could have been more convincing had the supply of needles increased.[69]

In the summer of 1916, the Government acted on the concerns of legitimate suppliers and dispensers and, no doubt influenced by press reports, established a committee headed by Chester Jones, thereafter known as the Chester Jones Committee. Under the Defence of the Realm (Consolidation) Regulation, No. 40B (Cocaine and Opium), the remit of the Committee was primarily to examine 'permits to purchase Cocaine or Opium'. Its focus was on authorised traders and dealers, particularly Dental Depots, where registered and unregistered practitioners could purchase cocaine, and how, if at all, the regulations needed to be improved or amended.[70]

While the Chester Jones Committee met at the Home Office, after a few but embarrassing false starts, the Committee for The Supply of Nurses finally convened at the War Office, although *The British Journal of Nursing* noted that all interests were represented except those of the 'rank and file'.

The Society for the State Registration of Trained Nurses was exercised by the developments within the profession and was deeply unhappy about the aims and objectives of The College of Nursing. Due to irreconcilable differences, competing demands and professional agendas, the Committee for the State Registration of Trained Nurses broke off its negotiations with the College. In a statement issued by the Central Committee, it claimed, 'The Nursing Profession must understand that it was a Breach of Agreement by the autocratic Council of the College of Nursing, Limited, which made a conjoint Bill impossible, and led the Central Committee to discontinue negotiations.'[71]

On the Western Front the battles on the Somme made enormous physical and psychological demands on everyone and, for the nurses, the politics of the Nurse Registration Bill, while important, were not of paramount concern. However, from College documents it would appear that in 1916 some nurses working at the front felt it was important to join and support the new College of Nursing.

In Maud McCarthy's end-of-year report a glimmer of hope was given to the ongoing contentious subject of trained nurses and VADs:

> Much has been written and said at different times about the relationship between the trained and untrained, but anyone who has seen them working together during the weeks following the Battle of the Somme, would have realised that any feeling there might have been was only of the most superficial character, and that each was only too anxious to help the other.[72]

According to her report, in 1916 there were four deaths within the nursing services; she was wrong, because her report only focused on the deaths on the Western Front. Unfortunately, any similar reports compiled by the Matrons-in-Chief in the other fields of military operations do not exist; it is not known if they were lost, destroyed, not compiled or censored.

In all theatres of war, the total deaths for 1916, inclusive of all nursing services, was forty-one. The cause of death quite often reflected the environment in which the nurses were working; the deaths of Matron Jaggard and Sister Munro, for example. They died of dysentery at Mudros, where the sanitary conditions were always problematic and, tragically, led to the deaths of patients and personnel.

The emotional strain of caring for the Somme casualties was evident in Sister Brander, who was sent to No. 5 CCS.

> My first weeks at Corbin I shall never forget, dying all around, gas-gangrenes, and the smells! – The CCS was made up of a few different buildings. Schools, cinemas, council chambers, etc. I started work in the two acute surgical wards for a fortnight. Then I went through to the big hall where it was even worse, the yard full of stretchers, not an inch to put your foot down on. Dying all around, gas-gangrenes and the smells more than you could bear. The fact of the matter is every few days we have attacks of diarrhoea. Head cases quite mad, tied on to stretchers, abdominal cases, with faecal matter oozing out with the awful mess of it. Morphine was given continuously, I was about three weeks or a month in this awful hell no other name. I really thought I should collapse. The yard outside full lines of them waiting on stretchers to go & lines waiting to be dressed. We did our best reverently picking out the dying to another line to pass away. Head cases, some all the brains hanging out, abdominals intestines hanging out. After this awful time I went on night duty and it immediately quietened down regarding patients, but air raids started and hardly a night passed without bombs being dropped.[73]

At the start of the Somme offensive, *The Nursing Times* wrote:

> Nearly all the military hospitals are working their hardest owing to the large number of wounded that have arrived as a result of the new offensive. Nurses are urgently wanted for service both at home and abroad, and the next few weeks will be a time of strain and incessant work.[74]

In the Somme battles of Albert, Bazentin Ridge, Delville Wood, Poziers, Guillemont, Ginchy, Flers-Courcelette, Morval, Thiepval, Transloy Ridge and Ancre Heights, the belligerents fought each other to a bloody and exhausted standstill. But the Gods deemed that a 'time of strain and incessant work' was far from over.

NOTES

1. Carver, Field Marshal Lord (2004), *The Turkish Front 1914–18*, London: Pan Books.
2. Ibid., p. 154.
3. Pope, S. and Wheal, E. (1995), *The First World War*, London: Macmillan, p. 41.
4. Birrell, I. J., Unpublished Papers, Women at Work Collection, Imperial War Museum, BRCS25.2/4.
5. Blair, M., Unpublished Papers, QARANC Archives, pp. 11–13.
6. Myres, C. S., 'A Contribution to the Study of Shell Shock', *The Lancet*, 13 February 1915, pp. 316–20.
7. McCarthy Papers, 'Summary of Annual Report of the Work of the Nursing Service in France, 1916'.
8. *Hansard*, House of Commons Debate, 15 March 1916, vol. 80, c. 2191.
9. *Hansard*, House of Commons Debate, 15 March 1916, vol. 80, cc. 2120–33.
10. Oram, E., Report, 'Nursing in Egypt and Palestine', QARANC Archives, p. 2.
11. Wilson, K. (2004), *Lights Out!: The Memoir of Nursing Sister Kate Wilson, Canadian Army Medical Corps, 1915–1917*, Ottawa: CEF Books, p. 66.
12. 'Australian Army Nursing Service During the Great War', Reports and Biographies, Imperial War Museum, Documents 10603.
13. Oram, E., p. 2.
14. Lea, E. W. B., Private Papers, Imperial War Museum, Documents 510.
15. Wilson, K., *Lights Out!*, p. 66.
16. McEwen, Y. T. (2000), 'The Occupational Lives, Health and Deaths of Nurses in the Great War', MSc Unpublished Dissertation, University of Edinburgh; *It's a Long Way to Tipperary*, p. 201.
17. Butler, A. G. (1938), *History of the Australian Army Medical Service, 1914–1918*, Part 1, 2nd edn, pp. 390–2.
18. Wilson, *Lights Out!*, pp. 107–8.
19. Cameron, Private Papers, BRCS, 25.4/5.
20. *The Scotsman*, 4 February 1916.
21. *The Times*, 11 February 1916.
22. Ibid.
23. *The Times*, 16 February 1916.
24. *The British Journal of Nursing*, 11 March 1916, p. 222.
25. *The British Journal of Nursing*, 25 March 1916, p. 272.
26. *The Times*, 14 March 1916.
27. Ibid.
28. Hodgins, F. M., 'Nursing in Mesopotamia', Nurses' Accounts, QARANC Archive.
29. MacPherson, W. G. (1931), *Medical Services General History*, vol. 4, ch. X, p. 248.
30. *The Times*, 15 March 1916.
31. *The Times*, 12 May 1916.

32. Ibid.
33. *The Times*, 22 June 1916.
34. *Hansard*, House of Commons Debate, 22 June 1916, vol. 83, cc. 300–2.
35. McGann, S., Crowther, A. and Dougal, R. (2009), *Voice for Nurses: A History of The Royal College of Nursing 1916–1990*, Manchester: Manchester University Press.
36. McCaul, E., Private Papers, Syracuse University, Special Collections Research Centre.
37. Wellcome Library, Archives and Manuscripts, RAMC/1922: O/S79.
38. McGann et al., *Voice for Nurses*, p. 23.
39. Horne, A. (1962), *The Price of Glory: Verdun 1916*, London: Macmillan.
40. Gardner, B. (1962), *The Big Push*, London: Cassell
41. McCarthy, M., 'Summary of Annual Report', 1916, pp. 1–2.
42. McCarthy, M., War Diary, 1 May 1916.
43. MacAuley, E. L., National Archives, WO372/23/25980.
44. Birrell, p. 3.
45. McCarthy, M., 'Summary of Annual Report', p. 31.
46. Birrell, p. 5.
47. Luard, K. E., 'Work at a Casualty Clearing Station', Unpublished Report, D/Dlu55/13/4, pp. 1–2.
48. MacPherson, W. G., vol. 3, ch. I, p. 30.
49. Gameson, L., 'Diary, 1916–1918', Imperial War Museum, Documents 612, vol. 1, pp. 52–6.
50. Voigt, F. A. (1920), *Combed Out*, Oxford: Swarthmore Press Ltd, pp. 70–1.
51. Voigt, pp. 93–5.
52. Luard, K. E., 'Work at Casualty Clearing Station', p. 4.
53. *British Journal of Nursing*, 6 May 1916, p. 393.
54. Black, C. (1930), *King's Nurse–Beggar's Nurse*, London: Hurst and Blackett, p. 92.
55. Ibid., p. 92.
56. Adrian, E. D. and Yealland, L. R., 'The Treatment of Some Common War Neuroses', *The Lancet*, 9 June 1917, pp. 867–72; Yealland, L. R. (1918), *Hysterical Disorders of Warfare*, London: Macmillan and Company.
57. McCarthy, M., 'Summary Report. Report of Sickness Amongst the Nursing Staff, 1916', p. 2.
58. National Archives, WO32/9342.
59. National Archives, WO32/9342/19A.
60. *British Journal of Nursing*, 30 September 1916, pp. 272–3.
61. National Archives, WO32/9342, Letter, The Irish Nurses Association, 7 October 1916.
62. National Archives, WO32/9342/45A.
63. National Archives, WO32/9344.
64. *Hansard*, House of Commons Debate, 18 October 1916, vol. 86, c. 536.
65. *Hansard*, House of Commons Debate, 21 August 1916, vol. 85, cc. 2298–9W.
66. Mitchell, J. and Smith, G. M. (1931), *Casualties and Medical Statistics of The Great War*, HMSO, p. 148.
67. *Hansard*, House of Commons Debate, 12 July 1916, vol. 84, cc. 340–1.
68. *Hansard*, House of Commons Debate, 26 July 1916, vol. 84, cc. 1705–50.
69. Gameson, L., Diary, p. 56.

70. National Archives, HO45/10814.
71. *British Journal of Nursing*, 2 December 1916, p. 453.
72. McCarthy, M., 'Summary Report', p. 32.
73. Brander, M., Diary, undated (September 1916).
74. *The Nursing Times*, 15 July 1916, p. 838.

5

Casualties, Consolidation and Cameos of War

IN 1916, THE MILITARY operations on the Somme cost the belligerents dearly. There were vociferous concerns about the military strategy and the commanders' inability to stem the loss of lives which were writ large in the casualty lists published daily in national, regional and local newspapers. The human cost of the Somme battles was now glaringly obvious. In a letter to *The Daily Telegraph*, Lord Lansdowne questioned the way the War was being prosecuted: 'We are slowly but surely killing off the best of the male population of these islands. Can we afford to go on paying the same sort of price for the same sort of gain?' According to official statistics, the BEF alone sustained 1,295,583 casualties on the Somme.[1] The figure includes all ranks as represented in battle and non-battle casualties. As can be realised, the demands on the medical and nursing services were excessive, and unfortunately were made worse by the shortages of trained staff and accommodation at the Base Hospitals. By the end of the year it was a case of taking stock, professionally and personally. Lessons from previous offensives, particularly the Somme, had to be consolidated into effective practice. The new system of grouping CCSs and admitting cases in rotation proved successful. The CCSs and Advanced Forward Units set up to deal with chest and abdominal trauma began to produce better survival outcomes.

At Étaples in 1915, No. 26 General Hospital was a new unit not yet functioning at full capacity and admissions were 7,493, of which 2,746 were wounded;[2] in 1916, No. 26 admitted 31,667 casualties, and of those 12,007 were wounded. In the space of one year the hospital had 'come of age' and was treating a variety of injuries and conditions. By 1917, it was a specialist treatment centre for fractured femurs, Dakin's therapy, shell shock and skin conditions.

The hospitals at Étaples were situated along the road and railway line bordering the River Canche, but No. 26 was situated on the inland side of the road. According to a VAD working at No. 26:

> Other hospitals sprang up and were staffed and opened but, since these were along the lower road, near the railway line, and little save a visit to the post office led us in that direction, our ideas concerning them were vague.[3]

The other hospitals established at Étaples in 1915 were No. 23 and No. 24 General Hospitals, No. 6 BRCS Hospital, the St John's Ambulance Brigade

Hospital and No. 51 General Hospital. By the end of 1916 there were eight British General Hospitals, two Canadian and four Voluntary Hospitals. In 1917, No. 56 General Hospital and the Sick Sisters' Hospital were added to the complement.

The history of No. 26 General Hospital could be the story of any number of Stationary or General hospitals at Étaples or elsewhere but its short life came to represent all that was best in the growth and development of casualty care, professionalism and *esprit de corps*.

On 18 June 1915, No. 26 GH mobilised for France and on 22 June the hospital arrived at Étaples. The 1,000-bed hospital was under construction when an all-male contingent arrived to take up duty. The Commanding Officer, Colonel Cree, remembered the difficulties they went through trying to establish the hospital: 'before the ladies arrived ... the wards were without cupboards of any kind and the men set to work with clasp knives and stones as hammers to make poison cupboards etc., no carpenter being provided, nor any carpenters' tools'.[4] On 12 July, the Matron, Miss Stuart, and a party of QAIMNSR Sisters joined the hospital; one week later, TFNSs and VADs arrived. At this point everyone lived under canvas but in early 1916 they moved to wooden huts. The hospital eventually evolved into several buildings made from either corrugated iron or wood. The largest building was constructed from corrugated iron and was divided into four surgical wards each containing twenty-three beds. Additionally there were two operating theatres and an X-Ray Department located in the building. The Reception hut, CO's office and Matron's office were located in buildings constructed from the same material, as were the kitchens, laboratories, pharmacy, stores, latrines and washhouse. There were thirty-one wards housed in free-standing wooden huts, each hut 120 feet in length and accommodating twenty-seven beds. The wards were heated by stoves, two per ward, and they had an electrical supply. Both the water and electricity were pumped from Paris Plage. However, the water did not go directly into the wards; they were served by stand-pipes established between the rows of hutted accommodation. Only the operating theatres, kitchens, dispensary and laboratory had tap supplies.

The sanitation arrangements were not ideal; as there were no drainage systems, all liquids including body fluids had to be disposed of in eight-feet-deep soak pits that required regular maintenance by the sanitary squads. All refuse, including body tissue and faecal matter, was destroyed in Horsefall incinerators, which were very effective as they did not produce noxious smells or gases, but they did require high maintenance. The latrines and ablutions rooms were some distance from the hutted wards and proved to be both impracticable and inconvenient, particularly during periods of inclement weather. There were three bathhouses: the Reception bathhouse, used only for arriving convoys of casualties; the main bathhouse for patients; and a specially designated bathhouse for the Skin Department.[5]

The exigencies of war demanded preparedness, and personal and unit discipline. It had taken three years of hard-earned experience for the AMS to establish an effective casualty care and evacuation system on the LOC and, by 1917, it was well suited for the care and treatment of most injuries and conditions. For the system to work effectively everyone had to know their place and follow strict sets of rules and instructions; to remind those who were in any doubt, there were copious instructions and memoranda, not to mention compulsory forms that had to be signed indicating 'willingness' to adhere to the rules and regulations. It can be imagined that many people reluctantly signed the forms and muttered under their breath as they did so. At any hospital on the LOC there were well-rehearsed admission and discharge procedures, and the MO, Matrons and Sisters worked under strict protocols. The Orderlies and VADs took their instructions from everyone.

By 1917, the work and patients at No. 26 were extremely diverse. Apart from the usual medical and surgical wards, a Skin Department was established as well as a special centre for the management of fractured femurs. The effectiveness of the Carrel–Dakin continuous wound irrigation treatment was monitored at a special Observation Unit and a 'shell shock' centre was developed. There was an eclectic mix of therapies and treatments in the hospital, and some were under trial. Furthermore, the patients came from a variety of cultures. According to Colonel Cree:

> No. 26 General Hospital was made thoroughly International and Cosmopolitan with many and various centres of interest. It has become a centre for Portuguese and

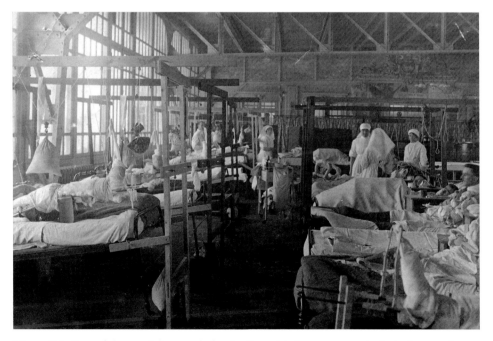

Figure 5.1 One of the specialist wards for dealing with fractures, particularly fractured femurs. General Hospital. QARANC Collection.

Australians, sick and wounded, and we constantly have Indian, Japanese, Maoris and men of many nationalities with many languages being spoken in the wards.[6]

No matter where the casualties came from, they all entered No. 26 General Hospital by the same procedures:

CONVOY ADMISSIONS – PROCEDURES

There were two types of convoy: the general and the emergency.

The general convoy consisted of men who had reported to the Regimental Medical Officer with a specific condition, been classed as temporarily unfit for duty and then sent down the line to a treatment facility. The wounded on the emergency convoy had been seen and treated at a CCS then, when deemed fit for transportation, evacuated to Base. However, during a major offensive convoys of wounded came straight from the front because the CCSs were overwhelmed and unable to meet the needs of all casualties.

The convoys of the sick and wounded invariably arrived during the night. It was considered advisable to move casualties on the LOC at night because of the threat of aerial bombardment and because the railway lines were allegedly less congested then. The hospital usually had a one-hour notice of incoming casualties, and when the convoy neared the hospital the alarm was sounded, usually a bell accompanied by shouts of 'Convoy, incoming convoy'. Once the convoy arrived, in order to triage the casualties with minimal delay, pain and discomfort and to comply with the admissions regulations, a reception centre was designated, usually near a bathhouse. At No. 26 a special reception area was set aside which included a convoy bathhouse.

To facilitate an efficient admissions process, six clerks and the night clerk attended to the administration, leaving the medical staff and orderlies sufficient time to deal with the casualties. To achieve this, three tables were placed at intervals down the admissions room, each with two clerks holding supplies of pre-prepared forms which were copied from the 'Admissions and Discharge Book', and they also had patient diet sheets. A fourth table was placed near the exit door, with a single clerk who held the prescription book and the list of wards to which patients were being admitted. The admissions procedure was simple; the doctors did the assessments, the clerks did the paperwork and the orderlies carried out all the labour-intensive duties. Not all casualties were stretcher cases and many of the sick or walking wounded were fit for baths and a meal. In No. 26 a special ward was designated for such patients. After the assessment they would be washed and fed before spending the night resting on or in beds with blankets and pillows but without sheets until it was time for their evacuation to the UK. It was considered uneconomical to use sheets for overnight stays.[7]

The stretcher cases were given a preliminary examination by a MO and their diet sheets were marked with the appropriate ward; in theory, they were immediately transported by orderlies to the designated ward, though with large convoy intakes it was not always possible to adhere to timescales.

WARD ADMISSIONS – PROCEDURES

Once the casualties reached the wards they had their first encounter with the nursing staff, usually the Sister, and she directed the ward admissions. Each patient arrived with his diet sheet and, if anything required immediate attention, with a set of instructions for the ward Sister from the admissions MO. A complete hospital kit was kept by each vacant bed and, on arrival, casualties, now classed as patients, undressed, washed and changed into hospital clothing. If they were able, they tied up their dirty clothing in one bundle and attached a slip showing their name and regiment and would then take their kit to the disinfector. They retained their boots, cap and toiletries. In the case of helpless patients, the ward orderly was responsible for ensuring kits were correctly marked and sent to the disinfector. Once the kits were passed through the disinfector, the NCO in charge of the Pack Store was responsible for their removal to the Pack Store, where they were examined and classified into the following groups:

a. Serviceable and clean kit. Placed in the racks marked distinctly with Regimental No., Rank and Regiment of the patient.
b. Serviceable and dirty kit. Sent to the dirty clothing store and sorted for Laundry. On return from Laundry taken to clothing store for reissue.
c. Unserviceable kit. All unserviceable articles inspected by the Quartermaster before final disposal.[8]

SURGICAL ADMISSIONS – PROCEDURES – CAPTAIN (DR) GREAVES

Consulting Surgeon: Sir George Makins

If the patients required surgery they were seen by the ward MO and a decision was taken on the best type of intervention, if any was needed. The policy on the treatment of wounds was described by Captain Greaves, one of the resident surgeons:

> By far the most important function of the surgical officer has been that of dealing vigorously with the septic condition of wounds. The methods tried to combat sepsis have been varied but the general principle of free drainage has always been adhered to. We never get a serious case in, whose wound has not already been opened and drained, haemorrhage arrested, and often a foreign body removed, the work at the CCSs always increasing and improving. All abdominal cases now being admitted have already been operated on except those in which no operation was likely to be beneficial, for example perforating wound of the liver.[9]

Not long after the outbreak of the War, Sir Anthony Bowlby surprised, perhaps shocked, his colleagues by telling them the *status quo* treatment of war wounds required some serious reconsideration. Throughout the War he immersed himself in the treatment of trauma and vociferously argued that the best chance the wounded had of surviving death or disability was to be treated immediately at forward units. He was the staunchest advocate of CCSs and their ability to deliver effective trauma care. From the earliest days of the War, abdominal surgery was pioneered in forward areas. In March 1916, questions were raised in the House of Commons about the treatment of abdominal injuries. Harold Tennant informed the House, 'there is an organisation of clearing stations so near the front that they are constantly under shell fire in which these operations can and do take place at all hours of the day and night'.[10]

In the same month, Maud McCarthy referred to the specialist units: 'The staff from 26 Field Ambulance arrived looking well in spite of their hard work and being under shell fire on several occasions.' The following day she inspected a chateau at Coupigny where 69 Field Ambulance established a new Chest and Abdomen centre: 'the nurses from 26 Field Ambulance will be joining. Beautiful building in beautiful grounds ... Splendid cellars where they and their patients will be able to seek refuge if shelled.'[11]

In the opening days of the Battle of the Somme, Sister Luard worked in a CCS with a special unit for abdomens and chests and commented on the strain of nursing patients with abdominal trauma:

> We have that ward full of abdominals in all stages, recovering, hovering, are going to die or dying. It is sometimes rather overwhelming to all our nerves. The Sister who runs it is made of real gold of quite a rare kind, and was made especially for it, but it will wear her out in time.[12]

By the following year Sister Brander attested to the vast improvement in the management of abdominal trauma: 'Came on day duty in acute surgical and had some excellent work, abdominals they did splendidly. I was proud indeed of the results, we never had such results. Major Gordon-Taylor is abdominal specialist.'[13] There were three recognised abdominal specialists: Owen Richards, Cuthbert Wallace and Gordon Taylor. And there was of course Sir Anthony Bolby, who was a great advocate of pioneering surgery and lectured extensively on the subject from his direct experience of working on the Western Front. However, there were other pioneers with specific interests such as John Fraser and Hamilton Drummond who wanted to understand more about the pathology of violent injury, particularly perforating wounds of the abdomen. With an agreement between the War Office, Sir Alfred Keogh and the Medical Research Committee, specialist centres for the rapid treatment of abdominal trauma were established near the front, usually CCSs or Field Ambulances. The results were collected in data-recording books supplied by the Medical Research Committee.

In order to classify as a legitimate Abdominal Centre and if a unit wanted to undertake research, specific criteria had to be met. In the first instance, they were required to have experienced medical and nursing staff. Other essential factors were:

- Immediate access to operating theatres.
- The unit had to be reachable within 30 minutes by motor ambulance.
- Specialist post-operative care had to be available.[14]

It is clear that in tandem with the research, nursing skills and practice were being enhanced, and many Sisters became specialist practitioners in their own right. By 1917, in addition to the abdominal units, specialist 'Preparation for Theatre' wards were established and 'Resuscitation' wards were becoming more prevalent. According to Sister Luard, it was not uncommon for those units to function without a MO: 'It often happens that no MO can be spared for this tent, so a great responsibility is thrown on to us, and only the Sisters with nerve, experience and sound judgement are any good here.'[15]

There was certainly a consensus between the forward units and Base Hospitals that traumatic wounding required rapid surgical intervention and intensive care. If a variety of skilled personnel including the Sisters contributed, there was a better chance of the patients' survival. One of the big problems the surgeons at the Base Hospitals faced was casualties arriving from the CCSs without their case notes. Dr Greaves rightly commented, 'when operations of ever increasing number and importance were performed the absence of notes with the patients was a very serious deficit. Urgent and repeated representation of the position produced a very decided improvement in this respect.' For the success of surgical cases, the doctors believed 'the rapidity of operation depends greatly on there being no confusion and eighteen to twenty operations can be performed in the two theatres in one day without undue hurry and upset'.[16]

The outcome for the patients was in part dependent on a successful surgical regime and this was predicated upon by the allocation of tasks.

THEATRE DUTIES – SISTER AND STAFF

From the ward to the operating theatre a chain of stringent protocols existed, but in times of high demand every member of staff had to demonstrate a willingness to be flexible. When patients required surgery that was not immediately life threatening, they were 'prepared' in the ward. They were bathed or bed-bathed depending on their physical state and mobility. They were given aperients to assist with a bowel movement, and a soap-and-water enema. The rationale behind the bowel 'purge' was two-fold: when patients were anaesthetised they no longer had control over their bowels with the obvious consequence and, post-surgery, patients could not be exerted with the problem of constipation, particularly if they had undergone abdominal surgery. Fasting was also a requirement for at least six hours before the operation. In the hour before surgery, patients were encouraged by the nurse to pass urine as the bladder, like the bowel, had to be empty. If patients had false teeth these were removed and if there was any indication of loose teeth the theatre staff were informed, particularly the anaesthetists. In the last stage of the preparation procedure, patients were dressed in a 'theatre shirt' and warm woollen socks. Just before they were taken to the operating theatre, the nursing staff ensured patients were wrapped in a warm blanket to protect against heat loss from the body, which was considered detrimental to the outcome of the surgery. Throughout the pre-op procedures the nursing staff – Sisters, staff nurses and VADs – worked to encourage and reassure their patients. Furthermore, should patients have a religious or spiritual requirement it was the job of the Sister or staff nurse to ensure that, if possible, it was respected and met. Most units had or shared Army Chaplains, but not all patients were of the Christian faith and all beliefs required respectful consideration. The philosophy was supported and reinforced in the *British Journal of Nursing*; it was important for nurses to 'cultivate the spirit of wisdom and understanding' because, as never before, nurses were dealing with a diversity of views, races and religions.[17]

Obviously, all the pre-surgery procedures were carried out in the controlled environment of a Base Hospital further up the LOC. However, this regime did not apply to the CCSs where, due to the volume of emergency admissions, it was impossible, if not impracticable, to implement the pre-op regime; only the minimum amount of preparation was carried out in the forward units.

At Base Hospitals it was the role of the theatre Sister to oversee the care of the patient as well as attend to the surgical instruments and assist the surgeon. The VADs collected lotions, dressings, bandages and whatever else was required. The theatre orderlies were responsible for clearing up and disposing of any surgical detritus but, unlike the rest of the theatre team who had well-defined roles, the orderlies were expected to do whatever was required of them.

From hospital admission to operating theatre, it was all very organised but, as one of the Sisters from No. 26 attested, the efficacy and efficiency of the plans were tested when a 'big push' was on:

> Days and still more nights, became nightmares of taking in and sending out. Stretcher beds appeared in every available corner, wards were littered with soiled and stained khaki and muddy boots which added themselves to the growing piles outside the wards as order was gradually restored within. The men, washed, fed, and with their wounds re-dressed, fell like logs into a slumber which, unless disturbed, often lasted for twenty-four hours or more. These were the days when the theatre staff was working continuously.[18]

ANAESTHETICS – CAPTAIN (DR) HORNE

Dr Horne claimed the preferred choice of anaesthesia was a light dose of chloroform followed by ether administered through a Schimmelbusch mask, a device consisting of a wire frame covered with several layers of gauze. The mask was applied to the patient's face, ensuring the mouth and nose were covered, then ether was dripped onto the gauze and the patient inhaled until anaesthetised. If patients showed signs of anxiety prior to surgery then, half an hour before the operation, they were given an injection of atropine along with a quarter grain of morphine.[19] However, anaesthctics were in their infancy and there was much trial and error. It was not unusual for patients to become violently sick after the administration of chloroform or ether and, if they were not administered with great care and skill, patients could choke. Some patients became so distressed and agitated they made strenuous efforts to tear the mask away from their face. Major side effects were loss of body heat from patients and post-operative respiratory problems. The alternative was gas, nitrous oxide, probably the most merciful anodyne, but it could only be used for short operations. Under its influence, patients became unconscious quickly without a struggle and they recovered consciousness without the dreadful retching and vomiting that nearly always accompanied the use of chloroform or ether. Because of the very unpleasant, sometimes lethal, side effects of ether, the Shipway's warm vapour apparatus was used. The benefit of this apparatus was that it allowed patients to breathe warm vapour at a known concentration, which minimised lung irritation and post-operative respiratory complications.[20]

Vapour anaesthetics were problematic for everyone. The theatre staff were not immune from the lingering effects of vapours, which were everything from headaches, nausea and vomiting to long-term conditions such as liver failure and kidney problems.

The other anaesthetics in use were stovaine, a spinal anaesthetic, and novocaine, used for local application.

After a patient recovered from the general anaesthetic, he was taken back to the ward. While he was at the operating theatre the nurses prepared the bed for the patient's return; sheets were changed and, in the event of any problems with body fluids, wound seepage or sickness, a rubber draw sheet was placed on the bed; the pillows were removed and the sheets drawn back. Prior to the patient's arrival, the bed was warmed with hot-water bottles. To ensure no loss of body heat, particularly in shock patients, a body blanket was placed over a radiator or near an open fire and wrapped around the patient as soon as he was placed on thc bed. If shock was present, the end of the bed was elevated on wooden blocks. A towel and a receptacle for sickness were also placed at the bedside. It was the job of all the nursing staff vigilantly to observe the patient for haemorrhage, shock, sickness or restlessness. By 1917, at the CCSs and Base Hospitals, as a matter of routine tourniquets were hung on beds of patients likely to develop haemorrhage after surgery to a limb.[21]

MEDICAL ADMISSIONS – CAPTAIN (DR) MACCORMACK

Consulting Physician: Sir John Rose Bradford

Following admission at the Reception hut, medical cases were sent direct to the medical blocks and were seen by the on-duty physician; the medical wards dealt with everything from pneumonia to scabies. Eventually, a Skin Department was established and skin conditions were segregated from general medical conditions.

Also, until a separate facility was created at the hospital, shell-shocked patients were taken to the medical wards.

The picture of medical admissions was not consistent. In 1915, the dominant condition was myalgia. According to Dr MacCormack, 'the types differed considerably from those met with in civil practice, in that they failed to respond to remedies commonly employed with success'. The doctor also observed that the condition, unusually, was affecting younger men. Diarrhoea was a frequent cause for admission but generally it was not uncommon in patients; laboratory test results proved negative for paratyphoid. Older soldiers were admitted with bronchitis, arteriosclerosis and Disordered Action of the Heart (DAH).

The skin conditions were generally scabies, impetigo and psoriasis. Cases of impetigo were unusually slow to respond to treatment, sometimes taking six to eight weeks, and cases of acne and boils were frequent. Soldiers returning from the Gallipoli Campaign were admitted with dysentery, relapsing fever, cerebro-spinal meningitis and malaria. Other conditions treated at the medical wards were trench fever, diphtheria, German measles, scarlet fever and mumps.[22]

One casualty, Stuart Dolden, who was suffering from impetigo, was reluctant to be admitted to No. 26 but was pleasantly surprised:

> If the motor ambulance went to the right, it went to No. 26 General Hospital, if it went to the left, it was going to the Canadian Hospital, where the troops had a wonderful time and a sporting chance of getting home to Blighty. This is where my luck let me down for my ambulance turned right ... After our particulars had been taken in the reception hut, I was sent off to Ward 32. On entering the hut a wonderful sight met my eyes, for behold there were beds with white sheets. A glorious wash in warm water followed then clean shirt and nightclothes, and then a nestle between the sheets ... Life passed very peaceably and, compared with the trenches, was like living on another planet. We spent the time mostly in reading, and indulging in endless arguments.[23]

The patients helped the nursing staff whenever and however they could. Stuart Dolden was allocated the impossible, if not ill-conceived, task of cleaning the windows: 'I was detailed to clean the windows of the ward, but as my hands were swathed in bandages this would have been no easy job.' He confirmed there was a problem with the latrines being so far removed from the wards because while he was there, 'an epidemic of diarrhoea swept through the hospital, and calls of nature became very pressing. Unfortunately, the latrines were about two hundred yards away, and this was too far in some cases.'[24]

The medical wards were by far the busiest in the hospital for, it has to be remembered, the hospitals not only cared for the casualties of war, they also treated everyday conditions and ailments.

SHELL-SHOCK WARDS – CAPTAIN (DR) H. YELLOWLEES

The Shell-Shock wards at No. 26 were part of a larger, specially designated network of treatment facilities that dealt with the psychological problems of warfare. In 1916, Charles Myres, Consulting Psychologist to the BEF, argued that specialist treatment centres should be established for the 'mental conditions of the war'. The first specialist centre was established at No. 8 Stationary Hospital. By the autumn of 1916, the term shell shock had become very contentious within the military, and military commanders were convinced it was an excuse for malingering or cowardice. Although the specialist centres were established, the majority of patients were sent back to Britain. According to Dr Yellowlees:

> It was difficult to work with patients diagnosed with acute confusional states, whether associated with shell-shock or not, and the cases suspected of malingering. These cases were by far the most difficult and perplexing in every way ... particularly because of the large number in which it was impossible to obtain a satisfactory history. Surprisingly, few cases of shell-shock showed symptoms which made their admission to a special mental ward really necessary and, of those which did, the majority were fit to be transferred to an ordinary ward in a few days.[25]

Part of the problem with cases of psychological breakdown was that there was no consensus among the burgeoning 'specialists' as to what actually caused psychological trauma.

There were doctors who were sympathetic to the problem while others saw it as a discipline issue. When there were suspected cases of malingering, nurses were drawn into the controversy and were requested to give evidence at courts martial. There is no way of knowing how prevalent the practice was, but Maud McCarthy refers to it in her War Diary.[26] Interestingly, Dr Yellowlees did not have trained nurses working in his wards; instead, he had 'the intelligent assistance of four orderlies attached to the wards. One was a regular RAMC mental attendant, and the others had been thoroughly trained in civil asylums. All four were most reliable and satisfactory.'[27]

THE X-RAY DEPARTMENT – CAPTAIN (DR) S. E. MCDONALD

Clinical Laboratory – (Dr) S. Rowland

Dr McDonald reported that the X-Ray Department was vital for the management of fractures and dealt with every type of case, from skull and femur to pelvic and rib fractures. Referring to limb injuries, he said, 'the pictures are always taken before and after setting'. He cited one case where the reduction of the fracture was carried out on the X-ray table and the doctors very quickly could 'see it on screen'. He claimed the ward trolley was a very valuable piece of apparatus because patients did not have to be transferred to X-ray tables. He did, however, point out that 'no screen examination is trustworthy'; presumably he was implying that doctors should also use their skills and common sense and not solely rely on X-rays.

The report from Dr Rowland was very short but interesting: 'beside the routine work of the hospital, research work is being carried on, with matters of military importance'.[28]

It was vital for the efficiency of the hospital that members of the medical and nursing staff had protocols and instructions to work with. Everyone had to know what was expected of them and they had to live up to expectations.

'Those' Rules and Regulations were:

SPECIAL INSTRUCTIONS FOR MEDICAL OFFICERS IN CHARGE OF WARDS

All 'Seriously ill' and 'Dangerously ill' reports were referred as a matter of urgency to the Statistical Office. Advice was given on whether SI and DI patients should be visited by their relatives. Alterations from SI to DI had to be reported immediately. A patient progress report had to be submitted through the Officer in Charge by noon on Sundays of all cases on the SI and DI lists, noting any cases to be removed from the list.

SPECIFIC CONDITIONS AND WOUNDS

All cases of jaundice, nephritis, arsenical poisoning and trench foot had to be notified immediately on admission or diagnosis, on forms obtained through the Statistical Office. All diagnoses had to be listed in medical terminology and each ward had orders and guidance on how to record injuries officially; wounds such as gunshot wounds were recorded as GSW.

Debility, trench foot and trench fever were officially recognised diagnoses and had to be recorded as such. After November 1916, shell shock was prohibited as a diagnosis and was substituted with Not Yet Diagnosed Nerves (N). All cases of NYDN had to be referred to the Officer in Charge of the NYDN wards or to the Statistical Office before a case could be transferred or discharged.

No alteration of 'Sick' to 'Battle Casualty' or vice versa was allowed to take place without reference to the Statistical Office. Medical Case Sheets (AFI 1237) had to be made out for all fatal cases, and if a PM was required it had to be notified within the desired time and the death reported to the Statistical Office.[29]

DISCHARGE FROM HOSPITAL

As soon as patients were classified for convoy, their army kit was drawn from the Pack Store and any additional clothing and necessities they required were drawn from the Clothing Store. Walking cases for the UK, having been approved by the Officer in Charge, were paraded at the CO's office at 2 p.m. on the same afternoon, with the suggested mode of disposal entered in the bottom left-hand comer of the Index Card which accompanied them and which had to be completely up to date. The office stamp on the top right-hand corner of the diet sheet denoted the patient's name on the convoy list. Patients for local discharge, either to convalescence or back to their regiments, received their kits at 2 a.m. Names of patients for evacuation, with time of evacuation, were submitted to the wards. At times of high pressure, demands were made on the transport system and it was not uncommon for patients to be transferred or evacuated back to Britain at very short notice. The Field Medical Card (FMC) had to be completed in every case and had to accompany the patient, with any other documents connected with him enclosed in the FMC waterproof envelope. For patients being sent back to Britain or Ireland, the AFW 3083 Ship Label had to be completed and signed by the MO and attached to the patient as soon as he was informed of his evacuation. The AFW 3110 had to be completed in duplicate and submitted for all infectious cases not transferred to an Isolation Hospital.[30]

THE NURSING STAFF – RESPONSIBILITIES AND REGULATIONS

Matron: Miss Hartigan, 1915–17

The Matron, Miss Helena Hartigan, QAIMNS, arrived at No. 26 in October 1915. She took over from Miss Stuart, RRC, who was the first Matron of the hospital. Miss Hartigan had held several positions since her arrival on the Western Front, firstly at a Base Hospital and then on an Ambulance Train, until, in February 1915, she was charged with running the Enteric Hospital at Malassise after an outbreak of enteric fever within the civilian population.

In a speech made by Captain Clayton in the Sisters' quarters at Christmas 1916, he reminded the assembled nurses and doctors that they were all 'one in the family life of the hospital – that family life of which Mama – the Matron – is Head'. There is no doubt Miss Hartigan and Colonel Cree were well loved by their staff; Major Dickson described them in very affectionate and respectful terms:

> I cannot begin to speak of what Colonel Cree and Miss Hartigan meant to us, all of us, who tried to live up to their standards of what a hospital should be; each ever ready to help in difficulties, and valuable help it always was, and I can testify, having tapped both sources frequently, they were entirely typical of well-balanced minds in all essentials.[31]

Helen Hartigan was affectionately described as 'mother' of the unit and she embraced her important role at No. 26 with discipline and humanity.

Matron's Duties

The Matron kept a register of her unit showing the names in full of each Sister; the Training School date of joining the ANS and the date of arrival in France were recorded and any special training such as fever-nursing was also listed.

A confidential report was kept on the efficiency, capability and moral conduct of each nurse. When a nurse transferred to a new unit, the Matron of her hospital sent the Matron-in-Chief, BEF (Maud McCarthy), a report on the nurse's work along with the dates of joining, departure and any other comments she believed to be relevant to the transfer. Unless there were any serious infringements, the reports tended to be brief. The Matron had to make sure that all her staff were inoculated and had to notify the Matron-in-Chief if any members were not inoculated or refused to be inoculated; refusal could result in being sent back to the UK. Unlike the anti-inoculation lobbyists, trained nurses did not have a choice but VADs were given the refusal option. All official applications from the nursing staff had to pass through the Matron of the hospital to the CO, and all matters of importance and sensitivity in connection with the nursing staff had to be reported to the Matron-in-Chief. Any member of the ANS unfit for work through ill health was sent to specially appointed hospitals where accommodation was provided for sick Sisters. Details of any member of the nursing staff on the DI list had to be telegraphed to the Matron-in-Chief and in every case the next-of-kin had to be informed. Matrons in charge of units where sick Sisters were nursed had immediately to notify the Matron of the Sister's unit when she was about to be discharged or transferred to the UK, and this information had to be transmitted immediately to the Command Paymaster at Base. A member of the ANS who was not ill but did need a short rest could, after making application, go to one of the many Rest-Convalescent Homes for nurses which were located at Hardelot, Le Touquet, Étaples and Étretat; in ordinary circumstances the rest period was limited to ten days, though an extension could be granted when a medical certificate was produced.[32]

Sister in Charge – Administrative Duties

The Sister in Charge had to report to the Matron's office at a fixed time daily; she had to produce in writing a list of off-duty times for staff nurses and orderlies, as well as a list of the operations for the day and a brief written report on recent operation cases. Moreover, she had to report on the progress of the patients on the SI and DI lists.

In the case of a patient being placed on the DI list, the Sister had to inform the Commanding Officer and the Matron. Furthermore, she had to report whether the patient had been seen by a representative from the religious denomination to which the patient belonged. Additionally, the Matron or Sister had to write to the nearest relative and, if the patient died, a second letter was sent giving all the available details; an official record of the correspondence was kept in the Matron's Office. Generally, it fell to the Sister to write the 'break-the-news letters'. Furthermore, it was the Sister's responsibility to see that any personal belongings of the deceased patient were handed over to the Quartermaster.

Additionally, the Sister was mentor, advocate and the general guiding light of her ward. She had the welfare of patients and staff alike to consider and had the unenviable and onerous task of trying to keep everyone happy in the chain of patient care.[33]

GENERAL REGULATIONS FOR NURSING STAFF – PROFESSIONAL AND MORAL CONDUCT

1. Regulations governing on- and off-duty times must be strictly adhered to, and no member of the Nursing Staff, whether on or off duty, must visit stores, kitchens, offices, etc. Should any deficiency or irregularity occur which needs attention, she should report it immediately to the Matron.
2. At all times on Active Service, regulation uniform only must be worn, and Matrons will be held responsible that all uniform is in good condition and worn according to the season. Winter uniform should be worn from October 1st to April 1st.
3. No member of the Nursing Service must absent herself from meals without the permission of the Matron, and all should return to their wards five minutes before the times specified, so that the hour of meals can be strictly adhered to.
4. Whilst on Active Service, in order not to create an unfavourable impression, or give any opportunity for adverse criticism, it is not desirable for members of the Nursing Staff to go to public places of amusement without permission. Neither is it permissible for them to accept invitations to dine or go out driving, etc with officers, either patients or friends.
5. Lest there should be any doubt on the matter it must be understood that members of the Nursing Staff are not permitted to visit other areas; they are not permitted to visit Officers' Messes.
6. That dances are not permitted and are against the regulations. It must be thoroughly understood in all units that great pressure of work will feasibly demand longer hours of service, and will necessitate at times the foregoing of off-duty hours for some period. It should be understood that any member of the Nursing Staff who is in any difficulty or doubt whatever should be given an opportunity of seeing the Matron.
7. Cigarette smoking and the consumption of alcohol are banned.[34]

If rules were made to be broken, then No. 26 was culpable. It was a very close-knit unit, primarily fostered by the warmth of Colonel Cree's and Miss Hartigan's personalities, and at times the rules were definitely relaxed. One nurse commented that two days after the Christmas Day festivities, the medical and nursing staff had their celebrations, each acting in turn to host or hostess the other: 'Those evenings remain a pleasant memory with the rendering of "Old King Cole" by the medical staff as an outstanding feature.' However, the prize that Christmas went to Captain Clayton for his speech in the Sisters' quarters; he addressed the assembled group, nurses and doctors:

> Colonel Cree and Brother Officers, I address myself to you individually and collectively, because what I have to say concerns you alone. If any ladies here present happen to overhear my remarks, that must be regarded as an accident of time and place and not a matter of design. I call you brother officers but I am going to speak about our Sisters.

He then went on to talk about the Sisters and asked his brother officers:

> What are her peculiar characteristics? When I was a boy, girls were made up of sugar
> and spice and all things nice. No doubt this is true but as they grow older, some of
> the sugar undergoes fermentation, and that is why they have so much spirit. The spice,
> well that is the flavouring, one has a spice of severity, one has a spice of humour, one
> has a spice of mischief. You know that kind, we rather like them. But it is not on
> the rounds of chemical analysis that we can determine the qualities of a real nurse ...
> Major Rowland [chemical laboratory] has, at my request, kindly undertaken some
> research in this direction ... I don't want to weary you with figures, but his findings
> are very briefly these. I have the laboratory report. Common sense, 90%; Training,
> 3 years; Good health, all the time; Good looks; keenness, a little above the normal.
> Patience, tact and sympathy, these unfortunately at the approach of pure science flew
> out the window, and would not be estimated, but they left a considerable vacuum.
> Certain accidental impurities – such as hair falling from under the cap, and more than
> one dimple on the chin. Please send another specimen.[35]

There is no doubt there were respectful and affectionate bonds between the
nursing and medical staff to the point of breaking the rules. It was prohibited for
officers and other ranks to socialise with the nursing staff. In the case of No. 26,
not only were the medical officers socialising with the nursing staff, they were
doing so in the nurses' quarters. Furthermore, alcohol consumption was not
allowed but it is evidenced from No. 26 and other war diaries and letters that
when doctors and nurses had social events alcohol was consumed.

But there were also bonds of affection and admiration between nurses, and
between nurses and orderlies. One VAD at No. 26 was so moved by the devotion of her ward Sister she felt compelled to write to the Matron-in-Chief to ask
for recognition for the Sister. The VAD was referring to Sister Davis who, during
the first few days of the Somme engagement, not only worked under the pressure
of insufficient staff to care for the casualties but, privately, had concerns about
her mother's health. She was informed that her mother was seriously ill but as
all home leave was cancelled it would be at least three days before a special
dispensation was granted:

> I am writing to bring before your notice the case of a Sister, to whom I'm sure you
> would wish to award the RRC did you know the circumstances of her great heroism.
> The Sister to whom I refer belongs to the QAIMNS Reserve. She was left single-
> handed (save for two VADs of whom I am one) with two huts each containing forty-
> two beds under her care, at the busiest time of this great crisis. Through it all she
> worked with untiring energy, quite forgetting herself for the sake of those around her.
>   During this trying time Sister worked with her usual bright inspiring tempera-
> ment, and never once lost patience or control. Not the least thing was forgotten in
> her trouble ... Such courageous self-effacement and noble sacrifice seems to me the
> greatest service a woman can render the cause of humanity.[36]

In the awfulness of the War, companionship, female and male, was important
for sustaining morale, a sense of normality and survival. By 1917, against the

backdrop of unspeakable traumas and scandals, the men and women serving on the various fighting fronts found ways to accommodate the depth of their feelings that would help mitigate the breakdown of their physical and mental health. Difficult, stressful and traumatic situations and conditions were confronted and negotiated by means of a variety of belief and support systems. Interpersonal relationships were invaluable and *esprit de corps* was vital. In the midst of the War's collective trauma, inspiring and spiritual experiences gave nurses and soldiers, sailors and airmen the strength to face the horrors and terrors of bloody and distasteful campaigns; they were supported and emboldened by humour, religion, music, literature, lucky charms and talismans, and also by compassionate interaction with animals. As early as the first year of the War, animals were unofficially integrated into medical and military units. By December 1914, cats, dogs and birds were mascots on Ambulance Trains, the most famous being two canaries rescued by soldiers at the first Battle of Ypres. They were given to the staff of an AT and christened Sausage and Mash. Additionally, Base and Clearing Hospitals took in animals that had been abandoned by fleeing refugees.

But it wasn't only the War that wore down morale and broke spirit; there were the ancillary problems – the environment, billeting arrangements, dietary needs, endless rules and regulations, censorship of mail, and anxiety about families at home. The winter of 1916–17 was particularly dreadful and was a great test of morale and ingenuity. At No. 26 and elsewhere, the hospital standpipes froze, the ward thermometers froze in a solid block of carbolic, wet glass and bowls froze to tables and bed tables. The nurses wore gumboots and several pairs of socks and, according to one Sister, 'the regulation indoor uniform was hidden under layers of sports coats and woollies, surmounted by the thickest uniform coat available'.[37] Sister Effie Garden was assigned to temporary duty at Rouen. She said the winter was awful: 'ink was frozen and raw eggs could not be cut in half with a knife'. Keeping the patients warm was a major problem; their hot-water bottles had to be thawed out before refilling and towels were frozen. Snow drifted into the tent Sister Garden slept in and one nurse woke to find the top of her blankets covered in snow.[38] The troops suffered badly with the re-emergence of frostbite and trench foot; these conditions were by far the leading causes of admission to hospitals. However, nephritis, chest conditions, dysentery and communicable diseases such as rubella and diphtheria were also problematic for 'the conservation of manpower'.

While the nurses on the Western Front struggled with the appalling weather conditions and the ailments inflicted on troops and staff by the cold weather, on the Eastern Front the casualty care arrangements had improved significantly. The scandal in 1916 and the subsequent Dardanelles and Mesopotamia Commission had forced the AMS to take immediate action. By 1917 the arrangements were less than perfect but they had a Matron-in-Chief, Miss Beatrice Jones, QAIMNS, who was formidable, highly efficient and much respected. It would appear that Beatrice Jones had a very stabilising effect on everyone; within a month of her arrival in 1916 the doctors marvelled at her ability to manage a chronic

situation. But the situation was fragile, and the hostile environment required vigilance of the sanitation arrangements and water supplies for hygiene and hydration. The one area of success was transport; new river steamers were introduced
and were specially equipped for the removal of casualties. Each vessel carried
two nurses and, according to Miss Hodgins, 'there was every convenience for
the sick and wounded on the boats, and they were quickly evacuated'.[39] The
nurses in Mesopotamia were highly regarded because it took a particularly stoic
individual to last in such demanding conditions. Dr Maurice Nicol, RAMC, was
effusive about the Sisters:

> They remained untouched by any kind of pessimism, nor were they greatly interested
> in the campaign as a military affair. All their interest was in their work. They were a
> wonderful stimulus. Where a man unwittingly tended to let things slide they exhorted
> and energised ... Naturally they suffered sickness, but not nearly so much as one
> might have expected; for discipline pays a tremendous part in the avoidance of sick-
> ness ... The sickness amongst the medical staff became rather serious, and at times we
> had to look after far more cases than we could treat adequately. But in these moments
> of temporary dislocation the presence of nurses made all the difference.[40]

The stoicism of the nurses is referenced in various wartime texts, and their
power to endure broke all the long-held prejudices and shibboleths about the
physical and emotional frailty of women. Unfortunately, it had taken the War
to demonstrate to the bigots and disbelievers that women, not just nurses, were
equal to the task and the realisation added a new dimension to the tea rooms,
public houses, parlours and parliamentary debates on women's suffrage.

In Salonika, since their first arrival in 1915, the medical and nursing services
expanded considerably and by 1917 there were seventeen General and four
Stationary Hospitals, five CCSs, two rest camps (one for officers and one for
nurses), two Ambulance Trains and one Field Ambulance. The nursing services
were represented by regulars, reserves, TFNSs, VADs, Canadian and Australian
Sisters. The British Salonika Force waged a battle with diseases as well as the
enemy; dysentery, enteric and malaria were rife. The non-battle casualties far
exceeded the battle casualties and the Sisters' skills were primarily taken up with
nursing infectious and fever cases. Salonika was not a popular posting, so much
so that a ditty was compiled about it:

> There's a little place out East called Salonique,
> Where they're sending British Tommies every week.
> When you view it from the sea,
> It's a fine sight all agree,
> And you think you'll have a spree in Salonique.
>
> When you're dumped upon the quay at Salonique,
> And the smell that meets you there seems to speak,
> You begin to feel quite glum,
> And to wish you hadn't come,
> For there's every kind of hum in Salonique.[41]

The nursing services in Salonika primarily dealt with infectious and communicable diseases, and the work was steady, physically taxing and professionally demanding. Infectious cases required labour-intensive nursing. Also, as the nurses were constantly exposed to the conditions they were trying to contain, it is surprising that so few nurses were afflicted by disease. Clearly, the policy of 'Control and Contain' had an impact, particularly on those most at risk. The highest numbers of hospital admissions within the British Salonika Force were due to malaria, dysentery, diarrhoea, influenza, venereal disease, scabies, pyrexia of unknown origin (non-attributable high temperature) and pneumonia. In the early part of the Macedonian Campaign, frostbite and trench foot were problematic, but nothing on the scale of what was treated on the Western Front.[42] The dominant condition was malaria, and so it continued throughout the campaign. In May 1916, nurses were assigned to No. 28 and No. 40 CCSs; however, the numbers were small in comparison to those working in the General Hospitals and only seven were allocated for CCS duty. In the same year, the first nursing deaths took place when two nurses died of dysentery and, in early 1917, two staff nurses working at No. 37 British General Hospital, Vertekop, died in bombing raids. Of the 1,574 nurses serving on the Macedonian Front, the largest contingent came from the QAIMNS and Reserve, 595 in total. The remainder belonged to the TFNS, VADs and the Australian nursing service. There were also the independent units of the Scottish Women's Hospital serving in Macedonia.

On 9 April 1917, on the Western Front, the British and Allied forces launched their spring offensive at Arras. It was preceded by a 2,800-gun preliminary bombardment. In 1916, in advance of the Somme offensive, a similar tactic had been

Figure 5.2 Two QAIMNSR nurses at Salonika. QARANC Collection.

carried out, with disastrous consequences: the element of surprise had gone and the Germans were prepared for the attack. This was recent history repeating itself. The medical and nursing services were preparing for the new offensive and they perhaps had a better idea than anyone about the cost of the War in pain, grief and misery. In one brief and chilling line in her diary, Kate Luard wrote, 'The CO and the QM are making preparations for possible thousands: so am I.'[43]

On day three of the offensive, it was apparent that things were going badly wrong as the wounded streamed into the CCSs. At Warlencourt, where Kate Luard was stationed, the CCSs were overwhelmed: 'The three CCS filled up in turn and then each filled up again, without a break in the convoys: we take in and evacuate at the same time. The Theatre, Dressing Hut, Preparation Hut and wards and tents are all humming.'[44]

In the midst of all this trauma, a General Staff Officer who had been injured in the Somme offensive decided to write to the medical services laying out his ideas as to how the casualty care arrangements could be improved. He started his memo by saying, 'I noted a few little points in respect of which I think it should be quite practicable to diminish the discomfort suffered by the more severely wounded.' He then listed the shortcomings noted on his trip in the ambulance to the Ambulance Train and the Hospital Barge. Nothing pleased him: 'The barges were too hot and needed more electric fans, there should be mosquito netting over the hatches, there was a total lack of provision of cool drinks and ice should be made available so should soda siphons.' Finally, on the delicate subject of bowels, he said, 'I do not think the nursing staff gave enough attention to this matter, I had to bring up this matter myself. I was refused an aperient because it might choose to act when I was being moved.' Clearly, this officer had not served in Gallipoli or Mesopotamia, and it is unfortunate that no copy of the official response appears to exist.[45]

The Arras offensive brought a different strategy from the enemy; they started aerial bombing and the Base Hospitals and CCSs were not exempt. On the night of 3 May, the first hospital was hit and the bombing campaign continued through to December, leaving 44 dead and 136 wounded. Sister Brander described what it was like to be caught up in the raids:

> We had a very lively time with air raids. When the moon was full, we never undressed, for we dwelt in the cellars. In fact 6 nights out of 7 we practically spent in the cellars, shrapnel bursting all around, and bombs falling all around. At times we should have thought they were gone, no sooner into bed than we had to hop out again and descend in all kinds of attire.[46]

The British Journal of Nursing ran an Editorial headed 'Barbarous War on the Wounded', stating it had the unimpeachable testimony of eye-witnesses that the bombing of hospitals by Germans was done 'deliberately' and that 'helpless sick and wounded are murdered in cold blood, and doctors, nurses or other humane people liable to share their fate'.[47] The *Journal* then went on to list all the bombings, not just of the British hospitals, but of the French and American

Base Hospitals also, and pointed out that Germans were killed in the bombing raids while being cared for in Allied hospitals. In those bombing raids, nurses distinguished themselves with acts of bravery and were duly recognised by being Mentioned in Dispatches or being awarded the Military Medal, sometimes both (see Appendix 1).

According to Sister Duncan, the raids were almost nightly and no Sister went on duty without her gas mask and shrapnel helmet. She said that on one occasion the CCS next to hers was bombed and many of the patients were killed outright. Eighty casualties were brought to her CCS for treatment but, in many cases, 'the efforts were in vain'. Many of the casualties had been in the hospital recovering from surgery when the CCS was attacked, a point Sister Duncan felt had to be made: 'How dreadful to see these once wounded men wounded again and in many cases making the supreme sacrifice. I wonder if many realize what it sometimes costs the Sisters in courage, energy and sympathy at a time like this.'[48]

Because of the increased bombing, all medical units were asked to update their evacuation plans. The COs of Base Hospitals and CCSs had to produce an evacuation plan based on two scenarios: evacuation with forty-eight hours' notice and with seven days' notice. The CO had to explain how he would move patients, nurses, tents and hospital medical and surgical equipment. The letter requesting the evacuation plan stated, 'it will not be possible to remove everything, hence only the articles considered indispensable to improvise a new unit should be dealt with'. At No. 26, Colonel Cree submitted his evacuation plans: he estimated they would have 500 lying cases and 500 sitting and would require sixteen motor ambulances and four charabancs, each vehicle making eight journeys in twenty-four hours. One nurse would be allocated to each vehicle until there were no nurses remaining at the hospital. Each nurse would leave with a satchel of dressings and a supply of morphine. The concern was the safety of the patients and the nurses, and in his notes Colonel Cree wrote, 'they can rejoin the unit later'. The hospital would have to abandon a quarter of its contents and only vital supplies would be evacuated. Approximately 125 tons of material had to be removed and this would involve forty trucks and twelve lorries. A list of articles considered indispensible was drawn up, but 75 per cent of tables, bedsteads, bedside tables and baths were to be abandoned. The staff of each ward were responsible for their own packing, and boxes were to be labelled by ward accordingly. The operating theatre had to salvage as much material and equipment as possible. All glass had to be wrapped in the theatre linen. Bottles of liquid that had been opened were to be disposed of and 'no attempt' was to be made to salvage them. All unopened boxes in the hospital stores were to be transported. Under the heading 'Time for each Operation', Colonel Cree wrote, 'It is suggested that packing, evacuation of patients and loading up should go on simultaneously until the whole is finished. Time and labour is economised.'[49]

While the fighting and bombing raids continued to kill, wound and maim on the Western Front, at sea the death rate was escalating and the nursing service was not immune. On 3 March the *Asturias* was torpedoed by a U-boat and one

Figure 5.3 Air-raid damage to a ward in the St John's Ambulance Association Hospital at Étaples, the largest voluntary hospital for the BEF in France. National Library of Scotland.

Figure 5.4 External damage by an air raid at the St John's Ambulance Association Hospital at Étaples. National Library of Scotland.

sister lost her life. On 10 April the Hospital Ship *Salta* was sunk and eight nurses were killed; and at the end of the year the *Osmanieh* was hit by a mine and 200 lives were lost, including eight nurses.[50]

Wherever nurses were deployed they faced very difficult professional and personal challenges. One Sister was willing to share her experiences and give advice to those nurses considering a temporary military nursing career. She described the hardships and miseries to be endured and expressed very clearly her opinion of the personal, mental and physical strengths required by nurses to survive in such circumstances:

> Anyone intending to volunteer for active service should spend a 'thought hour' of self-examination and see if she can answer such questions as these. Are you ready to give up many of the personal comforts which, upon the present time, you may have looked upon as mere necessities, but which will become impossible luxuries? Are you prepared to face damp and cold so intense and persistent some days you will seriously doubt if undressing will be possible? And when this difficulty has been overcome and you have tucked yourself under as many covers as you can stand, you begin to wonder if you will ever be able to get up and dress when the morning comes! Your hot water bag becomes cold in a very short time, your tent walls and bed covers are soon covered with frost, and you are lucky if your discomfort is not made worse by chilblains which are 'punishing' you dreadfully for having covered them up and tried to make them warm. The cold may be so intense that your hands are blue and numb, but the work has to be done and sometimes you will have to check tears of real suffering and do your duty. Your laundry will be a great problem, for weeks at a time you may not be able to have any done.

The Sister then listed further concessions: 'food fads … eat what is put before you'. There was loss of independence and rights. Nurses needed strength to endure 'the physical and mental strain that accompanies war nursing'. Tact, which she considered second only to endurance, was a prerequisite, particularly with doctors: 'In dealing with the medical profession it will be news to no one if I say that you will need much tact.' She claimed that 'good health' and a 'bright disposition' were absolute essentials. Finally, she listed patience: 'bring it all with you and if you have not much of it, beg, borrow or steal some'. She concluded her words of wisdom with the inspirational comment, 'in spite of all the hardships, you will find it the most satisfying work you have ever done and you will never regret having undertaken it'.[51]

The comments read like a survivor's charter but it was important that potential recruits understood the demands that active service would make on them. Surrendering the 'self' to the war effort required great sacrifices and personality, individuality, likes and dislikes were to be left at home.

By 1917, nurses on the various fighting fronts had gained considerable experience of caring for casualties with complex diseases and injuries. Professionally they developed skills that would not have been possible to achieve in civil practice. However, this left them in the position of being professionally strong but physically and psychologically vulnerable.

Their professional strength, however, was evident in politics. The Nurse Registration Bill drafted by the Central Committee for the State Registration for Nurses was being discussed again in political circles. In the opinion of Bonar Law, Chancellor of the Exchequer, the Bill should not wait until the War was over before submission; this was a coup for the pro-registrationists. However, after the 1916 split with the College of Nursing, there appeared to be little chance of reconciliation. It was clear the profession was heading for division and *The British Journal of Nursing* reported:

> The Central Committee for the State Registration of Nurses, having severed negotiations with the College of Nursing, Ltd on questions of principle, and revised its own Bill is prepared to take steps to represent these points effectively whenever the Government permits or undertakes the introduction into the House of Commons of a Nurses' Registration Bill.[52]

In the nursing press, the negative rhetoric towards the VADs was less obvious. For two years they had been serving in military hospitals without incident. All the scaremongering claims about them being a liability to the patients were without foundation.

After the debacle on the formation of The Supply of Nurses Committee, it finally produced its recommendations. Having taken comments and opinions from a variety of representatives and interested parties, the Committee's recommendations, twenty-three in total, focused on nurse training, further support being sought from the Dominions, the employment of more VAD and probationer nurses, increased salaries and bonus payments; also included were grading of VADs, particularly those who had over thirteen months' service, accommodation and travel for nurses, expenses, uniforms, and cost of medical examinations for potential recruits. It also recommended that nursing authorities were brought together by establishing one central committee to act as a clearing house during wartime and that there should be a census of all women suitable for nursing and willing to undertake it for the period of the War.[53]

The most damning report of the year was the publication of the findings of the Mesopotamia Commission and the explosive evidence from Major Carter of the Indian Medical Service. He cited an incident which occurred when he was the medical officer in charge of the Hospital Ship *Varela*; when a river barge full of sick and injured came alongside, he could not believe what he saw and could smell:

> We found a mass of men huddled up anyhow, some with blankets, some without. They were lying in a pool of dysentery about 30 feet square. They were covered with dysentery and dejecta from head to foot. With regard to the first man I examined, I put my hand into his trousers and I thought he had a haemorrhage. His trousers were full almost to his waist with something warm and slimy. I took my hand out and thought it was a blood clot. It was dysentery. The man had a fractured thigh, and his thigh was perforated in five or six places. Many cases were almost as bad. There were a certain number of cases of terrible bad bedsores.[54]

The report concluded that, knowing the medical services to be deficient for the type of campaign, Sir William Babtie had made no effort to improve the defects so as to equip the medical services in a manner suitable for the care of the sick and injured.

The revelations could hardly have been worse, barring the Black Ships at Gallipoli. The Dardanelles Commission concluded that a military attack on the peninsula was severely under-estimated and insufficient resources were diverted from the Western Front to ensure its success. Both of the Allied landings on the peninsula in April and August 1915 were fatally flawed. The Commission also censured a number of high-ranking military figures, most notably Sir Ian Hamilton, and the medical services were censured for being as ill prepared for the campaign as were the military authorities. The constant power struggles and disputes in and between the services only served to hamper effective decision-making.[55] However, no jobs were lost as a result of the findings.

At the end of 1917, *The Times* stopped publishing complete casualty lists. Since the outbreak of the War the paper had published endless lists of those Killed in Action, Died of Wounds, Wounded, Shell-Shocked, Prisoner in Enemy Hands. There could be as many as 5,000 names printed and the number never fell below 1,000 per day. The 1917 campaigns at Arras, Messines, Passchendaele and Cambrai had cost the British and Allied forces dearly: the total casualties for France and Flanders, which included battle casualties and non-battle casualties, were 1,792,515, the figure higher than in the Somme offensive. But, despite the increased technological capacity for killing and maiming and the high attrition rate among young able-bodied men who fought to the death, the War was not yet over and a new harvest was required for the coming year.

NOTES

1. Mitchell, J. and Smith, G. M. (1931), *Casualties and Medical Statistics of The Great War*, London: HMSO, p. 148.
2. Anon., *No. 26 General Hospital in France*, Privately Published by No. 26 VAD Association, p. 7.
3. Anon., *No. 26 General*, p. 11.
4. Cree, H. E., in *No. 26 General Hospital*, p. 9.
5. War Diary, No. 26 General Hospital, Wellcome Archives and Manuscripts, RAMC/728/2.
6. Cree, H. E., in *No. 26 General*, p. 8.
7. War Diary, Admission of Patients to Hospital, undated.
8. War Diary, Ward Admissions, undated.
9. Greaves, F. L. A., War Diary, Surgical Report, undated.
10. *Hansard*, House of Commons Debate, 9 March 1916, vol. 80, c. 1722.
11. McCarthy, M., Diary, 25–26 March 1916.
12. Luard, K. E. (1930), *Unknown Warriors*, London: Chatto and Windus, pp. 88, 89.
13. Brander, M., Diary, undated, March 1917.
14. *British Medical Journal*, 1916; 1: p. 863.

15. Luard, K. E., *Unknown Warriors*, p. 150.
16. Greaves, F. L. A., No. 26, War Diary, undated.
17. *British Journal of Nursing*, 14 November 1914, p. 393.
18. Anon., *No. 26 General Hospital*, p. 15.
19. Horne, M., Anaesthetics Report, No. 26, War Diary, undated.
20. *The Lancet*, 1916, 1: pp. 70–4.
21. Thurstan, V. (1917), *A Text Book of War Nursing*, New York: G. P. Putnam's Sons, pp. 104–5.
22. MacCormac, H., Medical Report, No. 26, War Diary, undated.
23. Dolden, A. S. (1980), *Cannon Fodder*, London: Blandford Press, pp. 52–3.
24. Ibid., 54.
25. Yellowlees, H., Shell Shock Report, No. 26, War Diary, undated.
26. McCarthy, M., War Diary, 29 June 1917.
27. Yellowlees, H., Shell Shock Report, No. 26, War Diary.
28. McDonald, S. F., X-Ray Report, and Roland, S., Laboratory Reports, No. 26, War Diary.
29. Rules, Medical Officer, No. 26, War Diary.
30. Discharge Rules, No. 26, War Diary.
31. Dickson, Speech, No. 26, War Diary.
32. Standing Orders, Nurses, No. 26, War Diary.
33. Sister Duties, No. 26, War Diary.
34. 'General Duties', No. 26, War Diary.
35. Clayton, Sisters, Supplementary Papers, No. 26, War Diary.
36. Anon., Women's War Work, Imperial War Museum, BRCS 25.2/13.
37. Anon., *No. 26 General Hospital*, p. 17.
38. Garden, E., in 'Australian Army Nursing Service During the Great War', Reports and Biographies, Imperial War Museum, Documents 10603.
39. Hodgins, F., Nurses' Accounts', McCarthy Papers, Box 10, QARANC Archives.
40. Swayne, M. (1918), *In Mesopotamia*, London: Hodder and Stoughton, p. 11.
41. McCarthy, M., Unlisted Collection, Box 10, QARANC Archive.
42. McPherson, W. G., vol. 4, ch. III, pp. 102–3.
43. Luard, K. E., *Unknown Warriors*, p. 150.
44. Ibid., p. 157.
45. McCarthy, M., Extracts, Letter General Staff Officer, Unlisted Collection, Box 10.
46. Brander, M., Diary, undated, February 1917.
47. *British Journal of Nursing*, 7 July 1917, p. 2.
48. Duncan, A., Nurses' Accounts, QARANC Archives.
49. Confidential Report, Evacuation, No. 26, War Diary.
50. McEwen, Y. T. (2006), *It's a Long Way To Tipperary: British and Irish Nurses in the Great War*, Dunfermline: Cualann, pp. 201–7.
51. Ibid., p. 170.
52. *British Journal of Nursing*, 29 December 1917, p. 424.
53. Bridgeman, W. C., Conclusions, Supply of Nurses Committee.
54. National Archives, HO45/10838/331607 (1917).
55. National Archives, CAB19/1 (1917–18).

BOOK III

In the House of the Gods

Contentment I have learned from suffering, and from long years, and nobility.

Sophocles

6

Daughters of Arête

I$^{T\ WAS\ OVER,\ OR}$ so they said, on the eleventh hour of the eleventh day of November 1918. By the final year of the War, there were 2,060,254 casualties in the BEF, but there were consequences that would last well beyond human comprehension.[1] Behind the doors of Britain, Ireland, our allies and our enemies, the trauma, grief, anger and despair would linger and foment. Would peace bring peace? Not to everyone, particularly those moving into the physical and psychological aftermath zones – and that included nurses.

At Rouen, on that day, the large hospital centre was transformed: an Australian band played the national anthems of the Allies; not to be outdone, a Scottish piper came forth and after a few bars of 'Auld Lang Syne' played a rousing rendition of 'Hielan' Laddie'; Australian, Portuguese, French, Chinese, South African, Canadian and Indian troops fell in behind the piper. The able and not so able, dressed in their 'hospital suits', were inspired to sing, march, dance, to forget the War and to look forward to the peace.[2] Observing the evolving carnival were nurses from the Base Hospitals. After four and a half years of warfare their role was coming to an end.

What would be the feelings on Armistice Day of the nurses at Rouen, the nurses in CCSs, Base Hospitals, Ambulance Trains, barges and Hospital Ships on all the fighting fronts? We can only imagine how their relief was tempered by their experiences of four years of war. The Matron-in-Chief for France and Flanders, Maud McCarthy, gave no indication of her personal feelings in a brief reference to the Armistice in her diary: 'Armistice with Germany signed at 5 a.m. to take effect from 11 a.m. Mons taken at 4.30 a.m. Great excitement and rejoicing in the town.'[3] The low-key response was very much in the fashion of Maud McCarthy. Since her deployment to the Western Front in 1914 her daily diary entries reveal very little about herself; there are very few commentaries on the prosecution of the War, sentiments on the suffering of the troops, or the health, welfare and deaths of nurses. Barring the occasional display of anger or annoyance, it would appear that every word was carefully crafted. From what little evidence does exist in the nurses' testaments, the perceptions of her vary from adoration to indifference, with one Sister describing her as a 'cold fish'. It would appear from her diary entries and reports that Maud McCarthy operated at a high level of efficiency but, in the absence of contemporaneous papers from senior figures within the nursing service and the War Office, there is little, if any, rebuttal evidence. Nevertheless, it is clear she was generally regarded by senior medical officers within the AMS as being a highly effective Matron-in-Chief with impeccable judgement on all matters relating to the nursing services. She clearly enjoyed a degree of personal autonomy hitherto denied any previous Matron-in-Chief in the QAIMNS. In 1918 her professionalism was duly rewarded with the Order of the British Empire Dame Grand Cross. In her public persona she presented as the consummate professional, but, in order to safeguard her reputation, and presumably spare her emotions, she exercised great restraint of feelings to the point of appearing detached and aloof. Yet, perhaps the real Maud McCarthy was revealed in an exchange of letters with the Director of Princess Victoria's Rest Club for Nurses, Lady Algernon Gordon-Lennox, during the demobilisation process in 1919:

My Dear Dame Maud,

Before leaving France where I have been since September, 1914, I want to express to you my great gratitude for the constant kindness I have received from yourself and all the Members of the Nursing Service with whom I have had the happiness to come in contact ... Amidst all the sadness and suffering with which the past years have been fraught, this will always remain a beautiful memory, and I feel the debt of gratitude we owe the nurses can never be repaid.

You and I have been in such constant intercourse, that I know full well how great your responsibility has been; but it must be a source of infinite satisfaction to you, that you have been able to carry through your great work to the very end and to take with you when the time comes, the affection and admiration of all who have served under you in France ... I am laying down my work with a full heart, and can only say I hope most earnestly that the bond which has been forged between us in War will be cemented in Peace, and that we shall meet in the days to come.

Believe me, dear Dame Maud,
Yours affectionately and gratefully,
Blanche Gordon-Lennox[4]

As her war diaries and reports are the only major primary sources of insight into the character of Maud McCarthy, unusually some of her innermost thoughts and sentiments are revealed in her reply to Lady Gordon-Lennox.

My Dear Lady Algernon,

I write at once in acknowledgement of your letter which arrived today and for which I feel it will be quite impossible for me to attempt to thank you adequately, or to express in any way my deep feeling of pride, for the very high tribute you have paid to the work of these wonderful women who I have had the good fortune to work for me from the very beginning ...

For myself I am very proud to feel I have been permitted to serve my country and am deeply grateful to those in power, who placed sufficient confidence in me to let me try and carry on my department in my own peculiar way, under the Director General of the Medical Services; but all the success you are kind enough to say I have made is entirely due to the extraordinary assistance, advice and support which I have always received, not only from him, but from all the departments with which I have come in contact, coupled also with the extraordinary loyal and devoted service of those dear workers whose numbers increased so rapidly and who are now falling away.

Thank you dear Lady Algernon too, for all your goodness to everyone of them, and for all the delightful Rest Clubs which you organised for HRH Princess Victoria for the benefit of them all; but quite apart from all that, for your many personal kindnesses and special interest in so many of them which with the HRH's Clubs will be one of the outstanding bright spots which will be always a beautiful remembrance for them of the great War.

For myself well, words utterly fail me – you have been so much to me; and it is good to feel that it is only *Au Revoir* still not only for me, but for the others too.

My love, your affectionate
E. Maud McCarthy[5]

The clubs and rest homes were well received and appreciated by the many nurses who required sanctuary and emotional respite from the traumas and travails of war service. In addition to Princess Victoria's Rest Clubs for Nurses, in March 1915 Mrs Robertson Eustace opened a club at Boulogne and personally generously provided the funds for its maintenance. The club enabled the Sisters to have access to a reading room and a lending library, stationery, rest rooms and refreshments. Limited accommodation was also provided and by 1916 a dozen rooms were available for overnight stays. From the outset, the club established twenty-four-hour access to hot baths, a facility the Sisters working on Ambulance Trains particularly appreciated. The club grew in demand and popularity; by 1917 there were 1,957 members, 11,000 teas had been served, 3,707 hot baths had been provided and 819 Sisters and VADs had availed themselves of the accommodation.[6]

In addition to the clubs in France, rest and recuperation facilities were established on the home front. In 1918, The Canadian Nurses' Club was opened in London at 95 Lancaster Gate and, in Edinburgh, the Victoria League established a club for overseas nurses at 8 Rutland Square. The Duchess of Atholl, who officially opened the Edinburgh club, claimed the War had placed a great strain upon British and Dominion nurses, and they were deserving of facilities being made available to them for rest and recuperation. She also said that many overseas nurses were anxious to visit Scotland, particularly Edinburgh, and therefore the establishment of the club could be more than justified.[7]

For all that, the Queen Mary Hostels established in London for nurses on home leave or in transit held a special place in the history of welfare facilities for war-weary nurses. The first hostel was opened at Tavistock Place in July 1915, but in order to accommodate more nurses it moved to larger premises at Bedford Place. Over the next two years, two more hostels were opened at Russell Square and Warwick Square. From 1915 until the demobilisation of the nursing services, 8,000 nurses passed through Bedford Place. The Superintendent of the hostels was Mrs Kerr Lawson, who was described by Sister Cameron as 'the confidant of nurses, and very often the lifter of their burdens'. A Canadian Sister said of her, 'That dear woman knows her job, and puts grit and love into it.' When Mrs Kerr Lawson was asked what struck her most about nurses, her response demonstrated her empathy with their plight and reinforced why she was so adored by members of the nursing services:

> The way in which some of you are putting up a fight against desperate odds, bravely and alone; the tragedy of those who have lost or are losing their precious health through war service, and who have others dependent on their earnings; the sad and bitter loneliness of those pushed through circumstances from their special home niche which, once having left, they never quite regain; and above all, the scant means which so often renders them helpless when they should be independent.[8]

There can be little doubt that Mrs Kerr Lawson was the confidant of many nurses; only someone privy to the tragedy of their lives could so succinctly but sympathetically describe their professional and personal burdens.

In early 1918, the health and welfare of nurses on active service was raised in the correspondence section of *The Times*. In response, *The Nursing Times* expressed annoyance that 'at this critical time when our men are fighting to the death and our nurses are working night and day, should be chosen by some to complain of the conditions of Army nurses'.[9] The complainants were four years too late, and *The Nursing Times* too early with their condemnation of these concerns. The working and living conditions for nurses on active service had always been less than ideal and no doubt had made a sizeable contribution to the deterioration of the nurses' physical and mental health. Between 1914 and 1918, there was sufficient evidence to support the argument that some of the deaths within the nursing services could directly be attributed to the inadequacies of their living and working conditions. However, the journal reassured its readership that a representative of *The Nursing Times*, on a recent visit to France, could report that nurses were 'absolutely cheerful and happy, and loyal'. The journal missed the point, deliberately perhaps, for as the publication was well aware, not all nurses were serving on the Western Front.

In order to reinforce their assertions, the journal ran a series of articles entitled 'How the Nurses are Cared For'. The reporter who penned these was Gertrude Vaughan, a trained nurse, who mentioned nothing in her dispatches of the Sick Sisters' Hospitals and the many nurses admitted with pneumonia, septicaemia, cerebro-spinal meningitis, nephritis, sciatica, bronchitis, rheumatism, gastritis, enteric and para-typhoid, or the nurses who sustained traumatic injuries caused by the bombing raids and those suffering from shell shock. Moreover, the articles on 'How the Nurses are Cared For' contradicted a report *The Nursing Times* had carried three months earlier on the health of a Sister who became seriously ill after working for three years on the Western Front. That report claimed the Sister had 'collapsed under the strain of work and is at present lying dangerously ill at No. 2 General Hospital, Havre'. It also covered the history of the nurse's arrival in France until she became critically ill: apparently, at the end of August 1914, the Sister crossed in a 'cattle boat' to France, where during her first few months on active service she worked under very trying conditions and spent the winter of 1914–15 'under canvas at Rouen'. In 1915, the Sister was assigned to a CCS where 'she experienced the pleasures of being shelled as well as gassed'. She then contracted trench fever and spent her home leave recovering from the condition. After the Sister returned to France, she was considered unfit for the demands of a CCS and was sent to work in a hospital at Le Havre, where finally her health broke down.[10] The report was an exemplar of how nurses were not cared for.

Between 1914 and the cessation of hostilities, respiratory conditions such as bronchitis, pneumonia and tuberculosis were the most prevalent illnesses among the nursing staff. For example, one Sister, aged only twenty-eight, was invalided out of the service with war-acquired tuberculosis. The Medical Board report stated the nurse had 'contracted her condition as a result of nursing conditions in the hospital'.[11] The other leading causes of sickness and debility were cardiovascular disease, infectious diseases, gastric, renal and endocrine conditions. The remaining cases comprised gynaecological, ear, nose and throat, skin and eye problems, and musculoskeletal injury (see Appendix 2).

Susceptibility to sickness, disease or injury was often dependent on the environmental conditions and the climate nurses worked in. For example, Hospital Ships brought their own rewards and problems. Hospital Ships were vulnerable to enemy attacks and in ten separate incidents fifty-five nurses were lost at sea. The highest incidence of nurses' deaths took place on 27 June 1918 when HMHS *Llandovery Castle* was torpedoed. Fourteen nurses died in the attack.

There were other 'enemies' working against the health and effectiveness of nurses too. Infection-control procedures were difficult to implement on Hospital Ships, so diseases were more easily transferred, and nurses were not immune. Evidence from pension files suggests that some nurses were medically retired from the service within a year of working on Hospital Ships, particularly those involved in the Dardanelles Campaign.

In Salonika and Mesopotamia, malaria, dysentery and enteric were the leading causes of illness and death among the troops and the nursing services.

DEATHS IN SERVICE AND DISTRIBUTION OF ESTATE

When a nurse died on active service, in accordance with the Regimental Deaths Act (1893) a 'Court of Adjustment' was convened to handle the financial affairs of the deceased nurse. If the nurse made a will, the army distributed the bequests to the legatees, thus removing the need for an executor. If the nurse died intestate, the army authorities distributed her net estate equally between surviving parents and siblings. However, dependent on the nurse's country of residence before joining the service, the army had to fulfil all the legal procedures of the country before the estate of the nurse could be settled.

Many of the cases were quite tragic. One Sister had served since the beginning of the War and was involved in the retreat from Mons. In 1915 she was sent to

Macedonia. In 1917 she became ill and was operated on for a cancerous growth. In a letter from her next of kin, it was claimed the Sister was sent to Britain via Malta 'in a dying condition'. Two miles out of Malta, the ship she was travelling on, the *Goorkha*, was torpedoed. The Sister was rescued and spent four weeks in a hospital in Malta before being sent back to Britain on the Hospital Ship *Braemar Castle*. Four months later she died in the Sick Sisters' Hospital, Vincent Square, London. In a letter to the War Office, her sister wrote that she would 'greatly treasure my sister's Mons Medal, which she had hoped to receive'.[12]

Another tragic case involved a widowed Sister who died on active service, leaving two small children. According to the records, she died of peritonitis. The Court of Adjustment deemed the children were due £39 from their mother's estate and the sum was paid to their grandfather, who was to use the money for 'their equal and exclusive benefit'. However, the Ministry of Pensions granted a gratuity of £93 15 shillings to the children but the money was paid to their grandmother as guardian of the children.[13]

TRAUMA-RELATED DEATHS AND INJURIES

All accidental deaths were referred to a military Court of Enquiry. For example, in 1915 at Alexandria, a Sister was killed in a railway accident. According to a report from the office of the Director General Army Medical Services, nurses were being transported by an ambulance wagon from a hospital to their billets when it stopped at a railway crossing. One of the Sisters saw an oncoming train and jumped out of the ambulance to alert the other Sisters to alight from the ambulance; she was killed instantly and the other nurses survived. The report concluded that the nurse was 'killed while gallantly attempting to save the others', and then went on to say, 'Please express to the relatives the regret of every nurse and all other ranks of the Royal Army Medical Corps, and their admiration for her heroic death.'[14]

At Basra, in January 1918, three nurses from the QAIMNSR and one VAD from the BRCS were killed when the motor launch on which they were travelling collided with a steam tug. The nurses were all from No. 65 British General Hospital. In evidence to the Court of Enquiry, the Matron-in-Chief, Miss Beatrice Jones, said that twelve nurses along with the Matron, Miss F. M. Hall, were invited to spend the afternoon of 15 January at the Beit Naama Officers' Convalescent Hospital. Additionally, Lieutenant Colonel E. W. Skinner RAMC was invited to join the group. The collision took place on the return journey. The second witness to give evidence to the Enquiry was the Matron of No. 65 General Hospital, Miss Frances Mary Hall, who confirmed the facts as stated by the Matron-in-Chief. The third witness was Lieutenant Colonel Skinner, and his evidence did not differ from the accounts given by Miss Jones and Miss Hall. As well as being a witness, Lieutenant Colonel Skinner was chairing the Enquiry. The hearings concluded that it had been a tragic accident with no blame being apportioned to anyone.[15] Frances Mary Hall died of paratyphoid the following year.[16] Some years later, in 1924, following an enquiry to the office of the Director General, the Awards, Officers Branch, requested a copy of the Court of Enquiry report. The response was brief: 'It is regretted that there is no trace of the proceedings of the Court of Enquiry having been received in this office.'[17]

There were, of course, trauma deaths caused by bombing raids on hospitals on the Western and Macedonian fronts. Furthermore, the highest rate of trauma-related deaths within the nursing services was due to attacks on Hospital Ships and troop transporters. The sinking of the transporter *Transylvania* tells its own story of the dangers nurses and others faced. On 3 May 1917, the ship left Marseilles bound for Alexandria. The following day it was sunk by two enemy torpedoes just off the Italian coast near Savona. Sixty-five nurses were on board, as well as RAMC personnel, soldiers and crew. Sadly, 412 souls lost their lives but there were no deaths within the nursing services. Even so, the tragedy was not without consequence for some nurses, for recorded in their confidential reports were comments such as 'Shipwrecked *Transylvania*, returned to England, invalided neurasthenia.' Additionally, there were accidental drownings, usually caused by nurses swimming in unfamiliar waters during their off-duty time (see Appendix 3).

LESION OF THE WILL OR WOUNDS OF THE SPIRIT? PSYCHOLOGICAL INJURY AND SUICIDE

Throughout the War there were frequent references to the 'sterling work' of nurses. Furthermore, the nursing journals regularly referred to the 'good health and welfare' of nurses posted overseas. In the early days of the War, nursing journals boasted that cases of nervous breakdown among nurses on active service were 'remarkably few'. By 1916, they were referring to 'nurses broken in the war'.

The most consistent references to nurses suffering from nerve strain, neurasthenia, nervous debility and shell shock can be found in Maud McCarthy's diaries, in reports filed from CCSs and in Unit War Diaries. Entries refer to nurses being sent to hospitals or rest homes for treatment of nerve strain or shell shock, while some were sent back home as unfit for service.

A member of the QAIMNSR, who had been on active service for ten months, was assessed by a Medical Board held at No. 24 General Hospital, Étaples, for her suitability to continue to work in France. The Board concluded that although there was no evidence of disease and the nurse's health was good, she had 'a nervous temperament and has been entirely unfitted for her work during the bombing raids'. The Board recommended that she return to Britain for home service.[18]

A Sister who had arrived in France in 1917 and been demobilised in 1919 was described by 1920 as being extremely disturbed and suffering from hallucinations, delusions accompanied by violence, acute insomnia, refusal to eat and threats of suicide. Her hospital reports prior to joining up for military service claimed she was a willing, capable and reliable nurse, and her tone and discipline were good. The nurse was eventually transferred to Bethlem Hospital with a diagnosis of 'shell shock'.[19]

In one incident the Senior Sister at a CCS wrote that following the bombing around the hospital, three nurses developed shell shock and had to be removed very quickly by ambulance further up the LOC. In another incident, an Australian nursing Sister claimed that nurses, shelled out of their CCS, arrived at her Base Hospital 'in a state of collapse with emotional exhaustion'. Some, she claimed, had to be evacuated because they were suffering from shell shock. In a letter to Maud McCarthy, the Senior Sister at a CCS described the death of a nurse killed by shelling and said that four of the nurses involved in the incident had to be evacuated suffering from shell shock.[20]

Noted in some nurses' confidential reports are comments such as 'suffering from nervous debility' or 'debility caused from nervousness in air raids'; not surprising, given that they were constantly under threat. The tragic consequences of the raids on personnel and structures were listed in a report compiled by Maud McCarthy:

> During 1917, there were forty-two casualties among the nursing staff, forty-one due to enemy action. Nine nurses were killed by enemy aircraft, and six of these were members of the Canadian Army Medical Corps. Many had very severe wounds and were dangerously ill, while others had slight injuries. The enemy air raids which caused greatest loss of life and casualties among the nursing services were those of 19 and 31 May at Étaples, and 29 May at Doullens. The raid at Étaples on 19 May lasted three hours and the hospitals suffered greatly. At No. 1 Canadian General Hospital one Sister was killed, two were so severely wounded they died shortly afterwards and five others were wounded.[21]

Official reports suggest that, for the most part, nurses coped well under the strain of shell fire. For instance, the CO of No. 58 Scottish General Hospital wrote to the Assistant Director of Medical Services at St Omer recommending some of his nurses for awards. His report stated that on the night of 30 September/1 October 1917 the hospital was bombed, 'killing four nurses and 18 other ranks and two nurses and 58 other ranks were wounded'. He claimed that:

> The nurses displayed great gallantry and devotion to duty in that they performed their work of attending to the wounded promptly, calmly and without any consideration of self amid the most distracting and nerve racking surroundings. One nurse, Sister Climie was killed while sitting on the bed of a nervous patient and singing to him in order to try and calm his nerves.[22]

For some nurses the physical and psychological strain was a burden they were no longer prepared to carry and they committed suicide. The first official case to be recorded was a staff nurse who took her own life in 1915. The nurse was a regular in the QAIMNS and had two years' service before war broke out. Following mobilisation she worked at No. 10 General Hospital. According to the military Court of Enquiry convened to establish the circumstances surrounding

Figure 6.1 Funeral of Sister Wake, Canadian Army Nursing Service, who died of wounds after a bombing raid in 1918. National Library of Scotland.

her death, evidence was presented which suggested the nurse had undergone long periods of intense, hard work which resulted in a breakdown of her health. She was diagnosed with neurasthenia, but in addition to her health problems she suffered bereavement when her 26-year-old brother was killed on active service. A witness statement to the Court of Enquiry stated that on admission to hospital she was described as nervous and suffering from insomnia. Following a medical examination, she was not thought to have suicidal tendencies and it was decided to repatriate her back to Britain. On the day she was due to depart, she jumped out of a third-floor window, sustaining multiple injuries from which she did not recover. The cause of death was listed as neurasthenia and the findings of the Court of Enquiry concluded that she committed suicide while temporarily insane.[23] In other cases, a Matron hanged herself while on active service and a staff nurse drank the disinfectant Lysol to end her life. In a few cases, non-accidental drowning was listed as the cause of death. One unmarried Sister, fearing she was pregnant, attempted suicide. However, from personal information noted in service files it would appear that the pressure was cumulative, arising from war service and domestic circumstances.

The highest incidence of nervous breakdown and shell shock among nurses was during 1917 and 1918. This coincided with the increased bombing and strafing raids on CCSs and Base Hospitals. Even so, there were more awards for bravery and Mentioned in Dispatches (MID) granted to nurses in this period than there were reported cases of shell shock or nervous debility. Furthermore, throughout the period of concentrated enemy bombing on CCSs and Base Hospitals, the accolades recorded in confidential reports were numerous, with notes such as 'Excellent, worthy of accelerated promotion, specially mentioned for bravery during bombing' recorded in their confidential reports (see Appendix 1).

In the House of Commons between 1917 and 1919, several questions were raised regarding the care, treatment, compensation and pension rights of sick, disabled and 'shell-shocked nurses'. The allocation of war pensions for mental health problems both in women and men appears to have been almost arbitrary, and it would be difficult to know exactly what criteria were applied for awards to be made. The primary duty of the Ministry of Pensions was to decide whether or not compensation should be awarded for physical and psychological disability arising from injury or disease attributed to war. In the House of Commons, debates took place over the eligibility of nurses receiving wound gratuities and wound pensions, and there were also discussions concerning nurses' dependants. Deceased, invalided or debilitated nurses could no longer economically provide for their families and Sir Archibald Williamson asked the Minister for Pensions:

> Whether he was aware that many nurses have relatives dependent upon them, whether Army nurses are eligible for pensions if they suffer injury through the war in common with other branches of the Army, and, if so, will he take steps to put them on the same footing as other branches of the Army by making provision for dependants in cases where a nurse loses her life? [24]

The Minister informed Sir Archibald and the House that he had:

> no knowledge as to whether members of the Navy and Army Nursing services have relatives dependent on them. No such cases have been brought to my notice, but I will consider the question of making some provision for the dependent relatives of nurses who lose their lives through war service. [25]

According to preserved correspondence with the Ministry of Pensions, many of the sick, disabled and shell-shocked nurses and their dependants faced serious economic hardship and poverty because they failed to meet the war pensions criteria. However, in some case files there is evidence that pensions were awarded despite the cause of the illness or debility being classed as 'not known'; given the Ministry of Pensions' rigorous case-by-case assessment, this was most unusual, but it also reinforced what many believed to be true: that the awards assessments were unfair and were riddled with inconsistencies and ambiguities.

There can be no doubt that life and work on overseas duties had been physically and emotionally taxing for nurses, but it would appear that for the most part it was met with a mixture of irritation and good grace. However, consistent sources of annoyance, frustration and distress emerged from researching nurses' letters, diaries and memoirs: for example, interminable bureaucracy, movement from hospital to hospital or other casualty care facilities and the attendant problem of breaking established relationships, the frequency of inadequate diet and insufficient sleep, poor billeting, censorship of mail, concerns about the safety of family and friends also serving, and isolation from those at home. The antidotes to their pressures were humour, music, concert parties, hockey matches, golf and tennis. Some nurses wrote poetry while others found peace and joy in painting. Sightseeing and shopping regularly featured in what little off-duty time nurses had. Although forbidden, socialising with officers and other ranks was not uncommon. Animals too played a significant role in the lives of nurses on active service, and it was not unusual for stray dogs and cats to be 'adopted'. Normalising nightmare situations and conditions required creative thinking skills and the nurses sourced all manner of adjuncts to ensure they were physically and psychologically 'fit for duty'.

CONCLUSION

Following their mobilisation in August 1914, the QAIMNS and the Reserve were involved in every theatre of war: France and Flanders, the Dardanelles Campaign, Mesopotamia, Macedonia, Egypt, Palestine, Italy, India, North Russia and East Africa. They were ably assisted by the Territorial Force Nursing Service and VADs from the Joint War Committee of the British Red Cross Society. Furthermore, nurses from the Dominion military nursing services and Britain's allies strengthened the effectiveness of casualty care on all the fighting fronts. Between August 1914 and July 1919, the nurses gained extensive experience of working in a variety of climates, in unconventional surroundings and in different care facilities, while dealing with a multitude of diseases and conditions, quite often with limited supplies, equipment and comforts for their patients and themselves.

It is difficult to generalise nurses' motives for volunteering their services during the Great War and, arguably, putting themselves in harm's way, but humanitarianism, imperial loyalties, a sense of adventure, strong convictions, connections to the Women's Movement, the possibility of advancing the Nurse Registration Bill and enhancing their professional standing all appear to have been strong motivators. Additionally, but not obviously stated in their text, were religious conviction and societal influence and expectation. However, pre-war nurses were already inculcated with the importance of 'duty'.

There was of course that cadre of thrill-seekers who enjoyed vicarious living and they cannot be discounted. However, it would appear that for the most part the voyeurs worked in independent or self-funded units, away from the mainstream of military nursing.

In the historiography of nursing in the First World War, the occupational lives, health and deaths of nurses have received scant attention and, rather ironically, when reference is made to the 'casualties of war' it is generally not recognised that the casualty carers became casualties themselves. The historical neglect is perplexing but the subject may be perceived by some historians or nurse historians as 'too dry' or lacking the drama of 'Tommie's traumas'; the evidence, however, belies the perception.

In the House of the Gods the daughters of Arête had secured their place. From the outbreak of hostilities until the Armistice they had carried out selfless and noble work. However, questions have to be asked about the effectiveness of the nursing services. From 1915 onwards within the medical services, aversion and denial regarding the mismanagement of casualty care had become almost commonplace; the Dardanelles and Mesopotamia campaigns were disturbing examples. In the Commission's final reports, 'neglect' and 'failures' were frequently used, as was 'ill-prepared', and the medical services were not exempt from the criticism. In the absence of any official documentation from the Matron-in-Chief's office, it is impossible to know if the nursing services were also considered culpable in the shortcomings and mismanagement of the casualty care arrangements. Conversely, if the nursing services raised concerns there is no evidence to show how they were received or acted upon. Apart from the War Diaries of Maud McCarthy, which should not be regarded as definitive or singularly authoritative, there is an absolute dearth of official correspondence and papers on the administration of the QAIMNS.

In the nurses' personal communications there is little, if any, criticism of the medical and nursing administration, despite knowing full well the chaotic situations in which many of them were working. Also, nurses were not ignorant of the public's response to the controversies over the inadequacies of casualty care. Furthermore, the deficiencies had been debated in Parliament and in the national and nursing press. While DORA would have been a deterrent to adverse comments or criticism, nurses did have the facility of being able to send anonymous correspondence to their nursing journals. Some did, and wrongdoings and inadequacies of casualty care were exposed. The majority, however, remained silent. It is understandable that the regulars of the QAIMNS would not wish to appear critical of the service that employed them; however, it was different for the reserves, for after demobilisation they were not restrained from speaking out or writing about the deeply unfavourable conditions the casualties were nursed in, and in which nurses had to live and work. However, the risk of unemployment, particularly if jobs were at threat from untrained volunteer nurses, may have bought the silence of many. Conversely, many nurses may have decided to move on and put their war service experiences behind them. Additionally, there was the luxury of selective memory, only choosing to remembering all that was good about the war years.

Equally, there was an official silence on the in-service deaths and disabilities in the nursing services. Throughout the War, the terms 'missing in action', 'killed in action' and 'died of wounds' became tragically familiar and commonplace, but was there ever an expectation that nurses would be killed in bombing raids or lost at sea due to enemy action? Was consideration ever given to the fact that nurses could be sent home physically or psychologically traumatised, or crippled with debilitating illness or disease? Did the politicians and public ever consider that 'losses' included nurses who were also daughters, sisters and mothers?

Clearly the Prime Minister, David Lloyd George, did not give the impression of equal consideration when he spoke of 'a land fit for heroes to live in', referring of course to male veterans. But what could the daughters of Arête expect?

For their war service, the four great Matrons-in-Chief, Ethel Becher and Maud McCarthy (QAIMNS), Sydney Browne (TFNS) and Sarah Swift (BRCS), were all rewarded with the Order of the British Empire Dame Grand Cross. However, Katharine Furse was acknowledged well before the cessation of hostilities and received the Order of the British Empire Dame Grand Cross in 1917. Among the ranks of the nursing services, the Royal Red Cross (Member) and Royal Red Cross (Associate Member) were awarded. Because of the discrepancies in the figures of *The Army List* and a Register of Recipients held in the National Archive, Kew, the actual number of awards remains a source of dispute. However, the lowest estimates awarded to nurses during the war years were 844 Members and 2,768 Associate Members.[26]

Yet, despite the contribution of nurses and women generally to the war effort, after the Armistice, post-war settlements ended in compromise. The Representation of the People Act (1918) gave the right to vote to women over the age of thirty, an outrageous scandal considering the legions of women in their

Figure 6.2 Presentation of the Military Medal by General Plumer to nurses for their courageous conduct when their hospital was bombed. National Library of Scotland.

twenties who kept 'the home fires burning' and the wheels of industry turning. In 1919 the Nurse Registration Act was finally enacted but the nursing profession was left divided by years of political in-fighting. The frequently raised concerns in the columns of the nursing press about post-war employment and VADs 'taking over' the jobs of trained nurses never materialised. In fact, the VAD contribution to the war effort was surrounded in a mythology that still perpetuates. According to the papers of Katharine Furse, in a document titled 'List of Joint Commission VAD Members Who Have Served in France', approximately 1,587 VADs served, and 1,304 of the total came from England. Furthermore, out of the English total, 784 came from London. The VAD presence on the Western Front was not as large as commonly believed. Also, it would appear from the statistics that, by chance or choice, VADs at the front were dominated by English selection, particularly London.[27] In the other theatres of military operations, a total of 630 VADs served, bringing the total VAD overseas deployment to 2,217. Unfortunately there is no indication in the Furse papers from where in the UK or Ireland the 630 VADs came.

It was unfortunate too the VADs were given such a hard time in the nursing press and, rather unfairly, little distinction was made between their valuable work and that of the hedonists, the 'Limelighters' or VAVs, an acronym for vicarious and voyeuristic thrill-seekers. The War for them was just another avenue of excitement to be explored and exploited. Unfortunately, some of them published their wartime memoirs and their writings have been taken far too seriously by historians, nurse historians and the media. However, their prose belies their actual experiences, and their alleged excursions into the suffering of combatants were more imagined than real. Nonetheless their writings have unjustly influenced the public's perception of First World War nurses.

On 10 April 1918, a memorial service was held in St Paul's Cathedral for 'all the nurses who have fallen during the war'. Queen Alexandra, Princess Victoria and other members of the royal family attended the service. The Archdeacon of London, V. E. Holmes, concluded his eulogy with, 'You have had your chance and you have taken it – women who would be remembered with the soldiers in a never-to-be-forgotten page of history.' He then reminded the assembled Matrons, Sisters and nurses that they were entrusted with 'great work', and because of that work they were gathered in worship to the memory of their dead colleagues.[28] Unfortunately, the death rate among nurses was not over and 1918 would see the highest attrition rate within the nursing services. Even so, not all nurses died on active service; many nurses spent their last few days or weeks in military hospitals on the home front or died in the loving care of their families. Some died alone, with despair, loss of hope or feelings of abandonment causing some to end their own lives. In the post-war years, others died of war-related diseases or injuries. Moreover, as a direct consequence of war-acquired physical or psychological conditions, some died in poverty because they were unfit for employment.

The 'great work' referred to by the Archdeacon of London came at a high price.

Figure 6.3 Lowering the coffin of Sister Wake, one of many nurses to die due to enemy action during the War. National Library of Scotland.

In 1920, an article claimed:

> The veil of secrecy which hid the operations of the nursing sisters during the war has not yet been lifted. Lightening glimpses have come through from time-to-time chiefly in the telling little narratives recounting deeds which have earned distinction. But nothing approaching a detailed history of 'Nursing in the Great War' has been attempted.[29]

It is doubtful if an Official History of the QAIMNS can ever be written. While there are preserved selective sources and references to consult on the wartime work of the Service, official War Office papers, particularly those of Ethel Becher, do not exist. Furthermore, there is a dearth of official communications between the Matron-in-Chief of the Army Nursing Services and the Director General of the Army Medical Services. Moreover, many of the nurses' service files have been 'weeded', making it impossible to build up an accurate picture of the relationship that existed between the War Office and the regular and reserve services.

There is, however, a corpus of work on the development of professional practice. Advances in civilian medicine and surgery inevitably stem from the exigencies of wartime practice, and the Great War was no exception. With the assistance of nurses, pioneering work was carried out on infection control, orthopaedic surgery, abdominal and chest trauma, environmental exposure, bone- and skin-grafting, blood transfusion, and physical and psychological rehabilitation. The list is not exhaustive. In truth, nurses were at the forefront of those developments and it would have been impossible to make such advances without their involvement and cooperation. In their own right, nurses were pioneers, innovators and patient advocates.

The ancient Greek concept of *arête* was fulfilment of purpose, but also possession of courage and strength in the face of adversity. There can be little doubt that throughout the period of the Great War this was true of many nurses. However, because of the great – perhaps respectful – silence among the ranks of the QAIMNS and the associated nursing services, we are not yet fully acquainted with the personal and professional costs and implications for those who served. For the moment we have to be thankful for the small cameos we have of their war service. Until further primary sources come to light we can only generalise on the nurses' wartime experiences, and speculate why out of 24,000 active service nurses, so many chose to stay silent. The writer and journalist William Linton Andrews said 'the war years were the haunting years, for nothing in our time will haunt us like the war'. He wanted to forget and took all the advice that was given to him as to how he could move on with his life. Years later, he wanted to recall those traumatic years: 'Time has healed many wounds and many minds ... I am trying to remember the War I have tried so hard to forget.'[30] Perhaps nurses shared the same sentiments but despite their best endeavours, and for many valid reasons, they were never able to produce their historical narrative of the haunting years. Sister Luard was adamant that the nurses' contribution should not be forgotten, even if they chose not to speak for themselves:

> Surely Britain, for all of her losses must be for generations immeasurably a better country for the sacrifices, the brotherhood, the effort, the endurance and the devotion poured out over every mile in France and Flanders, Gallipoli, in Palestine, East Africa and in Mesopotamia, to which she sent all of her sons – and some of her daughters.[31]

In the First World War, the QAIMNS and Reserve, supported by the TFNS, VADs and allied nursing services, numerically did not make a sizeable contribution to the war effort, but professionally their contribution was significant. However, despite the paucity of nurses' historical narratives, the existing small but irrefutable and impressive body of evidence does inform us that the daughters of Arête served in 'The Great War for Civilisation' with professionalism, dedication, humanity and a great deal of self-sacrifice.

Unfortunately the nation and the nursing profession lost sight of the endeavours, sacrifices and professional achievements of the nurses who served during the First World War. Over the past few years there has been an attempt by a small cadre of historians and nurse historians to 'remember and record' the war work of trained and volunteer nurses. Perhaps, if the long-overdue epitaph for the Daughters of Arête is to be written, surely it should include:

In that long dark war of endurance they had a great capacity for optimism and in their compassionate ministrations recognised there is no quality of life without hope.[32]

Figure 6.4 Members of the QA regulars and reserve, and Territorial Nursing Force leaving Buckingham Palace after an investiture. QARANC Collection.

NOTES

1. Mitchell, J. and Smith, G. M. (1931), *Casualties and Medical Statistics of The Great War*, London: HMSO, p. 168.
2. Marlow, J. (1999), *Women and the Great War*, London: Virago, p. 381.
3. McCarthy, M. Diary, 11 November 1918.
4. Imperial War Museum, Women's War Work, McCarthy–Gordon-Lennox correspondence, BRCS16.3/6.
5. Ibid.
6. National Archives, WO222/2134, McCarthy, M., 'Report on Nurses' Clubs in France', 28 June 1919.
7. *The British Journal of Nursing*, 13 April 1918, p. 257.
8. *The Nursing Times*, 1 March 1919, p. 196.
9. *The Nursing Times*, 4 May 1918, p. 491.
10. *The Nursing Times*, 2 February 1918, p. 140.
11. National Archives, WO399/7943.
12. NA, WO399/7932.
13. NA, WO399/6921.
14. NA, WO399/3365.
15. NA, WO399/8352.

16. NA, WO399/3454.
17. NA, WO399/8836.
18. NA, WO399/3962.
19. National Archives, PIN 26/20035.
20. McCarthy, M., Papers, Correspondence, Sister Wood, 22 August 1917.
21. Annual Report of the Work of the Nursing Services in France, 1917.
22. McCarthy, M., Papers, Report, No. 58 Scottish General Hospital, 5 October 1917.
23. NA, WO399/6558.
24. *Hansard*, House of Commons Debate, 18 March 1918, cc. 2121–2.
25. Ibid.
26. *The Monthly Army List 1914–1919*.
27. Furse, K., Papers, DM1584/12.
28. *British Journal of Nursing*, 20 April 1918, p. 272.
29. *The Hospital*, 18 December 1920, p. 269.
30. Andrews, W. L. (1930), *Haunting Years*, London: Hutchinson and Co. Ltd, pp. 5–6.
31. Luard K. E., D/DLu/66/1.
32. McEwen, Y. T. Speech, Nursing Memorial Appeal, Edinburgh, 15 November 2013.

Appendix 1

Nurses Awarded the Military Medal

In a few cases, the citation was not available.

QUEEN ALEXANDRIA'S IMPERIAL MILITARY NURSING SERVICE

Broome, Acting Sister Florence, at Noeux-les-Mines
For conspicuous bravery and devotion to duty, in that on the afternoon of September 30th, 1917, when two people were killed and three wounded just outside the main wards, though shelling still continued and pieces of shell occasionally struck the building in which she was working. Miss Broome with perfect coolness and courage continued to attend and encourage the wounded regardless of her own danger. This is only one of the many occasions when shells and bombs have fallen in the neighbourhood of this hospital, and the consistent manner in which her coolness, bravery, and devotion to duty have been displayed, has been of the utmost service in the care of the wounded and an example to all with whom she has worked.

Foley, Sister Mary Gladys Connice, attd. 33rd Casualty Clearing Station
For her splendid behaviour and example as Sister-in-Charge in exhibiting great coolness on the 7th December, 1917 at Bethune, when the town was heavily shelled all day, in attending to the patients in the wards and in the cellars. Also for continuous good service during the past year under trying times, the town being shelled and bombed frequently.

James, Sister Laura, ARRC
On the night of 3rd May 1917, when Arras was being heavily shelled, Sister Laura James showed great courage, and by her coolness and devotion to duty succeeded in allaying the fears of the patients under her charge. She refused to leave the ward, although the hospital had been hit several times, 3 men being killed and 14 wounded. She was only prevailed on to leave when all the patients had been safely evacuated.

Maude, Acting Sister Etherinda
On the night of the 3rd May, 1917, when Arras was being heavily shelled, Sister Maude showed great courage and devotion to duty. An operation was in

progress and by her coolness under such trying circumstances she was of great assistance to the surgeon, refusing to leave her post until ordered to do so. The Hospital was hit several times, three men being killed and 14 wounded.

McGrath, Staff Nurse Annie Marie, attd. No. 26 General Hospital
For conspicuous gallantry and devotion to duty at Étaples on 31st May 1916, during an enemy air raid when in charge of a ward of serious cases, showed a confidence and set a fine example during the most critical period.

Robinson, Sister Charlotte Lillian Annie, ARRC, No. 10 Stationary Hospital
For conspicuous devotion to duty and courage when night sister at No. 10 Stationary Hospital, St Omer, on 23 May 1918. On the early morning of the 23 May when the building occupied by No. 10 Stationary Hospital was struck by four bombs from an enemy aeroplane and one wing was practically cut in two, many patients were buried in the debris. Sister Robinson at very great personal risk immediately went in amongst the ruins to assist in recovering the patients, quite regardless of the danger from collapse of the upper stories of the building which might have occurred at any moment. Her one thought was the rescuing of the patients, and throughout she displayed magnificent coolness and resource and an utter disregard of the danger involved in removing them.

Roy, Acting Sister Catherine Murray, attd. 47th Casualty Clearing Station
At Dozinghem at 9.15 pm August 20th 1917, during a bomb raid in which there were 68 casualties including 14 deaths, this lady showed remarkable presence of mind and amid the darkness and confusion gathered together the staff of Nursing Sisters in an extraordinary space of time to attend to the injured. Her attitude throughout the night is deserving of the highest praise, and her assistance was of the greatest value in restoring the order and comfort of the patients. She maintained her presence of mind in a wonderful way.

Toller, Sister (Acting Matron) Lucie Maud Mary
For conspicuous gallantry and devotion to duty on the night of 19/20th May 1918 at Étaples during an enemy air raid. When the Sisters' Quarters were wrecked and the Nurses wounded, Sister Toller collected the staff, and placed them in comparative safety. By her action and fine example she undoubtedly saved life.

Tunley, Matron Mabel Mary, RRC and Bar
At Bethune, on the 7th August 1916, she did exceptionally good work in assisting getting all the patients, 260, down to the cellars, so that when the Clearing Station was eventually hit not one of the patients received a scratch. Her cheeriness and courage were instrumental in keeping everyone who came in contact with her up to the mark. She was slightly wounded and remained at duty.

Wood, Sister Minnie, attd. 44th Casualty Clearing Station
For most courageous devotion to duty. On the 21st August, 1917 this lady was Sister-in-Charge at No. 44 Casualty Clearing Station, Brandhoek when it was shelled at short intervals from 11.00am till night, one Sister being killed. This lady never lost her nerve for a moment and during the whole of a most trying day, carried out her duties with the greatest steadiness and coolness. By her work and example, she greatly assisted in the speedy evacuation of the patients and the transfer of the Sisters.

QAIMNS RESERVE

Abraham, Acting Sister Maud Alice, ARRC, Civil Hospital Reserve attd. QAIMNS Reserve
No. 7 Casualty Clearing Station. At Noeux-les-Mines, Acting Sister Maud Alice Abraham, Civil Hospital Reserve. For conspicuous bravery and devotion to duty, in that on the morning of Sept. 19th 1917 during very active enemy shelling she continued in her work as operating theatre Sister with the greatest coolness and courage, though shells were bursting very near and pieces were frequently striking the hospital. On this day approx. 200 shells fell near the hospital between the hours of 1.30am and 1.30pm. It was absolutely necessary for surgical operations to be performed, and Miss Abraham's consistent courage and devotion to duty were not only of great advantage to the wounded but an example to and the admiration of all who worked with her. This is only one of the many occasions when shells and bombs have fallen near this hospital and whenever acts of courage have been called for she has behaved in a manner beyond the highest words of praise.

Agatha, Acting Sister Mary

Allsop, Sister Beatrice Alice
At Bethune on the 7th August 1916 she was present in the operation theatre when it was wrecked by the close explosion of a 15 inch shell which slightly wounded her. She remained at work and displayed great courage in continuing to attend to patients for five hours.

Bascombe, Staff Nurse Beatrice, attd. No. 24 General Hospital
For conspicuous gallantry and devotion to duty at Étaples 31st May 1918 during an air raid by the enemy. When her ward was destroyed by a bomb and herself wounded, insisted on remaining at her post and attending to wounded patients.

Bell, Sister Mary Agnes Crawford, attd. 20th Casualty Clearing Station

Blair, Sister Mary Alice Crawford, ARRC
No. 20 Casualty Clearing Station. On the evening of June 3rd, 1917, at Boisleux these three members of the Nursing Service remained on duty in the

shrapnel swept hospital attending to the severely wounded and helpless cases, and would not leave their dangerous position until the patients were in a place of safety. *See also* McLean and Panton

Bowles, Sister Linda
At Bailleul Ambulance Siding. This lady was on duty on the night of the 6/7th July 1917, at No. 11 Casualty Clearing Station. For about three hours bombs were repeatedly dropped in the immediate vicinity of, and eventually into the Casualty Clearing Station, which was under canvas. There were some 250 patients in the Hospital at the time, 27 were killed and 68 wounded amongst the patients and personnel as a result of seven bombs dropped on the Hospital. Throughout she continued her duties amongst the patients helping to calm them and attending to those wounded in the bombardment. She showed most remarkable coolness and devotion to duty, and gave a splendid example under very trying circumstances.

Boyd, Acting Sister Anna Georgina, ARRC
7 CCS. At Noeux-les-Mines. For conspicuous bravery and devotion to duty in that during the night of September 12/13th 1917, during very heavy enemy shelling, when pieces of shell were striking the hospital, and one of the personnel was wounded she carried out her duties with the greatest courage and coolness. Her bravery, cheerfulness, and devotion to duty during this horrible night were of the greatest advantage when the darkness and helplessness of the wounded made many of them seriously alarmed. Her presence of mind and absence of fear gave a much needed confidence to the patients. This is only one of the many dangerous occasions when Miss Boyd has acted up to the highest traditions of the Nursing Service.

Brown, Acting Sister Mary Agatha, attd. No. 53 Casualty Clearing Station
For marked bravery and devotion to duty on the evening of 21st March 1918, at 8.30 pm, during a hostile bombing raid on the adjacent railway station at Lillers. She was accompanying the Matron (severely wounded), and the late Sister Andrews (killed) when the first aerial bomb, which struck them, fell. Unwounded herself she remained with them, tending them, until help arrived. On return to the CCS she turned to and worked until 2.00am in the Theatre as though nothing unusual had happened, and until all wounded had been operated on, although an ammunition train close by had caught fire and 6-inch shells kept exploding for some hours, several fragments of which went through the Theatre.

Byrne, Acting Sister Ellen, attd. 47th Casualty Clearing Station
At Dozinghem at 9.15 pm August 20th, 1917, during a bomb raid in which there were 68 casualties, including 14 deaths, this lady showed remarkable coolness and gallantry under the most trying circumstances. Although she had been on

duty in the Theatre for 13 hours, she was foremost in attending the injured, and when work could be resumed, took her place at the table at which she remained throughout the night. As a Theatre Sister to this Clearing Station very considerable responsibility rested upon her. By her action and example she materially assisted in maintaining order and discipline.

Colhoun, Staff Nurse Annie Rebecca (later Mrs Crofton)
For conspicuous bravery and devotion to duty during an enemy air raid. She attended to, and provided for the safety of, helpless patients. She was assisting Staff Nurse Dewar and the latter was fatally wounded, and although the tent was full of smoke and acrid fumes, and she had been struck by a fragment of bomb, she attended to Staff Nurse Dewar and also to the case of a helpless patient.

Davis, Sister Mary Ellen, attd. No. 26 General Hospital
For conspicuous gallantry and devotion to duty on the night of 19/20th May 1918 at Étaples during an enemy air raid. When the Sisters' Quarters were wrecked and bombs falling, by her fine example materially assisted in averting panic amongst the Sisters and attended to the Sisters who were wounded.

Devenish-Meares, Sister Ethel Isabella, attd. No. 37 Casualty Clearing Station (RAMC)
On the occasion of the bombing of No. 37 Clearing Station at Godewaersvelde by the enemy on the night of October 20th 1917, Miss Devenish showed great heroism and devotion to duty under the following circumstances. At the first intimation of enemy aircraft, this lady instead of going to the bomb-proof shelter, provided for the Nursing Sisters, at once went to the wards for serious cases to look after the patients. By the time she got to the wards, bombs were falling in the vicinity, and she was on her way from the serious ward to the Officers' ward when she was struck by fragments of a bomb, which hit the ward she had just visited and wounded her in three places. Sister Devenish-Meares was evacuated wounded.

Easeby, Sister Norah, OBE, RRC
At Bethune on the 7th August 1916 she was wounded by splinters of glass caused by a shell which exploded outside the operating theatre. She remained on duty and did good work until all patients were evacuated.

Galvin, Acting Sister Nellie, No. 10 Stationary Hospital
For conspicuous coolness and devotion to duty at No. 10 Stationary Hospital, St Omer on 23/5/1918, during a hostile air raid. Four bombs were dropped on the building occupied by the Hospital in the early morning of 23/5/1918, carrying away the outer 1/3rd of the ward in which Sister Galvin was on night duty. She

remained in the ward attending to the sick, several of whom were wounded, and carried on her work as if nothing had happened. She displayed the greatest coolness and devotion to duty in soothing and calming the fear of the patients under her charge.

Garrett, Staff Nurse Ethel
For conspicuous bravery and devotion to duty during an enemy air raid. She rendered efficient first aid to a patient who was injured by a bomb and then fetched a Medical Officer. She did this although no less than fourteen bombs fell within a radius of 60–80 yards of the tent in which her patient was wounded.

Gilbert, Staff Nurse Mary, attd. No. 11 Casualty Clearing Station
At Bailleul Ambulance Siding, this lady was on duty on the night of 6th/7th July, 1917, at No. 11 Casualty Clearing Station. For about three hours bombs were repeatedly dropped in the immediate vicinity of and eventually into the Casualty Clearing Station, which was under canvas. There were some 250 patients in the Hospital at the time, 27 were killed and 68 wounded amongst the patients and personnel as the result of seven bombs dropped on the Hospital. Throughout she continued her duties amongst the patients, helping to calm them and attending to those wounded in the bombardment. She showed the most remarkable coolness and devotion to duty, and gave a splendid example under very trying circumstances.

Guerin, Acting Sister Minnie Maude de, No. 10 Stationary Hospital
For bravery and devotion to duty at No. 10 Stationary Hospital St Omer, during a hostile air raid on 23/5/1918. The building occupied by the Hospital was hit by four bombs, cutting in two the ward in which Sister de Guerin was on night duty. Several patients were wounded and buried in the debris of the destroyed building and Sister de Guerin remained on duty in her ward and displayed the greatest calmness and courage in attending to the wounded and helping to rescue the buried.

Hutchinson, Staff Nurse Ethel
At Bethune, on the 7th August 1916, although knocked down by the explosion of a 15 inch shell, she resumed her work until all the patients were evacuated showing exceptional courage.

Johnson, Staff Nurse Sarah, ARRC
For gallantry, consistent good work, and devotion to duty. When the casualty clearing station was struck by a bomb from an aircraft she displayed great courage and coolness, and set a splendid example to all, showing absolute disregard of danger.

King, Sister Eileen
At Bandaghem Sister King showed great courage and devotion to the wounded while on duty in her ward on November 29th 1917, at No. 63 Casualty Clearing Station. Four bombs were dropped by enemy aircraft in the vicinity of the ward. She was severely wounded in both legs and though suffering from shock and loss of blood, continued to give directions etc. as to care of the wounded. She showed great pluck and presence of mind.

Lutwick, Acting Sister Marie Daw, ARRC
For bravery and devotion to duty during an hostile bombing raid when in company with the Matron who was severely wounded and a Sister who was killed. She crossed the open bomb-swept ground alone in order to procure help. Subsequently she returned to the CCS and continued to work for many hours, under conditions of great danger.

Mahony, Sister Kate
For conspicuous bravery under fire on No. 27 Ambulance Train. On the night of the 10th November 1916, the train was carrying a full load of 450 sick and wounded, and entered Amiens as an aeroplane attack began which lasted an hour, and during which the Anti-Aircraft guns and Maxims were in hot action. Five bombs fell in the immediate neighbourhood of the train causing damage, and some patients to be thrown out of their cots. The Commanding Officer reports that this Sister, carrying a hand lamp, went about her work coolly and collectedly and cheerfully and that by her magnificent conduct she not only allayed alarm among the helpless patients and those suffering from shell shock but caused both patients and personnel to play up to the standards which she set.

McLean, Staff Nurse Christina, attd. 20th Casualty Clearing Station
On the evening of June 3rd, 1917, at Boisleux these three members of the Nursing Service remained on duty in the shrapnel swept hospital attending to the severely wounded and helpless cases, and would not leave their dangerous position until the patients were in a place of safety.

Munroe, Staff Nurse Susan Deverell, attd. No. 46 Stationary Hospital
For conspicuous gallantry and devotion to duty on the night of 19/20th May 1918 at Étaples during an enemy air raid in which three of her wards were wrecked. Nurse Munroe showed a coolness and contempt of danger, and solicitude for her patients, which were invaluable.

Spence, Sister Cissy
At Bailleul Ambulance Siding. This lady was on duty on the night of the 6/7th July 1917, at No. 11 Casualty Clearing Station. For about three hours bombs

were repeatedly dropped in the immediate vicinity of, and eventually into the Casualty Clearing Station which was under canvas. There were some 250 patients in the Hospital at the time, 27 were killed and 68 wounded amongst the patients and personnel as the result of seven bombs dropped on the Hospital. Throughout, she continued her duties amongst the patients, helping to calm them and tending to those wounded in the bombardment. She showed most remarkable coolness and devotion to duty, and gave a splendid example under very trying circumstances.

Thompson, Sister Ethel Kate

For conspicuous bravery under fire on No. 27 Ambulance Train. On the night of the 10th November 1916, the train was carrying a full load of 450 sick and wounded, and entered Amiens as an aeroplane attack began which lasted an hour, and during which the Anti-Aircraft guns and Maxims were in hot action. Five bombs fell in the immediate neighbourhood of the train causing damage, and some patients to be thrown out of their cots. The Commanding Officer reports that this Sister, carrying a hand lamp, went about her work coolly and collectedly and cheerfully and that by her magnificent conduct she not only allayed alarm among the helpless patients and those suffering from shell shock but caused both patients and personnel to play up to the standards which she set.

Trotter, Sister Jane Elizabeth, RRC

For gallantry and devotion to duty during an enemy air raid, which lasted from 11 p.m. till 3 a.m. Sister Trotter was in charge on night duty. During the raid she visited all the wards, reassuring the sick and wounded; her orderly being mortally wounded whilst standing by her in one of the wards. Her conduct during the whole of the raid was most praiseworthy.

Watkins, Sister Ethel Frances, ARRC

For gallantry and devotion to duty during an enemy air raid which lasted for four hours. Sister Watkins behaved with the utmost coolness. When wounded by a piece of shrapnel she made light of her injury and set a magnificent example to those who were with her.

Wilkinson, Sister Louisa Alice, attd. No. 24 General Hospital

For conspicuous gallantry and devotion to duty at Étaples on 31st May 1918 during an enemy air raid. Her ward was demolished. She continued to attend to wounded patients whilst the air raid was still in progress.

TERRITORIAL FORCE NURSING SERVICE

Brain, Staff Nurse Rose

For exceptional courage and devotion to duty during a hostile air raid, when bombs were dropped on the Hospital. One of the bombs wrecked the hut in which she was on duty, and, with the greatest coolness, she attended to all the patients in the ward, though she herself was wounded.

Carruthers, Staff Nurse Kate, ARRC

At Edgehill, during the night of the 14th–15th November 1916, enemy aeroplanes dropped three bombs on the Casualty Clearing Station, killing two men and wounding 14. Miss Carruthers who was on duty in a tent near which one of the bombs exploded, displayed great courage and disregard of danger in continuing to attend to the patients although she was herself wounded by a fragment of the bomb.

Dobbs, Miss Daisy Ellen

For conspicuous bravery, calmness and special devotion to duty in looking after the safety of the patients under her charge, even after she was wounded by a piece of a bomb and bleeding profusely, during an enemy raid. One patient was killed beside this Nurse and another wounded by the same bomb.

Eckett, Staff Nurse Elizabeth Jane, attd. 32nd Casualty Clearing Station

For great courage while in charge of her ward at Brandhoek on the 21st August, 1917. Although the ward was twice riddled by enemy aircraft, she continued attending the patients, and by her example, prevented many of them from injuring themselves.

Evans, Miss Mabel Louise

For conspicuous bravery under fire on No. 27 Ambulance Train. On the night of the 10th November, 1916, the train was carrying a full load of 450 sick and wounded and entered Amiens as an aeroplane attack began, which lasted an hour, and during which the Anti-Aircraft guns were in hot action. Five bombs fell on the immediate neighbourhood of the train causing damage and some patients to be thrown out of their cots. The Commanding Officer reports that this Sister, carrying a hand lamp, went about her work coolly and collectedly and cheerfully and that by her magnificent conduct, she not only allayed alarm among the helpless patients and those suffering from shell shock, but caused both patients and personnel to play up to the standard which she set.

Foster, Sister Dorothy Penrose, RRC

For conspicuous coolness and devotion to duty when supervising the transfer of patients from a CCS to an Ambulance Train while the locality of the CCS was being steadily shelled. She set a splendid example of calmness and composure.

Hawkins, Sister Winniefred, attd. 47th Casualty Clearing Station

At Dozinghem at 9.15pm August 20th, 1917, during a bomb raid in which there were 68 casualties, including 14 deaths, this lady was on duty in the Officers' ward, and was struck by two pieces of shell in the thigh. She continued to work and re-assure the patients until faint and dizzy, when she collapsed. Her action in remaining on duty through suffering considerable pain, is worthy of the highest commendation for this gallant action.

Herbert, Sister Julia Ashbourne
35 General Hospital: On the night of 3/4th September, 1917, after being wounded in the head by an aerial bomb, came on duty in the operating theatre, and continued to work there as Theatre Sister the whole night and all the next day.

Humphries, Matron Elizabeth Mountford, attd. No. 50 General Hospital
St Omer during the raid by hostile aircraft on the night of September 30th–October 1st 1917. While on duty during an air raid during which bombs were dropped on the Hospital, causing casualties (killed and wounded) amongst the Sisters, patients, and medical orderlies, by her cool, methodical and collected demeanour she inspired confidence in, and showed an outstanding example of calm fortitude to the nurses under her.

Jennings, Sister Mabel, attd. 33rd Casualty Clearing Station
For her excellent conduct at Bethune on the 7th December, 1917, as Theatre Sister, helping during operations while the Town was heavily shelled, and many shells bursting quite near, and all the time she performed her duty in a fearless manner. Also for her continuous good service during the past year, and devotion to duty at all times, the town being shelled and bombed frequently.

Laughton, Sister Dorothy Ann, RRC
57 Casualty Clearing Station: On the night of the 19th August 1917, the Asylum at St Venant, which is in part used as a Casualty Clearing Station, was hit by five bombs dropped by an enemy aeroplane; 5 female lunatics were killed or died of wounds, and fifteen injured. Miss Laughton, in spite of being knocked over by the blast of a bursting bomb, behaved with the utmost coolness, and it was mainly by her example and presence of mind, amidst a maniacal chaos, that order was restored, and that the wounded were speedily attended when extracted from the ruins.

Lowe, Staff Nurse Katherine Robertson, attd. No. 10 Stationary Hospital
For bravery and devotion to duty at No. 10 Stationary Hospital on 23/5/1918. During an air raid on the early morning of 23/5/1918, bombs struck the building occupied by the Hospital, destroying a large part of the ward in which Staff Nurse Lowe was on night duty, and wounding and burying in the debris many patients. She continued to carry out her duties in the ward with great composure and showed much resourcefulness in looking after the injured.

Maxey, Sister in Charge Kate, RRC
For gallantry and conspicuous devotion to duty displayed during a recent hostile bombing raid on a CCS. Although severely wounded herself, she went to the aid

of another Sister, who was fatally wounded, and did all she could for her. Later, although suffering severe pain, she showed an example of pluck and endurance which was inspiring to all.

Panton, Staff Nurse Helen Elisabeth, attd. 20th Casualty Clearing Station
On the evening of June 3rd, 1917, at Boisleux, these three members of the Nursing Service remained on duty in the shrapnel swept hospital attending to the severely wounded and helpless cases, and would not leave their dangerous position until patients were in a place of safety.

Parker, Staff Nurse Agnes Jack
For gallantry and devotion to duty under trying conditions when heavily bombed by hostile aircraft at night. The ward in which Staff Nurse Parker was on duty was badly damaged early in the raid by a bomb falling close to it. By her exceptional coolness and complete disregard for her own safety, she set a splendid example to all, and gave great confidence and comfort to the patients.

Thomson, Sister Leila Helen Ann, attd. 58th General Hospital
St Omer during raid by hostile aircraft on the night of September 30th–October 1st 1917 while on duty as Night Superintendent during an air raid in the course of which bombs were dropped on the Hospital, and casualties (killed and wounded) were caused amongst the Sisters, patients, and medical orderlies, she displayed great courage and devotion to duty.

Whyte, Staff Nurse Jean Strachan, ARRC
At Bethune on the 7th August 1916, was wounded by splinters of glass caused by a shell which exploded outside the operation theatre. She remained at duty and did good work until all patients were evacuated.

BRITISH RED CROSS SOCIETY

Alexander, Nursing Sister Annie, Queen Alexandra Hospital
Devotion to duty attending to the wounded and sick at this base. By her courage and presence in the wards while the town was shelled and bombed was the means of allaying the fears of the patients when several bombs dropped near the hospital.

Brampton, Winifred Addie, attd. No. 46 Stationary Hospital
For conspicuous gallantry and devotion to duty during an enemy air raid on Étaples on the night of 19/20th May 1918. This lady continued at duty throughout the raid. The ward in her charge was almost completely wrecked, several patients killed, and she was herself wounded.

Campbell, Nurse Mary Gwynedd, attd. No. 26 General Hospital
For conspicuous gallantry and devotion to duty at Étaples on 31st May 1918 during an enemy air raid, when buildings were set on fire, moved about in full glare of imminent danger, moving patients to safety, bearing inspiring confidence.

Cavanagh, Moyra, attd. No. 58 General Hospital
For conspicuous gallantry and devotion to duty during an enemy air raid on Étaples on the night 19/20th May 1918. Miss Cavanagh was in charge of four wards, two of which were entirely wrecked. She continued to perform her duty, and in addition, was very active in removing the wounded to a place of comparative safety.

Crewdson, Dorothea Mary Lynette, attd. No. 46 Stationary Hospital
For conspicuous gallantry and devotion to duty during an enemy air raid on Étaples on the night 19/20th May 1918. Although herself wounded, this lady remained at duty and assisted in dressing the wounds of patients.

Forse, Gillian Audrey

Freshfield, Katherine Margaret, attd. No. 24 General Hospital
For conspicuous gallantry and devotion to duty at Étaples on 31st May 1918, during an enemy air raid the ward in which she was working was destroyed by a bomb, she continued to attend to her patients and was herself very severely wounded.

Gregory, Lily Anne, attd. No. 24 General Hospital
For conspicuous gallantry and devotion to duty at Étaples on 31st May 1918 during an enemy air raid. Her ward was destroyed by bombs but she insisted on remaining at her post and attended the wounded during the progress of the raid.

Repton, Matron Helena Kate, Queen Alexandra Hospital
Devotion to duty, attending on the wounded and sick at this base. By her courage and presence in the wards while the town was shelled and bombed she was the means of allaying the fears of the patients when several bombs fell near the hospital.

Weir, Nurse Annie, attd. No. 58 General Hospital
St Omer during a raid by hostile aircraft on the night of September 30th–October 1st 1917. While on duty during an air raid, in the course of which bombs were dropped on the hospital, and casualties (killed and wounded) were caused amongst the Sisters, patients and medical orderlies, by her bravery and devoted attention to her patients she deserves the highest praise.

AUSTRALIAN ARMY NURSING SERVICE

Cawood, Nursing Sister Dorothy Gwendoline, attd. 2nd Australian Casualty Clearing Station
On the night of July 22nd, 1917 at Trois Arbres, when an enemy aircraft dropped bombs on the 2nd Australian CCS, Miss Cawoood was on duty in the operating theatre. She carried on during the disturbance with the utmost calmness and self-possession and was very active in assisting and treating the wounded.

Deacon, Nursing Sister Clare, attd. 2nd Australian Casualty Clearing Station
On 22nd July, 1917, about 10.25pm, at Trois Arbres, an enemy aeroplane dropped bombs on the 2nd Australian Clearing Station. The above ladies did excellent work and exhibited much courage and resourcefulness in reassuring the wounded and dressing their injuries.

Derren, Staff Nurse Mary Jane, attd. 2nd Australian Casualty Clearing Station
On 22nd July, 1917, about 10.25pm, at Trois Arbres, an enemy aeroplane dropped bombs on the 2nd Australian Clearing Station. The above ladies did excellent work and exhibited much courage and resourcefulness in reassuring the wounded and dressing their injuries.

Kelly, Sister Alicia Mary, attd. 3rd Australian CCS
For bravery and devotion to duty at Brandhoek on the 21st August, 1917. Being alone in the ward and in close proximity to a bursting shell, she made every endeavour to protect the patients from falling fragments, and when orders were given to remove the Sisters to shelter, she left her ward with great reluctance though shelling was still in progress.

Pratt, Sister Rachel, attd. 3rd Australian CCS
On the night of July 3/4th 1917 at 3.40am, enemy aircraft attacked this clearing station at Bailleul. Sister Pratt was on duty at the time and attending to a patient's wants. He was very ill, a bomb dropped exploding close to the tent. Sister was wounded in the right shoulder and the right lung, yet she completed her task for the patient, bringing him a drink. She was afterwards admitted to hospital and operated upon. Throughout the whole proceedings, she exhibited the utmost coolness and bravery and by so doing was a conspicuous example to the patients and others, whose confidence was absolutely maintained.

Ross-King, Nursing Sister Alice, attd. 2nd Australian CCS
On 22nd July, 1917 at 10.25pm an enemy aeroplane dropped bombs on the 2nd Australian CCS. Miss Ross-King was on night duty in charge of the ward wherein

the casualties occurred. She was of great assistance in removing wounded from beneath the wreckage, and controlling them with admirable judgement and excellent effect.

CANADIAN ARMY NURSING CORPS

The dates are not listed in the citations but they refer to the bombing raids on Étaples and Doullens between 18 and 29 May 1918, where six Canadian nurses lost their lives.

Campbell, Matron Edith, RRC

For gallantry and devotion to duty during an enemy air raid. Regardless of personal danger she attended to the wounded sisters, and by her personal example inspired the Sisters under her charge.

Herrington, Night Sister Leonora

For gallantry and devotion to duty during an enemy air raid. She remained at duty the entire night, and by her excellent example and personal courage was largely responsible for the maintenance of discipline and efficacy.

Hodge, Night Sister Meta

For gallantry and devotion to duty during an enemy air raid. Although injured by a falling beam, these Sisters displayed great presence of mind in extinguishing overturned oil stoves, and later rendered valuable assistance in the removal of patients.

Thompson, Night Sister Eleanor Jean

For gallantry and devotion to duty during an enemy air raid. Although injured by a falling beam, these Sisters displayed great presence of mind in extinguishing overturned oil stoves, and later rendered valuable assistance in the removal of patients.

Urquhart, Night Sister Lottie

For gallantry and devotion to duty during an enemy air raid. When four bombs fell on her wards, regardless of danger, she attended to the wounded. Her courage and devotion were an inspiring example to all.

Williamson, Night Sister Janet Mary

For gallantry and devotion to duty during an enemy air raid. When in charge of a ward badly damaged, she displayed exceptional coolness, and regardless of personal danger, sustained her patients and ensured their evacuation.

ST JOHN'S AMBULANCE BRIGADE

Balance, Sister Margaret Hendebourck
For conspicuous gallantry and devotion to duty at Étaples on 31st May 1918, during an enemy air raid. Her fortitude and courage were most conspicuous. She devoted herself entirely to her patients.

Bemrose, Sister Jane
For conspicuous gallantry and devotion to duty at Étaples on 31st May 1918 during an enemy air raid, showed disregard of danger, attended the wounded in her charge during the intense bombardment.

Chittock, Assistant Matron Mabel
For conspicuous gallantry and devotion to duty at Étaples on 31st May 1918 during an enemy air raid, displayed great presence of mind and instilled courage and confidence throughout a very terrible time.

Hounslow, Nurse Edith, ARRC, attd. No. 26 General Hospital
For conspicuous gallantry and devotion to duty at Étaples on 31st May 1918 during an enemy air raid. A bomb fell between two of her wards and injured many patients. She behaved with the utmost coolness and set a fine example attending wounded under most trying circumstances.

McGinnis, Sister Molly
For conspicuous gallantry and devotion to duty at Étaples on 31st May 1918 during an enemy air raid. Showed great courage, took charge of a ward and sustained her patients.

Todd, Matron Constance Elizabeth
For conspicuous gallantry and devotion to duty at Étaples on 31st May 1918, during an enemy air raid, with great bravery and presence of mind moved freely about the wards during the bombing, encouraging the Sisters and patients. The Hospital was severely damaged.

Warner, Sister Kathleen
For conspicuous gallantry and devotion to duty at Étaples, on 31st May 1918, during an enemy air raid, displayed the utmost coolness and maintained a cheery spirit throughout, showing the highest type of bravery and courage.

Appendix 2

Nurses' Disabilities and Pensionable Years

In order to build a picture of the occupational lives, health and deaths of British and Irish nurses, and to a lesser extent nurses from the Dominion Forces, the Public Record Office at Kew was sourced for Service records and any supportive data. Additionally, awards and citations were examined for references to wounding. Furthermore, from the 'Miscellaneous Sample of War Pensions Files', 300 cases relating to nurses' war pensions were examined and the *War Pensions Gazette* was consulted. However, the latter proved to be problematic. For example, while the September 1919 edition claimed that in the year to 30 June 1919, officers and nurses drawing retired pay numbered just under 20,000, it did not distinguish between the two groups.

Before any definitive conclusions could be drawn, more information would be required about the number of war pensions granted to nurses and the criteria required for their award, and the 'latency' factor would also have to be addressed. However, it is quite clear from the accessed files that there were some very sick nurses who died relatively soon after their war service. Conversely, there appears to be inconsistency in the awarding of pensions. Some nurses received lifetime pensions for what were classed as minor conditions, yet others who faced chronic disability had reduced awards or were not considered eligible. From the 300 random samples the following conditions were the most common.

Note: The terminology for the conditions remains unchanged and is written in the medical nomenclature of the era. To protect identities, first names only have been used.

CARDIOVASCULAR

Nurse	Condition	Pensionable Years	Nurse	Condition	Pensionable Years
Clara	Hemiplegia	1916–35	Alice	Heart disease	1916–32
Florence	Varicose veins/anaemia	1919–25	Bessie	Varicose veins	1919–49
Alice	Disordered action of the heart (DAH)	1919–27	Sarah	Heart disease	1915–52

Nurse	Condition	Pensionable Years	Nurse	Condition	Pensionable Years
Florence	Heart disease/thrombosis	1920–33	Blanche	DAH	1918–52
Blanche	Heart disease/nephritis	1919–29	Elsie	Heart disease	1919–59
Florence	DAH	1916–24	Beatrice	DAH	1918–20, 1956–59
Florence	DAH	1915–40	Florence	DAH	1920–50
Violet	DAH	1919–51	Mabel	Heart disease	1920–39
Sarah	Heart disease	1922–36	Annie	Varicose veins	1920–30
Jane	Cardiac hypertrophy/ neurasthenia	1921–31	Mabel	Myocardial degeneration	1921–40
Madge	Heart disease	1918–73	Maud	DAH	1916–51
Judith	Heart disease	1921–50	Estelle	Cerebral embolism	1919–40
Lydia	Heart disease	1892–1926	Gladys	Heart strain/debility	1920
Ethel	Heart disease	1920–46	Florence	Heart disease	1925–26
Pleasance	Cardiac enlargement/ anaemia	1918–56	Edith	Myocardial degeneration	1907–30
Georgina	Varicose veins	1919–35	Annie	DAH	1916–56
Ethel	Heart disease	1919–24	Martha	Myocarditis	1922–24
Jane	Heart disease	1918–36	Annie	Heart disease	1920–43
Christine	Heart disease	1918–32	Elsie	DAH	1919–54

DIGESTIVE

Nurse	Condition	Pensionable Years	Nurse	Condition	Pensionable Years
Annie	Duodenal catarrh	1920–47	Gertrude	Intestinal stasis/pyelitis	1912–47
Bessie	Atonic dyspepsia	1917–31	Johanna	Gastric ulcer	1923–42
Mary	Dyspepsia	1918–74	Jessie	Gastritis	1919–60
Kate	Intestinal stasis/ neurasthenia	1919–44	Rhoda	Appendicectomy/ Gastro-entersotomy	1918–50
Elsie	Abdominal adhesions	1918–44	Mary	Gastro-jejunosteomy	1918–20
Hannah	Intestinal stasis	1920–27	Agnes	Gastralgia/neuritis	1915–23
Rhoda	Mucous colitis	1916–55	Jane	Gastritis	1919–53
Annie	Duodenal ulcer	1917–48	Georgina	Effects of abdominal operations	1915–52

Nurse	Condition	Pensionable Years
Louisa	Gastritis/insanity	1918–58
Gertrude	Gastric ulcer	1919–57

Nurse	Condition	Pensionable Years
Marjorie	Debility following gastro-intestinal catarrh	1916–32

ENDOCRINE

Nurse	Condition	Pensionable Years
Ethel	Graves disease	1916–27
Annie	Exophthalmic goitre/tuberculosis	1918–41

Nurse	Condition	Pensionable Years
Mary	Graves disease	1918–59
Ethel	Graves disease	1916–72
Jennie	Goitre	1917–64

INFECTIOUS DISEASE

Nurse	Condition	Pensionable Years
Ethel	Malaria	1919–28
Olivia	Malaria	1918–20
Rosa	Malaria	1918–58
Winifred	Malaria	1919–22
Elizabeth	Malaria/eczema	1918–42
Ellen	Malaria	1919–27
Louise	Effects of dysentery	1918–58
Nora	Malaria	1922–29
Selina	Malaria	1919–20
Jessie	Gastritis	1919–60

Nurse	Condition	Pensionable Years
Hester	Dysentery	1916–29
Violet	Dysentery	1916–24
Helen	Malaria	1919–21
Jane	Gastritis	1919–53
Helen	Dysentery/malaria	1918–20
Rosemary	Dysentery/malaria	1919–30
Marie	Malaria	1919–28
Maria	Malaria	1918–30
Ada	Malaria/varicose veins	1918–22

MUSCULOSKELETAL

Nurse	Condition	Pensionable Years
Florence	Fractured femur	1917–42
Ann	Fractured femur	1917–48
Margaret	Rheumatism/hypertension	1918–32
Mary	Thumb injury	1916–55
Annie	Rheumatoid arthritis	1916–36
Marjorie	Knee injury	1918–69

Nurse	Condition	Pensionable Years
Margaret	Leg injury	1921–31
Rhona	Fractured pelvis	1919–74
Florence	Rheumatoid arthritis/deafness	1918–45
Ellen	Rheumatoid arthritis	1914–66
Mabel	Rheumatism	1917–37
Eileen	Old dislocation of shoulder	1920–23

Nurse	Condition	Pensionable Years	Nurse	Condition	Pensionable Years
Mary	Knee injury	1918–20	Ethel	Knee injury	1917–32
Lucy	Sarcoma of ilium	1920–25	Evelyn	Amputation (hand)	1918–38
Constance	Rheumatism	1920–21	Mary	Rheumatoid arthritis	1919–41
Helena	Polyarticular arthritis	1928–31	Eva	Fractured tibia and fibula	1918–65
Marjorie	Arthritis	1931–38	Mary	Arthritis	1917–40
Isa	Knee injury	1919–22	Carrie	Arthritis	1920–36
Annette	Osteomyelitis	1919–21	Marian	Rheumatism	1918–32
Kathleen	Rheumatism	1917–23	Isabella	Arm injury	1921–40
Agnes	Rheumatoid arthritis	1919–31	Lavinia	Osteo-arthritis	1907–42
Eva	Rheumatoid arthritis	1919–53	Charlotte	Rheumatoid arthritis	1918–36
Florence	Knee injury	1920–51	Isabella	Bomb wound/fractures	1917–20
Frances	Arthritis	1920–28	Jessie	Rheumatism	1917–40
Margaret	Rheumatism	1918–29			

PSYCHOLOGICAL

Nurse	Condition	Pensionable Years	Nurse	Condition	Pensionable Years
Julia	Debility	1915–49	Mary	Neurasthenia	1917–32
Joanna	Confusional insanity	1918–37	Sarah	Debility	1918–55
Lilian	Hysterical neurasthenia	1920–30	Jessie	Neurasthenia	1918–42
Florence	Debility	1919–23	Alice	Neurasthenia	1922–36
Eleanor	Neurasthenia	1922–23	Laura	Neurasthenia	1919–37
Bessie	Neurasthenia	1918–63	Materina	Neurasthenia	1920–41
Isma	Exhaustion psychosis	1921–30	Dorothy	Debility	1919–23
Sarah	Debility	1920–55	Marjorie	Nervous debility	1918–19
Edith	Nervous debility	1919–64	Agnes	Nervous debility	1918–69
Amy	Neurasthenia	1916–50	Nellie	Neurasthenia	1920–49
Florence	Neurasthenia	1917–64	Hilda	Debility	1919–38
Elizabeth	Neurasthenia	1919–78	Margaret	Neurasthenia	1916–34

Nurse	Condition	Pensionable Years	Nurse	Condition	Pensionable Years
Grace	Debility	1918–26	Gertrude	Neurasthenia/rheumatism	1925–26
Jennie	Manic depressive psychosis	1918–41	Mary	Debility	1915–31
Sarah	Neurasthenia	1921–26	Charlotte	Neurasthenia	1917–50
Ethel	Neurasthenia	1918–25	Louisa	Neurasthenia/chest contusion	1917–51
Mabel	Debility	1916–37	Frances	Debility	1922–23
Mary	Mental instability	1918–58	Mary	Neurasthenia	1919–28
Ethel	Nervous debility	1915–32	Elizabeth	Neurasthenia	1919–64
Gertrude	Neurasthenia	1917–63			

RESPIRATORY

Nurse	Condition	Pensionable Years	Nurse	Condition	Pensionable Years
Laura	Tuberculosis	1918–81	Agnes	Tuberculosis	1920–37
Alicia	Debility/tuberculosis	1902–48	Adelaide	Tuberculosis	1917–68
Violet	Asthma/nephritis	1918–38	Evelyn	Bronchitis	1924–39
Annie	Tuberculosis	1922–40	Beatrice	Phthisis	1919–21
Charlotte	Tuberculosis	1921–43	Jessie	Tuberculosis	1919–72
Daisy	Tuberculosis	1918–23	Annie	Tuberculosis	1920–50
Katherine	Asthma	1919–31	Ada	Bronchitis/asthma	1919–54
Edith	Tuberculosis	1920–33	Mina	Tuberculosis	1916–30
Pauline	Tuberculosis	1919–31	Mary	Chronic bronchitis	1921–28
Margaret	Tuberculosis	1919–24	Rubena	Bronchial catarrh/pharyngitis	1917–52
Beatrice	Tuberculosis	1918–33	Florence	Tuberculosis	1918–38
Madge	Tuberculosis	1918–21	Ernestine	Tuberculosis	1919–31
Jessie	Tuberculosis	1919–32	Ruby	Tuberculosis	1916–32
Winifred	Tuberculosis	1920–41	Isabella	Bronchitis/varicose veins	1920–40
Jean	Bronchitis/rheumatism	1919–29	Margaret	Tuberculosis	1918–67

Nurse	Condition	Pensionable Years	Nurse	Condition	Pensionable Years
Mary	Bronchitis	1919–55	Gertrude	Tuberculosis	1919–59
Alberta	Tuberculosis	1920–35	Agnes	Tuberculosis	1920–33
Eliza	Tuberculosis	1918–58	Marguerite	Tuberculosis	1920–53
Charlotte	Tuberculosis	1919–45	Emily	Tuberculosis	1920–21
Jane	Tuberculosis	1917–34	Beatrice	Tuberculosis	1919–48
Elizabeth	Bronchial asthma	1926–31	Charlotte	Tuberculosis	1920–22
Mary	Tuberculosis	1916–70	Mary	Bronchitis	1919–56
Florence	Tuberculosis	1917–37	Nelly	Pneumonia	1919–23
Dora	Tuberculosis	1918–31	Dora	Tuberculosis	1921–29
Emma	Tuberculosis	1918–57	Florence	Chronic bronchitis	1919–34
Mary	Bronchitis/sciatica	1917–25	Edith	Asthma	1918–36
Jane	Tuberculosis	1921–48	Harriet	Tuberculosis	1918–66
Eva	Tuberculosis	1919–45	Esther	Bronchitis	1919–62
Elsie	Tuberculosis	1919–77			

URINARY

Nurse	Condition	Pensionable Years
Ernestine	Nephritis	1916–68
Violet	Asthma/nephritis	1918–38
Evelyn	Nephritis	1917–65
Dorothy	Pyelonephritis	1920–31
Elizabeth	Movable kidney	1917–22
Constance	Tubercle of kidney	1916–36
Mary	Nephritis	1916–50
Florence	Chronic nephritis	1912–31
Marjorie	Debility following gastro-intestinal catarrh/nephritis	1916–32

Source: Public Record Office, Kew, *PIN 26 Subseries – Selected First World War Pensions Award Files.*

Appendix 3

Nursing Deaths

QUEEN ALEXANDRA'S IMPERIAL MILITARY NURSING SERVICE

Name	Status	Date of Death	Name	Status	Date of Death
Allen, Mary Ann	Staff Nurse	5 January 1920	Brown, Euphemia Lucy	Sister	19 February 1919
Armstrong, Eleanor	Sister	31 May 1920	Buckingham, Maud Amy	Matron	4 December 1915
Armstrong, Ellen R. R.	Sister	20 March 1919	Buckler, Annie Eleanor	Staff Nurse	17 October 1918
Bates, F. M.	Probationer	9 April 1916	Butler, Sarah Edith	Sister	14 April 1916
Beaufoy, Kate	Matron	26 February 1918	Callier, Ethel Fanny May	Sister	22 June 1919
Bennet, Helena Stewart	Staff Nurse	18 October 1918	Challinor, Elizabeth Annie	Staff Nurse	26 October 1918
Beresford, Rebecca Rose	Staff Nurse	26 February 1918	Chandler, Dorothy Maud	Sister	15 November 1917
Berrie, Charlotte	Sister	8 January 1919	Clough, Mary	Staff Nurse	12 October 1916
Bird, Laura Edna	Staff Nurse	19 August 1919	Cole, Emily Helena	Sister	21 February 1915
Blake, Edith	Staff Nurse	26 February 1918	Compton, Florence D'Oyley	Sister	15 January 1918
Bode-Blandy, Stella Rose	Sister	13 January 1919	Consterdine, Vivien Courtenay	Staff Nurse	6 November 1918
Bolger, Kathleen	Staff Nurse	5 March 1916	Cooke, Ella Kate	Staff Nurse	8 September 1917
Bond, Ella Maud	Sister	3 November 1918	Cooper, Ann	Sister	17 November 1919
Brace, Frances Ethel	Staff Nurse	21 September 1916	Corfield, Agnes Beryl	Sister	2 February 1916

Name	Status	Date of Death	Name	Status	Date of Death
Crowther, Lena	Sister	22 October 1916	Gledhill, Annie	Sister	17 October 1918
Croysdale, Marjorie	Probationer	2 March 1919	Gorbutt, Martha	Sister	28 July 1920
Cruickshank, Isabella	Sister	10 April 1917	Gray, Emily	Staff Nurse	16 January 1919
Dalton, Joan Glassfurd	Sister	20 March 1916	Griffiths, Janet Lois	Sister	30 October 1915
Danaher, Mary	Staff Nurse	12 October 1918	Grover, Alice Jane	Sister	6 February 1919
Dawes, Emily	Sister	23 October 1918	Gurney, Elizabeth Shepherd	Staff Nurse	10 April 1917
Dawson, Eveline Maud	Matron	10 April 1917	Hall, Frances Mary	Matron	7 July 1919
Dewar, Margaret Smith	Staff Nurse	12 March 1917	Hamilton, Margaret	Sister	Not known
Doherty, Mary Agnes	Sister	5 September 1916	Hannaford, Ida Durrant	Staff Nurse	14 March 1918
Donovan, Bridget	Staff Nurse	3 April 1916	Harkness, Bessie	Staff Nurse	11 April 1919
Duckers, Margaret Ellison	Staff Nurse	16 May 1918	Harrison, W. M.	Sister	3 April 1920
Duncan, Isabella Lucy Mary	Sister	1 January 1917	Hawley, Florence	Staff Nurse	20 June 1918
Edgar, Elizabeth	Staff Nurse	26 February 1918	Hawley, Nellie	Probationer	31 December 1917
Elliffe, Margaret	Sister	24 May 1916	Henry, Charlotte Edith	Staff Nurse	26 February 1918
Evans, Jane	Sister	26 February 1918	Hetterley, Helen	Staff Nurse	30 May 1917
Farley, Martha	Matron	1 June 1918	Hilling, Sophie	Sister	12 October 1918
Fearnley, Ethel	Staff Nurse	23 November 1914	Hobbes, Narrelle	Sister	10 May 1918
Ferguson, Rachel	Staff Nurse	26 June 1918	Hockey, Jessie Olive	Sister	14 August 1917
Foyster, Ellen Lucy	Sister	10 April 1917	Hodgson, Eveline Mary	Sister	21 December 1918
Garner, Annie Edith Curtis	Sister	12 March 1917	Hook, Florence Maud	Staff Nurse	10 November 1918
Gladstone, Elsie Mabel	Sister	24 January 1919	Hughes, Gladys Corfield	Staff Nurse	6 November 1918

Name	Status	Date of Death	Name	Status	Date of Death
Jack, Christina	Sister	22 October 1918	McRobbie, Jessie Elizabeth	Nurse	7 November 1918
Jay, C.	Sister	Not known	Meikle, Catherine	Nurse	14 October 1918
Johnson, Ada Marion	Sister	24 October 1918	Miller, Frances	Sister	Not known
Johnston, Margaret Hessie	Staff Nurse	5 September 1915	Milne, Helen	Sister	23 November 1917
Jones, Beatrice Isabel	Chief Matron	14 January 1921	Moreton, Ada	Nurse	7 September 1916
Jones, Gertrude Eileen	Sister	10 April 1917	Nicol, Christina	Sister	6 February 1917
Jones, Hilda Lilian	Sister	28 October 1918	O'Brien, Moyra	Nurse	21 February 1917
Kearney, I. M.	Sister	26 September 1916	Oxley, Edith Mary	Sister	12 December 1918
Kemp, Christine Munro Fuller	Staff Nurse	4 July 1918	Parker, Elsie Kelly Donaldson	Matron	16 October 1916
Kendall, Rose Elizabeth	Sister	26 February 1918	Partridge, Constance Harriet	Staff Nurse	5 January 1920
Kynoch, Alison Grace	Probationer	Not known	Pearse, Phyllis Ada	Staff Nurse	29 April 1915
Lea, Hilda Louise	Staff Nurse	10 May 1916	Pepper, Edith Dorothy	Probationer	7 April 1918
MacBeth, Margaret Ann	Staff Nurse	30 October 1918	Phillips, Jessie Josephine	Sister	21 March 1917
MacGill, Mary Mitchell	Matron	11 March 1915	Pilling, Doris Ellen	Probationer	28 March 1919
Mackenzie, Isabella	Nurse	2 November 1918	Radcliffe, Ethel Blundell	Sister	10 March 1919
Mann, Agnes Greig	Staff Nurse	10 April 1917	Reid, Anne Campbell	Staff Nurse	4 March 1919
Marmion, Margaret	Nurse	25 January 1919	Ritchie, Jessie	Staff Nurse	13 August 1916
Marshall, Mary Bethia	Staff Nurse	12 March 1917	Roberts, Annie Louise	Sister	28 September 1916
Mason, Fanny	Staff Nurse	10 April 1917	Roberts, E.	Staff Nurse	12 August 1917
McAllister, Clara	Staff Nurse	10 April 1917	Roberts, Jane	Staff Nurse	10 April 1917
McGibbon, Rosa A.	Sister	6 March 1919	Roberts, Margaret Dorothy	Staff Nurse	31 December 1917

Name	Status	Date of Death	Name	Status	Date of Death
Robinette, Caroline Amela	Staff Nurse	30 March 1917	Thomas, Lilian	Staff Nurse	14 August 1918
Robins, M. J.	Sister	4 November 1918	Thomson, Elizabeth Robertson	Sister	26 October 1918
Rodwell, Mary	Staff Nurse	17 November 1915	Tindall, Fanny	Sister	15 January 1918
Russell, Alice Maud	Staff Nurse	4 October 1916	Townsend, Martha	Staff Nurse	21 September 1918
Saw, Nellie	Staff Nurse	4 October 1919	Tulloch, Edith Sarah	Staff Nurse	8 October 1918
Seymour, Constance Mary	Probationer	12 February 1917	Turton, Alice Mary	Staff Nurse	7 May 1917
Shore, Florence Nightingale	Sister	16 January 1920	Wallace, Elizabeth	Staff Nurse	Not known
Smith, Frances Elizabeth	Staff Nurse	1 July 1918	Wallace, Lily	Staff Nurse	6 June 1916
Smith, Jeanie Barclay	Sister	28 April 1916	Walshe, Mary Alice	Staff Nurse	21 August 1915
Smith, Susie Marie	Staff Nurse	12 February 1916	Watson, Elizabeth Harvey	Staff Nurse	5 November 1918
Spindler, Nellie	Staff Nurse	21 August 1917	Watson, Mary	Nurse	6 November 1918
Stacey, Dorothy Louise	Staff Nurse	5 October 1918	Welford, Alice	Sister	15 January 1918
Stalker, M. B.	Sister	18 January 1921	Williams, Katherine	Staff Nurse	4 August 1919
Stephenson, Gertrude Annie	Sister	25 March 1918	Willson, Nellie	Staff Nurse	16 October 1918
Stevens, Lottie M.	Staff Nurse	15 March 1916	Wilson, Christina Murdoch	Sister	1 March 1916
Stewart, Elizabeth Grace	Staff Nurse	15 February 1916	Wilson, Myrtle Elizabeth	Sister	23 December 1915
Sturt, Kate Rosina	Staff Nurse	13 December 1916	Wright, Hannah Elizabeth	Staff Nurse	26 October 1918
Teggin, Eugene Elizabeth	Staff Nurse	25 December 1918			

QUEEN ALEXANDRA'S ROYAL NAVAL NURSING SERVICE

Name	Status	Date of Death
Ainsworth, G. G.	Sister	29 October 1918
Beard, Eva Gladys	Sister	14 March 1920
Chamberlain, Louisa Charlotte	Sister	10 August 1918
Edwards, Caroline Maud	Sister	30 December 1915
Elvens, Eliza Millicent	Sister	30 December 1915
Grigson, Mabel Edith	Sister	3 October 1918
Prevost, Annette Maud	Sister	19 November 1918
Robins, Mary Jannette	Sister	4 November 1918
Rowlett, Olive Kathleen	Sister	30 December 1915
Wilson, A.	Sister	5 November 1918

TERRITORIAL FORCE NURSING SERVICE

Name	Status	Date of Death	Name	Status	Date of Death
Andrews, Ellen	Sister	21 March 1918	Elliott, Elizabeth	Nurse	27 October 1918
Astell, Frances Ethel	Sister	17 December 1917	Elliott, Leila Mabel	Nurse	2 March 1920
Blacklock, Alice May	Sister	13 August 1916	Flintoff, Alice	Sister	9 November 1918
Blencowe, Mabel Edith	Sister	10 March 1917	Forbes, Beatrice Georgina	Staff Nurse	12 May 1918
Brett, Nora Veronica	Staff Nurse	20 May 1915	Garlick, Hilda Mary	Staff Nurse	12 August 1917
Brinton, Gertrude	Staff Nurse	30 October 1918	Gaskell, Lily	Staff Nurse	Not known
Cammack, Edith Mary	Staff Nurse	1 March 1918	Goldsmith, Amy Alice Victoria	Staff Nurse	5 March 1918
Carley, Bessie	Assistant Matron	26 April 1920	Grant, Mary	Sister	Not known
Climie, Agnes Murdoch	Staff Nurse	30 September 1917	Greatorex, Janet Mary	Sister	2 April 1916
Cole, Dorothy Helen	Sister	24 October 1918	Griffin, Lilian	Sister	5 September 1916
Cox, Margaret Annie	Staff Nurse	7 February 1919	Hastings, Helen Munsie	Sister	23 July 1918

Name	Status	Date of Death	Name	Status	Date of Death
Henshaw, Isabel	Sister	11 August 1919	Paterson, Jessie Jane	Staff Nurse	29 September 1916
Hills, Maud Ellen	Sister	22 July 1918	Robinson, Elizabeth	Sister	12 July 1919
Howard, Florence Gwendoline	Staff Nurse	18 November 1914	Rowlands, Helena May	Nurse	10 May 1919
Humphrey, Elsie May	Sister	19 April 1920	Saxon, Ethel	Staff Nurse	3 September 1917
Irwin, Winifred Haviland	Staff Nurse	18 November 1918	Simpson, Elizabeth	Nurse	10 May 1917
Jamieson, Jessie Smith	Staff Nurse	30 December 1918	Smith, C.	Staff Nurse	26 January 1920
Jinks, Mary	Nurse	29 September 1919	Smithies, Ellen Louise	Staff Nurse	22 February 1919
Kemp, Elsie Margaret	Sister	20 October 1917	Stanley, Ada	Staff Nurse	22 December 1915
Kerr, M. T.	Staff Nurse	17 January 1915	Stewart, Wilma Bridges	Staff Nurse	10 July 1918
Lancaster, Alice Hilda	Nurse	3 June 1918	Swain, L. M.	Staff Nurse	31 August 1915
MacKinnon, Mary	Staff Nurse	26 February 1918	Thompson, Minnie Bailey	Staff Nurse	18 September 1914
Mark, Hannah Dunlop	Nurse	10 October 1918	Trevethan, R.	Staff Nurse	4 September 1917
Marley, Grace Margaret	Probationer	12 October 1916	Vinter, B.	Staff Nurse	30 May 1918
Marnoch, Margaret Bella	Staff Nurse	13 November 1918	Wakefield, Jessie Emily	Sister	7 February 1919
McCombie, Christian	Nurse	15 January 1919	Watson, Dorothy	Staff Nurse	13 March 1917
Meldrum, Isabel	Sister	2 February 1918	Wheatley, Annie	Sister	1 August 1919
Milne, Mabel Lee	Sister	2 October 1917	Willis, F. A.	Sister	15 December 1919
Murray, Mabel	Staff Nurse	2 November 1918	Wills, Mary Elizabeth	Staff Nurse	30 March 1918
Nodder, Ruth Mary	Nurse	24 May 1918	Woodley, Ada Ann	Sister	10 January 1918
O'Gorman, Eileen Mary	Sister	20 November 1914			

JOINT WAR COMMISSION

BRITISH RED CROSS SOCIETY AND ST JOHN'S AMBULANCE BRIGADE

VOLUNTARY AID DETACHMENT

Name	Status	Date of Death	Name	Status	Date of Death
Arnold, Margaret Trevenen	Nurse	12 March 1916	Craggs, Mabel Olive	Nurse	20 January 1915
Bailey, W.	Nurse	23 September 1918	Crewdson, Dorothy Mary Lynette	Sister	12 March 1919
Bain, Annie Watson	Sister	1 June 1918	Dickson, Mary C.	Nurse	16 February 1917
Ball, Catherine	Sister	31 December 1917	Duncanson, Una Marguerite	Nurse	31 December 1917
Barker, Edith Frances	Nurse	3 April 1918	Faithfull, Florence Mary	Nurse	15 January 1918
Baron, Margaret Alice	Nurse	22 October 1918	Fraser, M. N.	Nurse	8 March 1915
Barrett, Sophie Violet	Nurse	10 October 1918	Hackett, V. C. H.	Nurse	13 October 1918
Bates, Madeline Elsie	Sister	22 December 1917	Hallam, Alice Violet	Sister	18 December 1916
Bolton, Grace Errol	Nurse	16 February 1919	Harding, Isabel L.	Nurse	15 February 1919
Bousfield, Mary Cawston	Nurse	24 February 1919	Hartman, Emily	Nurse	20 October 1918
Bowser, Ida Thekla	Sister	11 January 1919	Heritage, Audrey	Nurse	31 October 1918
Brown, Winifred Maud	Sister	31 December 1917	Hogg, Florence	Nurse	21 October 1918
Bytheway, Gertrude	Sister	31 December 1917	Horrell, Dorothy May	Nurse	9 January 1921
Chadwick, Hilda	Nurse	2 November 1918	Ingram, Edith	Nurse	14 August 1918
Chadwick, Mabel Elizabeth	Nurse	15 October 1915	Jones, Lilian Kate	Nurse	6 June 1916
Chapman, Marion Dorothy	Nurse	10 August 1918	Kinnear, Katherine Ferrars	Nurse	3 September 1917
Coles, Daisy Katherine Mary	Nurse	30 September 1917	Lambarde, B. A.	Nurse	5 March 1919
Consterdine, V. C.	Staff Nurse	6 November 1918	Langdale, Mary Agnes	Nurse	9 February 1917

Name	Status	Date of Death	Name	Status	Date of Death
Lee, Jeannie Smith	Nurse	30/03/17	Roskell, Gertrude Lucinda	Nurse	31 October 1915
Lever, Lady Beatrice Hilda	Nurse	26 May 1917	Ryle, Margaret Caroline	Nurse	21 February 1915
Liddell, L.	Nurse	29 September 1918	Samuelson, Lady Lelia Mathilda	Nurse	18 June 1915
Llewellyn, Gwynedd Violet	Nurse	3 November 1918	Smales, Florence Emily	Nurse	13 October 1915
Maltby, Phyllis May	Nurse	6 December 1918	Smyth, P. J.	Nurse	4 March 1919
Maunsell, M. J.	Nurse	7 January 1919	Taylor, Helen Batchelor	Nurse	15 November 1915
Midwood, Lilian	Nurse	31 December 1917	Thomson, Elizabeth	Nurse	30 September 1917
Palmieri, Alice Elicia	Nurse	15 May 1917	Warnock, Elizabeth McMath	Nurse	5 May 1918
Parrott, Amy Maud Augusta	Sister	24 October 1918	Williams, Jeannie	Nurse	31 January 1919
Pope, Cecily Mary Lee	Sister	25 June 1921	Young, Ada Elizabeth	Nurse	15 July 1918
Powers-Peel, A.	Nurse	31 December 1918	Young, Mary Ann Eliza	Nurse	13 February 1919
Richards, Ella	Nurse	14 October 1918	Young, Margaret Cameron	Nurse	30 July 1918
Rogers, Hermione Angela	Nurse	31 December 1917			

DOMINION FORCES

Australian Army Nursing Service

Name	Status	Date of Death	Name	Status	Date of Death
Bicknell, Louisa Annie	Staff Nurse	25 June 1915	Grewar, Gertrude Agnes	Sister	24 May 1921
Brennan, K. A.	Nurse	24 November 1918	Hennessy, May	Staff Nurse	9 April 1919
Clare, Emily	Sister	17 October 1918	Knox, Hilda Mary	Sister	17 February 1917
Dickinson, Ruby	Staff Nurse	23 June 1918	McPhail, Irene	Staff Nurse	4 August 1920
Gladstone, Emily Mabel	Sister	24 January 1919	Moorhouse, Edith Ann	Sister	24 November 1918

Name	Status	Date of Death	Name	Status	Date of Death
Moreton, Letitia Gladys	Sister	11 November 1916	Rothery, Elizabeth	Staff Nurse	15 June 1918
Mowbray, Norma Violet	Staff Nurse	21 January 1916	Stafford, Mary Florence	Staff Nurse	19 March 1919
Munro, Gertrude Evelyn	Sister	10 September 1918	Thomson, Ada Mildred	Staff Nurse	1 January 1919
O'Grady, Amy Veda	Sister	12 August 1916	Tyson, Fanny Isabel Catherine	Sister	20 April 1919
O'Kane, Rosa	Staff Nurse	21 December 1918	Walker, Jean Miles	Matron	30 October 1918
Porter, Katherine Agnes Lawrence	Sister	16 July 1919	Watson, Beatrice Middleton	Staff Nurse	2 June 1916
Power, Kathleen	Sister	13 August 1916	Williams, Blodwyn Elizabeth	Sister	24 May 1920
Ridgway, Doris Alice	Staff Nurse	6 January 1919			

Canadian Army Medical Corps

Name	Status	Date of Death	Name	Status	Date of Death
Alpaugh, Agnes E.	Sister	12 October 1918	Dussault, A.	Sister	27 June 1918
Baker, Margaret Eliza	Sister	30 May 1919	Follette, M. A.	Sister	27 June 1918
Baker, Miriam Eastman	Sister	17 October 1918	Forneri, Agnes	Sister	24 April 1918
Baldwin, D. M. Y.	Sister	30 May 1918	Fortescue, M. J.	Sister	27 June 1918
Bolton, G. E.	Nurse	16 February 1919	Fraser, Margaret Marjorie	Sister	27 June 1918
Campbell, Christina	Sister	27 June 1918	Frederickson, Christine	Sister	28 October 1918
Champagne, Ernestine	Nurse	24 March 1919	Gallaher, Minnie Katherine	Sister	27 June 1918
Cumming, Isabel K.	Sister	4 February 1921	Garbutt, S. E.	Sister	20 August 1917
Dagg, Ainslie St Clair	Sister	29 November 1918	Grant, Grace Mabel	Sister	12 September 1919
Davis, Lena Alloa	Sister	21 February 1918	Green, Matilda E.	Sister	9 October 1918
Donaldson, Gertrude	Sister	29 July 1919	Hennan, Victoria Belle	Sister	23 October 1918
Douglas, Carola Josephine	Sister	27 June 1918	Hunt, Myrtle	Sister	16 January 1918

Name	Status	Date of Death
Jaggard, Jessie Brown	Matron	25 September 1915
Jarvis, Jessie A.	Sister	23 May 1918
Jenner, L. M.	Sister	12 December 1918
Kealy, Ida Lilian	Sister	12 March 1918
King, J. N.	Sister	4 April 1919
Lowe, M	Sister	28 May 1918
MacDonald, Katherine Maud Mary	Sister	19 May 1918
MacIntosh, Rebecca	Sister	7 March 1919
MacLeod, Margaret	Sister	20 December 1919
MacPherson, A.	Sister	30 May 1918
McDiarmid, J. M.	Sister	27 June 1918
McDougall, Agnes	Sister	18 July 1919
McEachen, Rebecca	Sister	16 November 1918
McGinnis, Mary Geraldine	Sister	10 February 1920
McKay, E. V.	Sister	4 November 1918
McKenzie, Mary Agnes	Sister	27 June 1918
McLean, Rena Maud	Sister	27 June 1918

Name	Status	Date of Death
Mellett, Henrietta	Sister	10 October 1918
Munro, M. F. E.	Sister	7 September 1915
Pringle, E. L.	Sister	30 May 1918
Roberts, Jean O.	Sister	3 November 1918
Rogers, Nellie Grace	Sister	19 October 1918
Ross, A. J.	Sister	12 July 1918
Ross, Elsie Gertrude	Sister	26 February 1916
Sampson, Mary Belle	Sister	27 June 1918
Sare, Gladys Irene	Sister	27 June 1918
Sparks, E.	Sister	20 August 1917
Stamers, Anna Irene	Sister	27 June 1918
Templeman, Jean	Sister	27 June 1918
Trusdale, A.	Sister	12 September 1919
Tupper, Adruenna	Sister	9 December 1916
Wake, Gladys Maud Mary	Sister	21 May 1918
Whitely, Anna E.	Sister	21 April 1918

New Zealand Army Nursing Service

Name	Status	Date of Death
Brown, Marion Sinclair	Staff Nurse	23 October 1915
Clark, Isabel	Staff Nurse	23 October 1915
Fox, Catherine Anne	Staff Nurse	23 October 1915
Gorman, Mary	Staff Nurse	23 October 1915
Hawken, Ada Gilbert	Staff Nurse	18 October 1915

Name	Status	Date of Death
Hildyard, Norma Mildred	Staff Nurse	23 October 1915
Isdell, Helena Katherine	Staff Nurse	23 October 1915
Jamieson, Mabel Elizabeth	Staff Nurse	23 October 1915
Lumley, Corale	Nurse	25 November 1918
Rae, Mary Helen	Staff Nurse	23 October 1915

Name	Status	Date of Death		Name	Status	Date of Death
Rattray, Lorna Aylmer	Staff Nurse	23 October 1915		Tubman, Esther Maud	Staff Nurse	18 September 1918
Rogers, Margaret	Staff Nurse	23 October 1915		Whishaw, Mabel Helen	Sister	10 November 19/18
Thompson, Margaret Hepple	Staff Nurse	28 February 1921				

Nyasaland Nursing Service

Name	Status	Date of Death
Salvator	Sister	8 September 1918

South African Military Nursing Service

Name	Status	Date of Death
Baker, Edith Agnes	Staff Nurse	6 November 1918
Beaufort, Kate	Nurse	21 October 1918
Bernstein, Dora	Staff Nurse	6 November 1918
Bettle, Hilda Maud	Sister	7 February 1919
Dunn, Gertrude Eliza	Staff Nurse	14 December 1918
Edmeades, Constance Alexandra	Sister	17 October 1918
Fitzhenry, D. A.	Sister	1 December 1918
Flanagan, May Charlotte	Probationer	29 February 1920
Hearns, Beatrice	Staff Nurse	20 October 1918
Munro, Annie Winifred	Staff Nurse	6 April 1917
Wardle, Ida	Staff Nurse	13 October 1918
Watkins, J. K.	Staff Nurse	21 October 1918

As this information is in the public domain, the author did not see any breach of ethics in naming these women. All the dead of the Great War are named in the National Books of Remembrance at War Memorials.

Sources

Commonwealth War Graves Commission.
Scottish National War Memorial.
Roll of Honour of British Trained Nurses Serving Under the Joint War Committee of the Order of St John and the British Red Cross Society Who Gave Their Lives in the War of 1914–1919.
Royal College of Nursing Archives and Special Collections.
Imperial War Museum, Women's War Work Collection.
McEwen, Y. T., *WW1 British and Allied Nurses Rolls of Honour*, 2001.
The Honourable Women of the Great War and the Women's (War) Who's Who.

Bibliography

MANUSCRIPTS

Army Medical Services Museum – QARANC Archive

M. Blair Papers; A. Duncan Papers; F. Hodgins Papers; E. Killery; M. Loughran;
M. McCarthy Papers; E. Oram Papers; M. Philips Papers; A. V. Reay; J. Todd Papers;
A. L. Walker Papers; M. E. Webster Papers.

British Museum

Nightingale Papers.

Essex Records Office

Private Papers of Bramston and Luard families, Essex Record Office, Ref. D/Dlu55/
13/4.

Imperial War Museum, London

Australian Army Nursing Service During the First World War, Nurses' Accounts.
Private Papers of M. Brander; L. Gameson; E. W. Lea; J. Paterson; M. B. Peterkin.
The Women at Work Collection, British Red Cross Society.

National Archives, Kew, London

General

CAB19/1; HO45/10814; HO45/10838/331607; WO32/9342; WO95/3982; WO95/3988-
91; WO142/24; WO222/2134; WO372/23/25980; WO399/2668.

Pension Files (Selected)

PIN26; PIN2014; PIN20007; PIN20026; PIN20027; PIN20035; PIN20052; PIN20074;
PIN20104; PIN20110; PIN20273; PIN20119 l.
See Appendix 2 for an extensive sample.

Service Files (Selected)

WO/399/501; WO399/660; WO399/1260; WO399/2372; WO399/2887; WO399/3670; WO399/3962; WO399/4371; WO/399/5023; WO/399/6503; WO/399/6614; WO/399/8615; WO399/9177; WO/399/9836; WO/399/12912.

Service Files (Random Selection)

WO399/2299; WO399/2400; WO399/2668; WO399/3199/; WO399/3366; WO399/3788; WO399/3903; WO399/3962; WO399/4066; WO399/4177; WO399/4302; WO399/4531; WO399/5657; WO399/5622; WO399/5852; WO399/6449; WO399/6451; WO399/6560; WO399/7047; WO399/7080; WO399/7850; WO399/7879; WO399/7943; WO399/8079; WO399/8351; WO399/8773; WO399/8836; WO399/9033; WO399/9071.

National Library of Scotland, Edinburgh

Haldane Papers, MS 20233.

Royal London Hospital Archive

Ethel Hope Becher Papers RLHLH/N/1/4; Maud McCarthy Papers RLHLH/N/1/1–4.

University of Bristol Archives and Special Collections

John Addington Symonds Family Papers; Katharine Furse Collection, DM/1584/12/H.

Wellcome Trust

RAMC 523/14; RAMC/728/2 (MES); RAMC/1922: O/S79.

JOURNALS, PERIODICALS, OFFICIAL PUBLICATIONS

Daily News; Hansard; International Journal of Osteoarchaeology; Journal of the Royal Army Medical Corps; Kildare Observer; The British Journal of Nursing; The British Medical Journal; The Classical Quarterly; The Daily Express; The Daily Graphic; The Daily Telegraph; The Lancet; The London Gazette Army List; The New England Journal of Medicine; The Nursing Mirror and Midwives' Journal; The Nursing Times; The Red Cross; The Scotsman; The Tatler; The Times; Syston Parochial Magazine.

DATABASES AND ROLLS OF HONOUR

British Red Cross Society Archives.
Commonwealth War Graves Commission.
Historical Roll: Women of the British Empire to Whom the Military Medal has been Awarded During the Great War 1914–1918.

Roll of Honour of British Trained Nurses Serving Under the Joint War Committee of the Order of St John and the British Red Cross Society Who Gave Their Lives in the War of 1914–1919, British Red Cross Society Archives.

Scottish National War Memorial.

The Honourable Women of the Great War and the Women's (War) Who's Who.

Y. T. McEwen, WW1 British and Allied Nurses Rolls of Honour, 2001, Royal College of Nursing Archives and Special Collections.

GENERAL REFERENCES

Locations of Casualty Clearing Stations, BEF, 1914–1918, Ministry of Pensions, HMSO 1923.

Mitchell, J. and Smith, G. M., *Casualties and Medical Statistics of The Great War*, HMSO 1931.

Official Histories of the Great War: Medical Services, HMSO 1923.

Report of the War Office Committee of Enquiry Into 'Shell-Shock', 1922.

The Hague, Convention (II) with Respect to the Laws and Customs of War on Land and its annex: Regulations concerning the Laws and Customs of War on Land. Article 23, 29 July 1899.

The Times Diary and Index of the War, 1914–18, J. B. Hayward and Son, 1985.

CONSULTED SOURCES

Andrews, W. L. (1930), *Haunting Years*, Hutchinson and Co. Ltd.

Anon., *No. 26 General Hospital in France*, privately published by No. 26 VAD Association.

Anon. (1915), *Diary of a Nursing Sister on the Western Front*, William Blackwood and Sons.

Arnott, R. (ed.) (2002), *The Archaeology of Medicine*, British Archaeological Reports.

Ashworth T. (1980), *Trench Warfare*, Pan Books.

Australian Dictionary of Biography, vol. 10, Melbourne University Press, 1986.

Babington, A. (1997), *Shell-shock: a History of Changing Attitudes to War Neurosis*, Leo Cooper.

Bassett, J. (1997), *Guns and Brooches*, Oxford University Press.

Baynes, J. (1967), *Morale*, Cassell.

Best, S. H. (1938), *The Story of the British Red Cross*, Cassell.

Black, C. (1930), *King's Nurse–Beggar's Nurse*, Hurst and Blackett.

Bowser, T. (1917), *The Story of the VAD Work in the Great War*, Andrew Melrose.

Bradbury, J. (1994), *The Medieval Siege*, Boydell Press.

Brown, M. (1999), *Verdun – 1916*, Tempus Publishing Ltd.

Butler, A. G. (1938), *History of the Australian Army Medical Service, 1914–1918*, Part 1, 2nd edn.

Carew, T. (1971), *The Vanished Army*, Corgi.

Carroll, M. (1907), *Woman in all Ages and in all Countries: Greek Women*, Rittenhouse Press.

Carver, Field Marshal Lord (2004), *The Turkish Front 1914–18*, Pan Books.

Chapman, G. (ed.) (1937), *Vain Glory*, Cassell.

Chapman-Huston, D. and Rutter O. (1924), *General Sir John Cowans*, Hutchinson and Co. Ltd.

Churchill, W. (1933), *The World Crisis*, Butterworth.

Clark, A. (1961), *The Donkeys*, Mayflower.

Coppard, G. (1999), *With a Machine Gun to Cambrai*, Cassell.

Cuddeford G. M. (1976), *Women in Society*, Hamish Hamilton.

Dent, O. (1917), *A VAD in France*, Grant Richards Ltd.

Dionysus of Halicarnassus, *The Roman Antiquities*.

Dolden, A. S. (1980), *Cannon Fodder*, Blandford Press.

Dunn J. C. (1987), *The War the Infantry Knew 1914–1919*, Abacus.

Crankshaw, E. (1963), *The Fall of the House of Habsburg*, Sphere Books.

Edwards, E. B. (1891), *A Thousand Miles Up the Nile*, G. Routledge and Sons.

Eyre, Giles E. M. (1991), *Somme Harvest*, London Stamp Exchange Ltd.

Furse, K. (1940), *Hearts and Pomegranates*, Peter Davies.

Gardner, B. (1962), *The Big Push*, Cassell.

Gibbs, P. (1920), *The Realities of War*, Heinemann.

Gordon, C. A. (1887), *Medicine in Ancient India*, London.

Hay I. (1953), *One Hundred Years of Army Nursing*, Cassell.

Haldane, E. (1923), *The British Nurse in Peace and War*, John Murray.

Herodotus, *Histories*.

Homer, *Iliad*.

Horne, A. (1962), *The Price of Glory: Verdun 1916*, Macmillan.

Hurd-Mead, K. C. (1938), *A History of Women in Medicine*, The Haddam Press.

Keegan J. (1998), *The First World War*, Hutchinson.

King, E. J. (1934), *The Rules, Statutes and Customs of the Hospitallers 1099–1310*, Methuen.

Lane Fox, R. (2005), *The Classical World: An Epic History of Greece and Rome*, Penguin Books.

Lawrence, J. (2001), *Warrior Race: A History of the British at War*, Little, Brown and Company.

Lee, E. (1892), *Some Noble Sisters*, James Clarke and Company.

Leneman, L. (1994), *In The Service of Life*, Mercat Press.

Liddell Hart, B. (1970), *History of the First World War*, Cassell.

Livy, *History of Rome*.

Lloyd George, D. (1938), *War Memoirs*, Odhams.

Luard, K. E. (1930), *Unknown Warriors*, Chatto and Windus.

MacDonald, L. (1980), *The Roses of No Man's Land*, Papermac.

MacPherson, W. G. (1931), *Medical Services General History*, The Naval and Military Press, HMSO.

Majno, G. (1982), *The Healing Hand*, Harvard University Press.

Masefield, J. (1917), *The Old Front Line*, Heinemann.

McEwen, Y. T. (2006), *It's a Long Way To Tipperary: British and Irish Nurses in the Great War*, Cualann.

McGann, S. (1992), *The Battle of the Nurses*, Scutari Press.

McGann, S., Crowther, A. and Dougal, R. (2009), *Voice for Nurses: A History of The Royal College of Nursing 1916–1990*, Manchester University Press.

McLaren, B. (1917), *Women of the War*, Hodder and Stoughton.

Middlebrook, M. (1984), *The First Day of the Somme*, Penguin Books.

Mills, C. (1820), *History of the Crusade for the Recovery and Possession of the Holy Land*, Longmans.

Mitchell, P. D. (2004), *Medicine in the Crusades*, Cambridge University Press.

Montague, C. E. (1940), *Disenchantment*, Evergreen Books.

Moore, W. (1987), *Gas Attack*, Leo Cooper.

Moorehead, A. (1956), *Gallipoli*, Hamish Hamilton.

Moorehead, C. (1998), *Dunant's Dream: War, Switzerland and the History of the Red Cross*, HarperCollins.

Moran, Lord (1945), *The Anatomy of Courage*, Constable and Company Ltd.

Mumby, F. (1915), *The Great World War*, Gresham Publishing Company.

Nightingale, F. (1969), *Notes on Nursing*, Dover Publications.

Nutting, M. A. and Dock, L. L. (1907), *A History of Nursing*, vol. 1, G. P. Putnam's Sons.

Oldfield, S. (2001), *Women Humanitarians*, Continuum.

Pankhurst, E. (1914), *My Own Story*, Eveleigh Nash.

Piggott, J. (1975), *Queen Alexandra's Royal Army Nursing Corps*, Leo Cooper.

Plowman, M. (1927), *A Subaltern on the Somme*, Battery Press.

Pope, S. and Wheal, E. (1995), *The First World War*, Macmillan.

Purdom, C. B. (1930), *Everyman at War: Sixty Personal Narratives of the War*, Dent and Sons.

Reid, B. J. D., *The Story of the British Ambulance Train Service in France from August 1914 to April 1915*, Imperial War Museum, Department of Printed Documents.

Reminiscent Sketches 1914–1919 (1922), John Bale and Danielson.

Robinson, J. H. (ed.) (1904), *Readings in European History*, vol. 1, Ginn and Co.

Robinson, V. (1931), *The Story of Medicine*, New York: Tudor Publishing Company.

Shephard, B. (2000), *A War of Nerves*, Jonathan Cape.

Shepherd, J. (1991), *The Crimean Doctors: A History of the British Medical Services in the Crimean War*, Liverpool University Press.

Simpson, A. (1995), *The Evolution of Victory*, Tom Donovan Publishing.

Sorley Brown, W., *My War Diary 1914–1919. Recollections of Gallipoli, Lemnos, Egypt and Palestine*, John McQueen and Son.

Stanmore, Lord (1906), *Sidney Herbert, and Lord Herbert of Lea: A Memoir*, John Murray.

Stewart, J. C. (1983), *The Quality of Mercy: The Lives of Sir James and Lady Cantlie*, George Allen and Unwin.

Strachey, L. (1918), *Eminent Victorians*, Chatto and Windus.

Strauss, B. (2006), *The Trojan War*, Simon and Schuster.

Swayne, M. (1918), *In Mesopotamia*, Hodder and Stoughton.

Taylor, E. (2001), *Wartime Nurse*, Robert Hale.

Terraine, J. (1982), *White Heat: The New Warfare, 1914–1918*, Sidgwick and Jackson.

Terraine, J. (1972), *Morns*, Pan Books.

The Life and Times of King George V (1937), Odhams.

Theodorich (1896), *Description of the Holy Places*, Palestine Pilgrim Text Society.

Thurstan, V. (1917), *A Text Book of War Nursing*, G. P. Putnam's Sons.

Vansittart, P. (1998), *Voices from the Great War*, Pimlico.

Voigt, F. A. (1920), *Combed Out*, Swarthmore Press Ltd.

Waite, F. (1919), *The New Zealanders at Gallipoli*, Whitcombe and Tombs Ltd.

Whitehead, I. (1999), *Doctors in the Great War*, Leo Cooper.

Williams, H. S. and Williams, E. H. (1904), *A History of Science*, Harper Brothers.

Williams, J. (1972), *The Home Fronts*, Constable and Company Limited.

Wilson, H. W. and Hammerton, J. A. (eds), *The Great War (1915–1919)*, Amalgamated Press Ltd.

Wilson, K. (2004), *Lights Out!: The Memoir of Nursing Sister Kate Wilson, Canadian Army Medical Corps, 1915–1917*, CEF Books.

Winter, D. (1978), *Death's Men*, Penguin.

Winter, D. (1991), *Haig's Command*, Penguin.

Woodham-Smith, C. (1972), *Florence Nightingale*, Constable and Company.

Würzburg, J. (1896), *Description of the Holy Land*, Palestine Pilgrim Text Society.

Index

Page numbers in *italics* refer to figures

Army Nursing Board, 42–3, 131
Army Nursing Service (ANS), 9, 41–2, 58,
     59, 63–4, 65, 113, 114
Army Ordnance Department (AOD), 52
Army Service Corps (ASC), 46, 53
Arnold of Villanova, *Regimen Almarie*, 28,
     29
Arras offensive, 157–9, 163
Arrephoroi (Greek priestesses), 15
arsenical poisoning, 150
Artemis-Hecate (Greek goddess), 14
Artemisia (naval commander), 11
arteriosclerosis, 148
artificial respiration, 91
Artois–Loos offensive, 112, 114
Asclepiadae (Greek physician-priests),
     14–15
Asklepious (Greek god), 14, 14–15
asphyxiation, through gas inhalation, 87,
     88, 89–90, 90–1
aspirin, 78
Assyria, 16
Asturias, HMHS, 53, 159–61
Atholl, Katharine, Duchess of, 169
Aubers Ridge, battle for, 84
Augeas, King of Epeans (Greek mythological
     figure), 12
Augustinian Rule, 24
Augustus, Emperor, 21
Australian Army Nursing Service (AANS),
     94
Australian nurses, 48, 99, 113, 156, 174
Australian troops, 93, 94, 142
Avicenna (Ibn Sina), *Canon of Medicine*,
     29, 30
awards
   military, 76
   for nurses, 63, 159, 168, 175–6, 179,
     179, *183*

Babtie, Surgeon General Sir William, 101,
     102, 163
bacteria
   antibacterial remedies, 13, 18
   bacteriological investigations, 72, 84, 87
Bailleul, 62, 89–90, 90–1
barges, 60, 81, *81*, *82*, 113, 158, 162
Barton, Matron, 132
Base Hospitals (BHs)
   appointment of consultants, 72
   bombing of, 158, 159, 174, 175–6
   at Boulogne, 56
   during the Gallipoli Campaign, 99, 101
   shortages at, 139
   system, 91, 145, 146, 147
   transportation to, 60

Basra, 111, 119–20, 120, 172
bathhouses, 140, 142
battlefield medicine, 28
Beadsmore Smith, Anne (Matron-in-Chief,
     QAIMNS), 1
Becher, Colonel Arthur William Reddie (IA),
     41
Becher, Ethel Hope (Matron-in-Chief,
     QAIMNS)
   at the 1913 Nursing Officers' conference,
     37–8
   attitude towards release of information on
     nursing services, 3–4
   awarded Order of the British Empire
     Dame Grand Cross, 179
   career, 41–2, 44
   character, 41–2
   concern over employment of nurses, 61
   deployment of nurses to the
     Mediterranean, 99
   implementation of mobilisation, 41, 43–4
   lack of papers, 181
   member of the Joint VAD Committee, 83
   member of the Supply of Nurses
     Committee, 131–2
   during the Mesopotamia Campaign,
     120
   post during the war queried, 42–3
   responsibilities, 58
Becher, General Sir Arthur Mitford, 41
bedsores, 162
Beit Naama Officers' Convalescent Hospital,
     172
Belgian nurses, 82
Belgium, 38, 47, 48, 49; *see also individual
     places*
Bell Stretcher Tents, 103
Benedictines, in the Holy Land, 24–5
Bethlem Hospital, London, 174
bhang, 30
bicarbonate of soda, 89, 90
Bikaner, Maharajah of, 75
billeting arrangements, in France, 45–6
Birrell, Sister Jean (TFNS), 112, 126, 127
Birrell, Surgeon General William (MEF),
     101
bitterroot, 12
'Black Ships', 96–7, 98–9
Black, Sister Catherine (QAIMNSR),
     129–30
Blackie, James Stuart, 22
Blair, Sister Mary (QAIMNSR), 46, 86
Bloemfontein, 73
bombing raids, on hospitals, 158–9, *160*,
     173, 174, 175–6
bone-setting, 17, 30